Unequal By Design

Unequal By Design critically examines high-stakes standardized testing in order to illuminate what is really at stake for students, teachers, and communities negatively affected by such testing. This thoughtful analysis traces standardized testing's origins in the Eugenics and Social Efficiency movements of the late 19th and early 20th centuries through its current use as the central tool for national educational reform via No Child Left Behind. By exploring historical, social, economic, and educational aspects of testing, author Wayne Au demonstrates that these tests are not only premised on the creation of inequality, but that their structures are inextricably intertwined with social inequalities that exist outside of schools.

Wayne Au is Assistant Professor in the Department of Secondary Education, California State University-Fullerton and he is an editor for the progressive education journal, *Rethinking Schools*.

D0143851

The Critical Social Thought Series

Edited by Michael W. Apple,
University of Wisconsin—Madison

Unequal By Design

High-Stakes Testing and
the Standardization of Inequality

Wayne Au

Routledge
Taylor & Francis Group

NEW YORK AND LONDON

First published 2009
by Routledge
270 Madison Ave, New York, NY 10016

Simultaneously published in the UK
by Routledge
2 Park Square, Milton Park, Abingdon, Oxon OX14 4RN

Routledge is an imprint of the Taylor & Francis Group, an informa business

© 2009 Routledge, Taylor and Francis

Typeset in Minion Pro by EvS Communication Networx, Inc.

Library of Congress Cataloging in Publication Data
Au, Wayne, 1972-
Unequal by design : high-stakes testing and the standardization of inequality / Wayne Au.
p. cm. — (The critical social thought series)
Includes bibliographical references and index.
1. Educational tests and measurements—Social aspects—United States. 2. Test bias—United States. 3. Educational equalization—United States. I. Title.
LB3051.A86 2008
371.26'013—dc22
2008008799

ISBN 10: 0-415-99070-X (hbk)
ISBN 10: 0-415-99071-8 (pbk)
ISBN 10: 0-203-89204-6 (ebk)

ISBN 13: 978-0-415-99070-7 (hbk)
ISBN 13: 978-0-415-99071-4 (pbk)
ISBN 13: 978-0-203-89204-6 (ebk)

CONTENTS

SERIES EDITOR'S INTRODUCTION

When I began teaching in the some of the poorest schools in one of the poorest cities on the east coast of the United States, teachers faced a good deal of pressure to have students do well on the standardized tests that seemed so important to the central administration. I wasn't pleased that my students and I had to take a week out of our lives to complete what seemed like a never ending barrage of examinations, but we survived and went on. As unbelievable as it may now seem, that time seems almost Edenic to me now. My colleagues and I still had a good deal of autonomy and we could make major transformations in our curricula and in our models of teaching. And we could then connect that transformed content to the lives, cultures, and realities of the students and their communities.

Let me be honest. There were times when our practices were challenged politically. And there were times when no matter what we did and how hard we worked, many students still did not fully succeed (see, e.g., Apple, 1999, 2006). But, we still felt that there was space for serious and critical pedagogical work that could and often did transform the lives of dispossessed students. That was then; this is now. In a time of No Child Left Behind in the United States and similar "reforms" in other nations, the space of autonomy, the space of critical pedagogic work, has been lessened considerably—although many critical educators still struggle mightily to keep that space alive (Gutstein, 2006; Anyon, 2005).

The importance given to ubiquitous tests, now increasingly high stakes, has altered the conditions for policy making, for curriculum planning, and for teaching. What have been called *audit cultures* have now taken center stage (Apple, 2006; Leys, 2003). Demonstrating "success" in what are often reductive ways is the norm. Sanctions are very real if one fails to demonstrate continuous movement toward what are often nearly impossible to reach, or even simply rhetorical, goals. Indeed, as Smith, Miller-Kahn, Heinecke, and Jarvis (2004) so clearly show, a large portion of the avowed goals of current educational policy is part of political theater, since the means to actually reach them are never sufficient to come close to meeting the real needs of the institutions being audited and then attacked so vociferously.

Testing is so ingrained in our commonsense that even asking the question of what it is that tests actually do seems strange to all too many people. Aren't tests there to help us find those students who have talent? Who have the values of hard work and discipline? Who have the capacity to employ the benefits of our schools to go further than they would otherwise have?

There are, of course, a considerable number of critical analyses of the dangers of our overuse of high-stakes testing. Some have demonstrated that these instruments discriminate against poor people and people of color. Others have clearly shown that, even with the rhetoric of "leaving no child behind," the current economic and ideological context seems to create immense pressure for high-stakes testing to operate as a giant "push-out" program. Considerable numbers of poor children are formally or informally placed in programs where they do not have to take the tests, so that schools look better in the naming and shaming politics of school evaluation. At the same time, the very same tests reduce the curriculum that poor children (and not only poor children) receive to only that which is tested and reduce the teacher to someone who simply delivers the (usually low level) content that is measurable on the high-stakes tests (Valenzuela, 2005; Lipman, 2004). Entire organizations, such as Fair Test, have been built to rightly challenge the dominance of testing as the primary criterion of judgment about school and student success and to give us alternatives that actually do a better job.

All of these critical investigations have been essential—and they decidedly need to continue. But few have gone where Wayne Au takes us. He situates these necessary criticisms into a larger framework of analysis, one that stresses the school's role both in the reproduction of class and race differences and in possibly interrupting such reproduction. Drawing on an entire tradition of political economy and sociological theory and research, and in addition on Basil Bernstein's influential work on the sociology of the curriculum (Bernstein, 1977, 1990, 1996), Au engages with the history, educational and social effects, and implications of high-stakes assessment in very insightful ways. As befits one of the editors of the very valuable journal *Rethinking Schools*, however, he is not content to leave it at that. He opens the doors to a serious discussion of what might be done to alter this situation.

What Au accomplishes is striking. He recuperates parts of the critical traditions (the plural is important here) in educational and social analysis, ones that have all too often become sets of rhetorical slogans. He then applies these tools to give us a very different picture of the testing enterprise. The fact that I am employing a business metaphor is important here, since high-stakes testing is also a big business, once more documenting why political economy provides crucial insights into how testing functions. Indeed, the ways in which the evaluation of students, educators, and schools now goes on reminds me of the line in a rather famous book that argues that reality has increasingly become dominated by a set of institutions that have a sign hanging outside them. That sign says, "No admittance except on business" (Wheen, 2006, p. 71).

Wayne Au is the author of a widely read and discussed critical analysis of the empirical basis of support for high-stakes testing. There he undercut a number of the claims of the supporters of such widespread testing as simply a "technical" tool that helps all students and assists us in making crucial decisions (Au, 2007). In this book, he goes significantly further politically, empirically, and educationally. In the process, he shows what the stakes actually are in the use of high-stakes testing, and for whom the stakes are highest. In a time when significant parts of leftist scholarship have turned away from dialectical points of view, by applying these kinds of relational perspectives in a disciplined manner *Unequal By Design* helps restore the vitality of this tradition and offers us tools that progressives need if they are to interrupt dominance inside and outside of schools.

When combined with Au's talents as a scholar/activist, all of this makes *Unequal By Design* a book that deserves to be read by all critical educators who care deeply about what our educational institutions now do.

Michael W. Apple

John Bascom Professor of Curriculum and Instruction
and Educational Policy Studies
University of Wisconsin—Madison

REFERENCES

Anyon, J. (2005). *Radical possibilities*. New York: Routledge.

Apple, M. W. (1999). *Power, meaning and identity*. New York: Peter Lang.

Apple, M. W. (2006). *Educating the "Right" way: Markets, standards, God, and inequality* (2nd ed.). New York: Routledge.

Au, W. (2007). High stakes testing and curricular control: A qualitative meta-synthesis. *Educational Researcher, 36*, 258–267.

Bernstein, B. (1977). *Class, codes, and control III*. London: Routledge and Kegan Paul.

Bernstein, B. (1990). *The structuring of pedagogic discourse*. New York: Routledge.

Bernstein, B. (1996). *Pedagogy, symbolic control, and identity*. London: Taylor and Francis.

Gutstein, R. (2006). *Reading and writing the world with mathematics*. New York: Routledge.

Lipman, P. (2004). *High stakes education*. New York: Routledge.

Smith, M. L., Miller-Kahn, L., Heinecke, W., & Jarvis, P. (2004). *Political spectacle and the fate of American schools*. New York: RoutledgeFalmer.

Valenzuela, A. (Ed.) (2005). *Leaving children behind*. Albany, NY: State University of New York Press.

Wheen, F. (2006). *Das kapital: A biography*. New York: Atlantic Monthly Press.

ACKNOWLEDGMENTS

All writing, all thinking, is by nature social. The work contained herein was influenced by and may have not been possible without the support of my friends, family, colleagues, and comrades. While many, many people from different educational, political, and cultural communities have supported me over the years, I am indebted to the following individuals and collectives for their support on this specific project: My wife, Mira Shimabukuro, for being my best friend in joy and struggle; my father, Wilson Au, for providing me with incredible political leadership over the course of my whole life; my dear friend and adviser, Michael W. Apple, for his direction and continued support; my dear friends and colleagues from Friday seminar at UW Madison (too many to name you all), especially those who gave me feedback on various aspects of this manuscript, Kristen Buras, Edo Cavieres, Minerva Chavez, Taina Collazo-Quiles, Ross Collin, Hee-Ryong Kang, Tom Pedroni, Jen Sandler, and Keita Takayama; my comrades at Rethinking Schools; my other friends and colleagues who have supported this work in various ways, Bill Ayers, Patricia Burch, Mary Ellen Cardella, Benji Chang, Mark Ellis, Eugene Fujimoto, Luis Gandin, Fatma Gok, the Garcia-Gonzales family, Diana Hess, the Kumasaka family, Gloria Ladson-Billings, Zeus Leonardo, Corey Mead, Deborah Menkhart and Teaching for Change, the steering committee of the National Coalition of Education Activists, Sonia Nieto, Denise Oen, Puget Sound Rethinking Schools, E. Wayne Ross, Simone Schweber, Christine Sleeter, Paulette Thompson, Haunani-Kay Trask, Gail Tremblay, Sophia Ward, Anjela Wong; Routledge editors Catherine Bernard and Heather Jarrow; my family—my mother Priscilla Welles, stepmother Kathleen Au, sister Kendal Au, brother Tim Au and his family; the Shimabukuros—Bob, Zen, Alice Ito and the rest of the ohana; the DeWeese's, especially Cathie and Lynn DeWeese-Parkinson; my dear friends, Ken Matsudaira, Veronica Barrera, Chloé Barrera-Cloyd, and Yume Barrera-Matsudaira.

It should be noted that a portion of two chapters are adapted from previously published material:

Portions of Chapter 1 have appeared in: Au, W. (2006). Against economic determinism: Revisiting the roots of neo-Marxism in critical education theory. *Journal for Critical Education Policy Studies, 4*(2); http://www.jceps.com/?pageID=article&articleID=66.

A small portion of Chapter 4 has appeared in: Au, W. (2007). High-stakes testing and curricular control: A qualitative metasynthesis. *Educational Researcher, 36*(5), 258–267.

1

THE ZIP CODE EFFECT
Educational Inequality in the United States

> And your education! Is not that also social, and determined by the
> social conditions under which you educate, by the intervention,
> direct or indirect, of society, by means of schools, etc.?

Karl Marx & Frederick Engels (1848/1977, p. 55)

When I taught at Berkeley High School in California, administrators
and teachers there, myself included, often referred to a phenomenon
called the zip code effect. This effect was a crude approximation for
relative levels of academic achievement at Berkeley High. Graduation
rates, grade point averages, discipline rates, dropout rates, and standardized test scores could be relatively accurately predicted by a simple
analysis of where in the city of Berkeley a particular child lived.

To be sure, this zip code effect was an unsophisticated and perhaps
unfair analysis of the phenomenon of educational inequality at Berkeley High, and the vast majority of teachers there recognized this fact.
Most of us used it with a tone of despair and as a critique of the educational conditions that existed there. In reality, we teachers felt that
none of our students' academic achievement was totally predetermined
or completely pre-ordained no matter from which neighborhood they
hailed. We saw evidence to the contrary on most days, where individual
students from anywhere in Berkeley worked hard, sometimes against
overwhelming odds, and performed well in school. However, at the end
of the day, at the end of the school year, after all of the test scores had

1

been tallied, and after all of the statistics were processed and reported, students from some zip codes seemed to do well while students from other zip codes did not.

Zip codes, of course, are just numbers used to organize our mail delivery. However, because zip codes are geographical markers, in the case of Berkeley, California, they also serve to delineate between neighborhoods with distinctly different racial and economic class demographics, because in essence, Berkeley High School serves two largely disparate communities. The Berkeley "hills" are very rich and predominantly White; The Berkeley "flats" are mostly poor/working class and are predominantly African American and Latino. Even though the recent surge in gentrification in the Bay Area has changed the demographics of the flats to varying degrees, when I taught there during the 2001–2003 school years, the patterns were unmistakable. Kids from the hills generally did well in school, and kids from the flats generally did not—making the race and class disparities of the education of Berkeley High School students only that much more pronounced (Au, 2005a; Maran, 2000; Noguera, 2001, 2003a). In the end, the zip code effect was simply another name for the existence of deeply entrenched race and class inequality in the city of Berkeley generally.[1]

Unfortunately, Berkeley High's race and class based educational inequality cannot be relegated to Berkeley alone: It represents a trend that appears in public education in the United States generally, where, according to any number of markers, poor students and students of color[2] are simply less "successful" than their wealthy and/or White counterparts (see, e.g., Coleman et al., 1966; Hunter & Bartee, 2003; Sirin, 2005; The Education Trust, 2004). The debate over this inequality in the United States is similarly widespread historically, politically, and geographically. For instance, educational inequality has been a subject for research, discussion, debate, and action in the African American community for well over 100 years (see, e.g., DuBois, 1903; Washington, 1903; Woodson, 1990/1933). Educational and social inequality was the stated impetus behind the passing of the Elementary and Secondary Education Act (ESEA) of 1965 and remains the central theme for federal education reform in the United States since then (Jennings, 2000). However, despite various reform efforts, race and class based inequalities in public education persist today (Hunter & Bartee, 2003; Noguera, 2003a), with researchers noting that these inequalities seem to reflect similar inequalities that exist in society at large (Anyon, 2005; Barton, 2003).

In its most recent iteration, U.S. federal education policy—now referred to as the No Child Left Behind Act, or NCLB (U.S. Department of Education, 2002)—has taken the issue of educational inequality and stitched it together with standardized testing. Systems of standardized testing are now used to hold teachers, schools, districts, and states "accountable" if their students do not perform well on the tests (Apple, 2006a; Darling-Hammond, 2004; Kim & Sunderman, 2005; McNeil, 2000; Moe, 2003; Nichols & Berliner, 2007). Over the last 25 years, these "high-stakes," standardized tests have become the central tool for public education reform in this country (Kornhaber & Orfield, 2001), as politicians from both political parties, the business community (see Chapter 3 of this volume), and some segments of poor communities and communities of color have lent their support (Apple, 2006a; Apple & Pedroni, 2005; Karp, 2006b; Pedroni, 2007) to this purportedly neutral, fair, accurate, and meritocratic measure of educational performance (Berlak, 2000; Hoffman, 1962; Lemann, 1999; Popham, 2001). But is this final assumption, that high-stakes, standardized testing is neutral, fair, accurate, and meritocratic, actually true? Can high-stakes tests not only mark educational inequality but also prove to be the tool to fix such inequality as well?

Research on the outcomes of high-stakes testing would appear to answer, "No," to the above questions. The race and class based inequalities associated with the zip code effect at Berkeley High School seem to reproduce themselves nationally on high-stakes, standardized tests. A central finding of the research is that, while all students are feeling some effects, the weight of the high-stakes testing environment falls heaviest on the shoulders of low income students and students of color who are consistently found to be negatively and disproportionately affected by high-stakes, standardized testing (Amrein & Berliner, 2002b; Groves, 2002; Haney, 2000; Lomax, West, Harmon, Viator, & Madaus, 1995; Madaus & Clarke, 2001; Marchant & Paulson, 2005; McNeil, 2005; McNeil & Valenzuela, 2001; Nichols, Glass, & Berliner, 2005). This finding has caused some researchers to conclude that high-stakes standardized testing connected to grade promotion increases drop-out rates, produces no lasting educational benefits, and impacts Latino and African American children disproportionately in schools (Orfield & Wald, 2000).

The educational consequences of high-stakes testing have been particularly tangible for low income students and students of color. For instance, in Texas, whose state-level educational policy became the blueprint for the federal level No Child Left Behind Act, Black and Latino students have been feeling the brunt of the statewide testing program there (Hampton, 2005; Haney, 2000; McNeil, 2000, 2005; McNeil & Valenzuela, 2001; Sloan, 2005; Valenzuela, 2005b). The high-stakes testing and accountability movement in public education in Texas witnessed conservatively estimated school drop-out rates of 40% in 2001. This translates into Texas public schools losing between 90,000 and 95,000 students a year, the vast majority of which are African American and Latino (McNeil, 2005). The irony of Texas' drop-out rates is that the state claims to have made strong gains in test scores.

Darling-Hammond (2004) tells the story of the "Texas Miracle," where highly publicized gains in test scores were discovered to be the product of disappearing students, most of whom were students of color. For instance, Darling-Hammond explains how at Sharpstown High School in Houston, "a freshman class of 1,000 dwindled to fewer than 300 students by senior year—a pattern seen in most high-minority high schools in Houston, including those rewarded for getting their test scores 'up'" (p. 21). The miracle is that in Houston, not a single drop out was reported. This impossibly low drop-out rate came through the designation of missing students as incarcerated, transferred (with no follow up address), returned to Mexico, or having received a General Educational Development certificate, any of which would keep these disappeared students from officially counting as drop outs while simultaneously keeping these students, often low test scorers, from counting on the tests (McNeil, 2005). Ironically, despite these and other extremely disproportionate numbers associated with the education system in the State of Texas, some researchers still maintain that the Texas system of educational accountability is a success (see, e.g., Evers & Walberg, 2004; Winick & Kress, 2004).

Unfortunately, the Lone Star State of Texas is not alone in terms of high-stakes testing, inequality, drop-out rates and test-related scandal. Scores on the 2005 National Assessment of Educational Progress show White students outscoring African American and Latino students by 26 points in scaled reading scores, by 20 points in fourth-grade mathematics scores, by 23 points in eighth-grade reading scores, and by more than 26 points in eighth-grade reading scores. Further, these disparities are persistent over time (Ladson-Billings, 2006). High school exit exams produce similar gaps in performance (Darling-Hammond, McClosky, & Pecheone, 2006; Zabala, 2007), and while Beatty and colleagues (Beatty, Neisser, Trent, & Heubert, 2001) are reluctant in positing a causal relationship between high-stakes tests and high school drop outs, they do concede that:

> ...[T]here is reason to believe that high-stakes testing at any level may sometimes be used in ways that have unintended harmful effects on students at particular risk for academic failure because of poverty, lack of proficiency in English, disability, and member-

ship in population subgroups that have been educationally disadvantaged. (p. 7)

Other research analyzing data across eighteen states finds that 62% of states with high school exit exams saw an increase in drop-out rates when they implemented their exams (Amrein & Berliner, 2002a). Given that, according to the National Center for Educational Statistics, African American and Latino students are twice as likely as White students to drop out of school, and students from low-income families are five times more likely to drop out than students from high-income families (Laird, Lew, DeBell, & Chapman, 2006), these findings would seem to support a relationship between high-stakes testing, dropout rates, and a disproportionate impact on low income students and students of color (see also Nichols & Berliner, 2007; Roderick & Nagaoka, 2005).

For all of the high-minded rhetoric surrounding high-stakes, standardized testing and issues of equality in educational achievement, the empirical reality appears to be just the opposite. Systems of high-stakes testing damage the education of low income and students of color (Amrein & Berliner, 2002b; Darder & Torres, 2004; Darling-Hammond, 2007; Groves, 2002; Haney, 2000; Kane & Staiger, 2002; Madaus & Clarke, 2001; McNeil, 2005; McNeil & Valenzuela, 2001; Roderick & Nagaoka, 2005). Such findings raise serious, fundamental questions about high-stakes, standardized testing. Is it possible that systems of high-stakes, standardized testing only help (re)produce the very same inequalities they purport to measure?

In this book I explore the relationship between high-stakes testing, as part of broader school structure and education policy, and the (re)production of socioeducational inequalities. Specifically, my research hinges on the possibility that high-stakes testing produces classroom level changes in the educational experiences of students and teachers that increase inequality. Thus, in this book I focus on the question: *What is the relationship between high-stakes, standardized testing and the (re)production of educational inequality?* The essential reason why this question is important is that social and economic inequality has only increased in the United States (and the world) in recent years (Brown & Lauder, 2006; McLaren & Farahmandpur, 2005). Such increased inequality bodes poorly because there have been corollary increases in educational disparity (Anyon, 2005). Thus, an analysis of the relationship between high-stakes testing and the (re)production of inequitable educational-social relations, as this book hopes to achieve, can only help critical educators work toward a more just society within their educational contexts.

My central question, however, requires unpacking before proceeding. The rest of this chapter is devoted to this task. First, I explain the definition of "high-stakes testing" I use in this book. Second, I explain the conceptual ideas that guide and shape my analysis, and third, I sketch an overall outline of this book.

HIGH-STAKES TESTING

In very specific terms, high-stakes tests are a part of a *policy design* (Schneider & Ingram, 1997) that "links the score on one set of standardized tests to grade promotion, high school graduation and, in some cases, teacher and principal salaries and tenure decisions" (Orfield & Wald, 2000, p. 38). As part of the accountability movement, stakes are also deemed high because the results of tests, as well as the ranking and categorization of schools, teachers, and children that extend from those results, are reported to the public (McNeil, 2000), in turn shaping the reputations of states, districts, schools, principals, teachers and students. As part of a policy design, high-stakes tests represent one "*instrument* the State uses to implement the policy and to allocate its values" (M. L. Smith, 2004, p. 6) of "good" and "bad" schools, teachers, and students. Thus, the term "high-stakes testing" simultaneously implies two things: 1) Standardized testing as the technology and tool/instrument used for measurement, and 2) Educational policy erected around the standardized test results that usually attaches consequences to those results thereby making such tests "high-stakes." Any discussion of high-stakes testing therefore requires that we discuss policy and testing itself, as well as the curricular implications of the testing.[3]

SOCIAL REPRODUCTION IN CRITICAL EDUCATIONAL THEORY

The overarching arguments in this book regarding the relationship between high-stakes testing, educational inequality, and socioeconomic relations, recalls a broader argument amongst critical educational theorists regarding the role of schools in the reproduction of socioeconomic inequality associated with capitalism, one that can be traced back to Marx. In the *Preface to a Contribution to the Critique of Political Economy*, Marx (1968a) writes:

> In the social production of their life, [humans] enter into definite relations that are indispensable and independent of their will, relations of production which correspond to a definite stage of

development of their material productive forces. The sum total of these relations of production constitutes the economic structure of society, the real foundation, on which rises a legal and political superstructure and to which correspond definite forms of social consciousness. The mode of production of material life conditions the social, political and intellectual life process in general. It is not the consciousness of [humans] that determines their being, but, one the contrary, their social being that determines their consciousness. (p. 183)

These four sentences outline what is commonly referred to as the base/superstructure model in Marxism, where the "legal and political superstructure" rises out of the "relations of production" that make up the base "economic structure of society." Marx's formulation, having been interpreted in a variety of ways, has proved useful (if not controversial) for activists and scholars interested in understanding how social, cultural, and institutional inequalities relate to capitalist economic relations. Consequently, critical educational theorists have made use of Marx's conceptualization, or some related derivative, to analyze educational inequality in terms of economic inequality (Au, 2006a).

The modern contours of this theorizing were sparked by Bowles and Gintis (1976) and the publication of their book, *Schooling in Capitalist America: Education Reform and the Contradictions of Economic Life*. Bowles and Gintis generated a debate amongst critical educational scholars about the relationship between schools, society and the economy, one that generally revolved around the central question: Are schools completely determined by the structure of our economy, or do they have some amount of autonomy from economic forces? Bowles and Gintis answer this question with the "correspondence principle" of educational relations. According to this principle, in capitalist societies,

...the division of labor in education, as well as its structure of authority and reward, mirror those of the economy...[and] in any stable society in which a formal educational system has a major role in the personal development of working people, there will tend to emerge a correspondence between the social relations of education and those of the economic system. (Bowles & Gintis, 1988, p. 237)

Bowles and Gintis' formulation asserts that schools mainly function to serve the needs of capitalist production in nearly a one-to-one correspondence, and thus provide one explanation of how and why schools reproduce inequality.

Critical education theorists sharply criticized Bowles and Gintis' correspondence principle (also commonly referred to as "correspondence theory"), arguing that the correspondence principle ignores the role of teachers, culture, and ideology in schools, is too mechanical and overly economistic, and neglects students' and others' resistance to dominant social relations (see, e.g., Apple, 1979/2004, 1980–81, 1988a; Cole, 1988; Edwards, 1980; Giroux, 1980, 1983a; Moore, 1988). Arnot and Whitty (1982) provide a clear summary of these critiques when they state:

> [T]he political economy of schooling as presented by Bowles & Gintis... failed to describe and explain classroom life, the conflicts and contradictions *within* the school and the distance and conflict *between* the school and the economy. Further, it could not account for the variety of responses of teachers and pupils to the structures of the school—some of which were liable to threaten the successful socialisation of the new generation. (p. 98, original emphasis)

Instead of schools reproducing an exact reflection of norms of behavior, attitude, and ideological dispositions required for capitalist production, critics argue, individuals within those schools possess *agency* and *consciousness* which allows them to *mediate* and *resist* the dominant social relations reproduced through institutions. This critique, while suggesting that the transmission of inequitable social relations is not a mechanical one, still maintains that individuals do feel the effects of, succumb to, or are products of an unequal socioeconomic system. Put differently; that a message is communicated through an institution such as school does not mean that this message is heard and universally embodied by its intended recipients. Transmission is one process, acquisition is another process altogether, and the mechanisms of mediation between the two are critical (Bernstein, 1996).

The above critiques withstanding, I do not want to downplay either the importance of understanding the transmission of social relations via education or the importance of Bowles and Gintis' contribution to this debate. As Lankshear (1997) recalls:

> ...[H]indsight reveals that *Schooling in Capitalist America* and the debate it stimulated made an enduring contribution to our understanding of the extent to which, and ways in which, social relations, practices, and outcomes of formal education are enmeshed with the (re)production of economic life under capitalism. (p. 309)

Given the vast disparities in educational achievement along lines of race and class, it is fairly clear that schools do play a role in (re)producing social inequality through the (re)production of educational inequality (Apple, 1995; Bourdieu & Passeron, 1977; Carnoy & Levin, 1985). For most critical education scholars, the question is not, "*Do* schools reproduce inequality?" Based on the empirical evidence, discussed earlier, it is inarguable that schools generally maintain and reinforce the hierarchies associated with the social and economic status quo. But this is a general position that in some ways does not stray too far from Bowles and Gintis' original formulation. Rather, the more nuanced question has been: *How* do schools reproduce social inequality in a way that still accounts for the complexity of human agency, intervention, and resistance in this overall process? Indeed, students, teachers, and communities have resisted schooling's tendency toward social reproduction in very counter-hegemonic, and at times even revolutionary, ways (see, e.g., Apple & Beane, 2007; Gibson, Queen, Ross, & Vinson, 2007; Rethinking Schools, 2008).

In response to the mechanistic and deterministic analysis offered by Bowles and Gintis (1976) and others, critical educational theorists, particularly neo-Marxists, applied the concepts of "hegemony" (Gramsci, 1971) and "relative autonomy" (Althusser, 1971) to their analyses of schools and socioeconomic reproduction. These two concepts provide utility for critical educational theorists because they account for some level of control of education by the socioeconomic relations associated with capitalism, while simultaneously providing for forces within education to resist such control. Gramsci (1971), the Italian communist credited with the most elaborated formulation and application of hegemony, posits that power was maintained less often by direct, physical force and more often through the maintenance of consciousness that allows the masses to grant "spontaneous consent" to control by dominant elites. This consent, however, often relies upon offering compromises to the subordinate in order to maintain the legitimacy of the dominant (Apple & Buras, 2006b), even if these compromises act as "an umbrella under which many groups can stand but which basically still is under the guiding principles of dominant groups" (Apple, 2000, p. 64).

Applied to education, the concept of hegemony creates the space for an analysis of schools and social reproduction that allows for the contradictory role that public education in the United States has often played, thus challenging the economic determinism of Bowles and Gintis while still recognizing that capitalist production plays a significant part in the shaping of our common sense understandings of education and social relations (Apple, 1995). As Apple (1995) explains:

> On the one hand, the school must assist in accumulation by producing both agents for a hierarchical labor market and the cultural capital of technical/administrative knowledge. On the other hand, our educational institutions must legitimate ideologies of equality and class mobility, and make themselves be seen as positively by as many classes and class segments as possible...The need for *economic* and ideological efficiency and stable production tends to be in conflict with the other *political* needs. What we see is the school attempting to resolve what may be the inherently contradictory roles it must play. (pp. 52–53, original emphasis)

While schools play a key role in reproducing social inequality, their contradictory role in legitimating ideologies of equality also allows some room for resistance to this reproduction (Carnoy & Levin, 1985).

Similarly, Althusser (1971), a French communist and philosopher, is often credited with the concept of "relative autonomy." In his discussion of the relationship between the economic base and the superstructure, Althusser arrives at two conclusions: "(1) there is a 'relative autonomy' of the superstructure with respect to the base; (2) there is a 'reciprocal action' of the superstructure on the base" (p. 136). It is Althusser's conception of relative autonomy that has been taken up by critical education theorists. For instance, Apple (1995) explains that:

> ...[T]here was a dynamic interplay between the political and economic spheres which was found in education. While the former was not reducible to the latter—and, like culture, it had a significant degree of relative autonomy—the role the school plays *as a state apparatus* is strongly related to the core problems of accumulation and legitimation faced by the state and a mode of production...(p. 26, original emphasis)

Strands of Althusser's formulation can also be found running through the work of theorists such as Bourdieu and Passeron (1977) and Bernstein (Apple, 2002; Bernstein, 1990). The concept of relative autonomy holds a utilitarian value for resolving the problems posed by economic determinism and aids critical education theorists in developing theories of resistance (Dance, 2002; Giroux, 1983b; Willis, 1977), because it attempts to both acknowledge human intervention through cultural practices and to establish schools as relatively autonomous from the economic base, and thus as spaces where the possibility of social transformation might be created.

Arguably it is the intent of all Marxist, functionalist, and/or neo-Marxist formulations to analyze the relationship between schools and society—the empirical evidence connecting schools and inequality is too overwhelming to deny such a relationship. The devil, however, is in the details, in *how* we conceive of the interconnections between things within an organic, interrelated totality. Sayers (1990) provides a glimpse of such a conception in his summation of Marxist dialectical relations:

> Social processes have their own internal dynamic, their own inner contradictions. The different aspects of society—forces and relations of production, base and superstructure—are aspects of a single whole, internally and organically interrelated, in dialectical interaction and conflict. It is these interactions, these conflicts, these contradictions—which are internal to society—that lead to historical change. In the process, none of these aspects is inert or passive: the forces and relations of production and also the superstructure are all transformed and developed. (p. 164)

The importance of understanding social and economic processes as having their own internal dynamics cannot be overstated, for it recognizes that there are logics of development at play within these relationships, that there are social and economic systems in a sense have their own life *and* are made up of the lives of individual humans. As Creaven (2000) observes,

> The existence of such relationships of structural dependence (of polity, law, major cultural institutions, etc.,) upon economic production and exploitation is what justifies the Marxist view that societies are systems, or totalities, following their own logics of development, rather than a heterogeneous ensemble of "autonomous" structures or practices, moving in no particular direction. (p. 67)

The conception of these relationships as systematic, as processes that develop in particular directions and that exhibit particular characteristics, means they function in ways that can be interrogated, understood, and ultimately, changed.

Elsewhere I have argued that the neo-Marxist turn away from what was labeled as traditional or orthodox Marxism toward analytical tools such as hegemony and relative autonomy was fundamentally misguided because it was based upon a deep misunderstanding of Marxist dialectical materialism, and that Marx and Engels' original, dialectical materialist conception of the base/superstructure relationship was not only adequate, but provided the basis for both Gramsci's and Althusser's own conceptions (Au, 2006a).[4] The important piece of the neo-Marxist impetus, however, is to recognize that within a Marxist, dialectical analysis, human beings are not totally determined beings. As Marx

(1968b) himself asserted, humans "make their own history, but they do not make it as they please; they do not make it under self-selected circumstances, but under circumstances existing already, given and transmitted from the past" (p. 97). Or, in Engels' (1968c) words, "In the history of society...the actors are all endowed with consciousness, are [humans] acting with deliberation or passion, working towards definite goals; nothing happens without a conscious purpose, without an intended aim" (p. 622). Indeed, within a Marxist conception, humans do have agency, they can be and are subjects of history. This was the goal of both Lenin's (1975) and Vygotsky's (1978; 1987) conceptions of consciousness (Au, 2007c) and is the backbone of Freire's (1974) conception of "liberatory pedagogy" (Au, 2007a; Au & Apple, 2007): That humans, as subjects, as agents, as individuals, and as individual classes, develop consciousness of the imposition of structures on their lives and, based on that consciousness, take action to change it.

However, as Anderson (1980) explains, the terms "agent" and "subject" both are internally contradictory: "agent" signifies both "active initiator" and "passive instrument" (e.g., the agent of a foreign power), and "subject" signifies both "sovereignty" and "subordination." Such internal contradiction perhaps points to the appropriateness of both terms, for it provides analytic space, in a Marxist conception, for both individual consciousness and schools to be "relatively autonomous" from the relations of production associated with the economic base. Thus, while schools play a key role in reproducing social inequality, their contradictory role in legitimating ideologies of equality also allows room for resistance to this reproduction (Apple, 1979/2004, 1995; Carnoy & Levin, 1985). It is absolutely critical for us to recognize this room for resistance because students *do* resist the inculcations of schooling on many levels (Au, 2005a; Dance, 2002; McNeil, 1986; Shor, 1992; Willis, 1977), and teachers, as laborers within the political economy of education (Apple, 1986, 1995), also resist the reproduction of inequitable capitalist socialist relations in their classrooms and schools (Allman, 1999; Allman, McLaren, & Rikowski, 2000; Carlson, 1988a, b; Shor, 1987). In this way, a dialectical conception of the relationship between schools and capitalism, in a Marxist, dialectical materialist sense, poses a significant challenge to the economic determinism of Bowles and Gintis, one that still recognizes that the superstructure is emergent from, but not reducible to, the economic base (Apple, 2000; Creaven, 2000).

In a Marxist conception, schools, as part of the superstructure, have a contradictory relationship with the relations of capitalist production. Fritzell's (1987) explanation of the contradictory nature of the State's relationship with the economic base is apt for the present discussion about education, when he observes that:

[It] could be argued that in a functional context the autonomy of the State refers essentially to a *potentiality*, insofar as it is granted that even under empirical conditions of advanced capitalism the State cannot in the long run enforce policies and interventions that are basically destructive to the commodity form of economic production. (p. 27, original emphasis)

Fritzell roots the essential contradiction of the position of the State in the fact that it is fundamentally outside of the process of producing commodities—"autonomous from the commodity form," yet it still is required under capitalism to support the production of those commodities and thus "cannot...enforce policies...that are basically destructive to the commodity form." In relation to capitalist production and social reproduction, the State is required to work out this internal contradiction. Schools, on behalf of the State-superstructure, have to simultaneously accomplish the fundamentally contradictory goals of reproducing the social and material relations of capitalist production while hegemonically working to win the "spontaneous consent" of the students/workers through appeals to individual equality within the educational and social meritocracy (Apple, 1995). This contradiction presents a dialectical relationship between production of capitalist social relations and the maintenance of bourgeois hegemony vis-à-vis education.

ON (RE)PRODUCTION

In light of the above discussion, in this book I use the term "(re)production" to frame my analysis of the relationship between high-stakes, standardized testing and socioeconomic inequality. My use of this term is very specific. Clearly, there is the phenomenon of the "production" of inequality, and just as clearly there is the "reproduction" of inequality. These two verbs connote two different but related meanings. Production suggests origination. So, to say that high-stakes, standardized tests produce inequality suggests that inequality is originally produced by the tests themselves and that institutions of education are also a source of this production. On one level, I believe this to be true. As I argue here, schools are sites for the production of inequality as well as the production of resistance to such inequality in their own right, and deserve to be analyzed as such (Apple, 1995).

However, I do not think that schools are totally independent institutions either. The empirical evidence to the contrary outlined above is just too strong, as we see schools also reproducing inequalities that exist more broadly in society and the economy (Anyon, 2005). Thus, reproduction suggests a copying, imitation, or conduction of something that originates elsewhere—in this case, extant to schools. So, to say that high-stakes, standardized tests reproduce inequality suggests that the tests are operating as a conduit for a process or phenomenon that exists outside of education, perhaps as a mirror of socioeconomic relations. By using the term (re)production, I want to suggest that education, schools, and high-stakes, standardized tests do *both*: They produce inequalities in their own right *and* they reproduce inequalities that exist more broadly outside of schools.

Such relationships are dynamic, interactional, fluid, and relational and therefore do not allow for linear, mechanical, one-to-one chains of causality or correspondence (Allman, 1999; Engels, 1940; Ollman, 2003). In this sense my use of the term (re)production attempts to grasp at what I feel is the dialectical relationships that exist within schools themselves as well as between schools and socioeconomic structures. Indeed, this conception of (re)production is one of the central tenets of my analysis, and evidence will be provided to support this position in every chapter of this book

THE SCOPE AND LIMITS OF THIS BOOK

Scope

In this introductory chapter, I have discussed the issue of educational inequality in the United States, posed my central question, and reviewed the academic discussion surrounding social reproduction in education and critical educational theory. On the whole, the rest of this book consists of a series of critical analyses of the relationship between high-stakes testing and educational inequality that embody several approaches. In Chapter 2 I take up a critical historical analysis by examining the legacies of inequality and capitalist forms of production associated with the origins of high-stakes testing in the Eugenics, I.Q., and "social efficiency" movements in education in the United States. Such an analysis serves to demystify high-stakes, standardized testing as being rooted in marking socioeconomic inequalities, as opposed to being an objective, fair, and meritocratic measurements of humans. In Chapter 3 I provide a political-economic analysis of high-stakes testing by outlining both how ideologies of equality, as well as the economics of test-associated education policy, relate to contemporary capitalist production and politics. There, I trace the modern day high-stakes testing movement, including its origins in the publication of *A Nation At Risk* and its explicit, sometimes conflicted, relationship to the needs of capital. Through this analysis I connect the history of inequality associated with high-stakes testing with contemporary policy. In Chapter 4, I offer a more empirically based analysis of how high-stakes testing affects the curriculum and how its effects exert types of control over pedagogic discourse and identities. In this way I begin to illustrate how the inequalities embedded in these tests manifest in actual classroom practice. Then, in Chapter 5 I apply the critical sociology of knowledge to offer an explanation of high-stakes testing as a mechanism for the (re) production of dominant social relations. Using the conceptual framework provided by Basil Bernstein, I explain how high-stakes tests, as a manifestation of the "pedagogic device" in practice, embed inequality in the very structure of pedagogic discourse itself. Finally, in Chapter 6 I offer some conclusions and implications of my analysis, hopefully developing deeper understandings of schools, social reproduction, relative autonomy, and the curriculum.

Limits

One of the most difficult things for any researcher, in the field of education or elsewhere, is defining the limits of a study and bracketing any number of critical issues as existing outside the focus of a particular study. Therefore I must make clear that the focus of this book is quite specific. I will be looking at high-stakes testing, the curriculum, and their relationship to the most significant achievement gaps in education today—race and class. These gaps exist empirically, and I offer an analysis and explanation of a particular process, among others, that contributes to this educational inequality. Further, high-stakes testing is just one aspect of the entire educational system among others. There are an infinite number of possibilities for educational research, from classroom discourse, to hallway interactions, to staff meetings, to school board meetings, to school/community relations, etc., that impinge upon and influence relations in schools. For the purposes of this study, and to maintain a clear focus on a singular phenomenon, I am leaving these areas aside. Such a focus means that, for instance, I will be taking the race and class-based outcomes of high-stakes testing systems as an a priori fact, but will not necessarily be dealing with how high-stakes testing contributes to the process of *racialization* (Omi & Winant, 1994) of students of color or how class identities are constructed (Willis, 1977) through high-stakes testing.

My focus here generally also neglects the processes of masculinization and feminization in education, as well as other issues dealing with sexuality and disability studies. This is not to say that these processes are unimportant or unworthy of inclusion or analysis. Indeed there is good, critical work being done in these areas (see, e.g., Benjamin, 2001;

Erevelles, 2005). For instance, high-stakes testing, with its philosophically positivist claims to objectivity and comparison, embody particular historically gendered norms (Benton & Craib, 2001), and therefore must play a role in the construction of the identities and achievement of male, female, or intersex students. This is also not to say that testing, gender, race, and class, etc., do not overlap or intersect each other, and, while I may briefly touch upon how masculinity and race intersect in regards to testing (see Chapter 5) or the historical feminization of the teaching profession (see Chapter 2), a full treatment of the complexities of gender construction and high-stakes testing is not possible given the current focus—just as a full treatment of the processes of racialization and class constitution is not either.

Rather, I carry into my analysis an assumption that, when one discusses economic class, for instance, such a discussion inherently carries with it racial, gender-based, or cultural dimensions, and that such a focus does not necessarily deny the ways in which social, cultural and economic inequalities are intertwined and are often used to instantiate each other. Indeed, I do not want to fall prey to, nor do I uphold, a completely economic or economist view of race, gender, or culture—a longstanding and sometimes correct critique of Marxist analyses of society and the economy (Apple, 1995). In this sense I concur with Fraser's (1995) work on the complex relationship between economic/material redistribution and that of cultural/identity recognition associated with constructions of race and gender among others, who argues that:

> [T]his distinction between economic injustice and cultural injustice is analytical. In practice, the two are intertwined. Even the most material economic institutions have a constitutive, irreducible cultural dimension; they are shot through with significations and norms. Conversely, even the most discursive cultural practices have a constitutive, irreducible political-economic dimension; they are underpinned by material supports. Thus, far from occupying two airtight separate spheres, economic injustice and cultural injustice are usually interimbricated so as to reinforce one another dialectically. Cultural norms that are unfairly biased against some are institutionalized in the state and the economy; meanwhile, economic disadvantage impedes equal participation in the making of culture, in public spheres and in everyday life. (pp. 72–73)

Thus what I am after in this book is an explanation of the (re)production of race and class based inequality that are particularly pressing in education today (King, 2006). My intent here is to interrogate the relationship between high-stakes testing and the (re)production of social and economic inequalities *generally*, while leaving room for understanding that such inequalities are in fact multidimensional at every turn.

POSITIONING THE AUTHOR

As a critical educational theorist and activist academic, I realize it is important to position myself in relation to the project undertaken in this book. For this project, like all projects, the scope and limits of it are in part guided by my own autobiography, political commitments, beliefs, and worldview. My Chinese American grandfather and father were both active leftists. This has meant, to varying degrees, that I was raised within a milieu of social activism and critiques of capitalism, with the language of anti-oppression entering into my vocabulary at a very early age. For instance, I have very strong memories of being eight years old and participating in the 1980 May Day demonstrations in downtown Seattle, and at 13, participating in anti-apartheid demonstrations on Telegraph Avenue in Berkeley. Such participation was always accompanied by analysis, including long conversations about racism, imperialism, class exploitation, and women's oppression (sometimes too long in the mind of a young teenager). These aspects of my personal experience helped establish in me an internal drive to work for social change and contributed to my decision to become a public high school teacher.

My academic research followed my work in urban educational settings for 11 years, all of which were informed by my commitment to critical analyses of schools, economy, culture, and society. Over half of this time was spent working with students in Upward Bound, a program that serves low-income, first generation college-bound high school students. The two programs that I worked with served large populations of working-class African American, Native American, Asian American, and White students in the Puget Sound region. Upward Bound, and the incredible kids involved in the program, helped me conclude that I really did want to be a teacher, and so, after earning my credential, I spent seven years as a high school Social Studies and English/Language Arts teacher in both Seattle and Berkeley. My time in Seattle was mostly spent teaching at and running a small, alternative public school for "drop-outs," and my time in Berkeley was spent teaching at the infamous and heavily researched Berkeley High School (where I was fortunate enough to be able to teach courses in Ethnic Studies and Asian American Studies in addition to more typical courses). Like so many others, I was drawn to working with the students who struggled most in the public school system, and much of the impetus for my research stems from my drive to understand the mechanisms in schools and society that caused my students to struggle.

Because of my concern for issues of social justice, my teaching worked in tandem with my educational activism, which first manifested in my writing for the progressive education journal *Rethinking Schools*, where I now serve on the editorial board. Similarly, it was through *Rethinking Schools* that I became aware of and connected to the now dormant National Coalition of Education Activists (NCEA), where I also spent time as a steering committee member and co-chair. Both of these organizations are (or were, as in the case of NCEA) made up of committed, serious individuals who work for social justice through education, schools, and communities, and both organizations provided me with an overall orientation for my political work in the field. More locally, this resulted in my participation as a co-founder of the Puget Sound Rethinking Schools group, a Seattle area group of teachers organizing for educational reform, a co-founder of Education Not Incarceration in California—a Bay Area group of teachers, community activists, and youth organizers who challenge the state of California's prioritization of prison spending over education investment, as well as small schools reform work at Berkeley High, which, at its origins, was committed to closing the vast achievement gap that exists there.

My scholarly work stems from these political commitments and generally follows several of the tasks of the critical education theorist (Apple, 2006b; Apple & Au, in press). Thus, part of the task I undertake in this book is to "bear witness to negativity." That is, one of the primary functions of my work is "to illuminate the ways in which educational policy and practice are connected to the relations of exploitation and domination in the larger society" (Apple, 2006b, p. 681). However, more than just taking up a critique of socioeducational inequalities, I also seek to "critically examine current realities with a conceptual/political framework that emphasizes the spaces in which counterhegemonic actions can be or are now going on" (p. 681), something I highlight in every chapter of this book. In addition, my scholarly work is part of a larger project of keeping the tradition of radical theory alive; I see part of my project in this volume as bolstering the Marxist and critical educational theoretical tradition, illustrating the soundness, value, and explanatory power of such analyses. Finally, my work here seeks to act in concert with progressive social and educational movements, lending my expertise and research in support of an agenda of working toward social justice in schools and society (Apple & Au, in press).

2

WE ARE ALL WIDGETS

Standardized Testing and The Hegemonic
Logics of the Educational Assembly Line

Our schools are, in a sense, factories in which the raw products
(children) are to be shaped and fashioned into products to meet
the various demands of life. The specifications for manufacturing
come from the demands of twentieth-century civilization, and it
is the business of school to build its pupils according to specifications laid down.

Stanford University Professor Ellwood Cubberley (1916, p. 338)

As Schneider and Ingram (1997) observe, "Policy designs are produced through a dynamic historical process involving the social constructions of knowledge and identities of target populations, power
relationships, and institutions" (p. 5). As a policy design, high-stakes
testing has its own historical context from which it sprang, as well
as its own trajectory over time, and an understanding of the foundational context of high-stakes testing is crucial to understanding its
relationship within contemporary educational and social inequality. In this chapter I seek to contextualize and demystify high-stakes
testing by examining the material conditions that have shaped and
formed this policy tool during the 20th century. As such, the ideological, social, and educational history I relay here provides a foundational conception of the connections between schools and capitalism
that have stretched over the last 120-plus years. In doing so, I place
high-stakes testing specifically within the context of evolving social

19

and economic relations as well as illustrate how this type of education is associated with the (re)production of inequality.[1] Thus, as I argue in this chapter, we can see how the incorporation of capitalist ideology in school reform, as well as the application of elitist testing, illustrate high-stakes testing's legacy of inequality, where both school organization and standardized tests enabled the maintenance of strict institutional and social hierarchies.

I begin here with a look at the social efficiency movement of the early 1900s, tracing the application of the principles of "scientific management" to education, specifically the effects of the application of these principles on school organization and the curriculum. I then explore why this particular vision of education, one associated with the logics of industrial capitalist production, came to be instituted as the dominant model for schooling in the United States.[2] I further argue that, looking back to its origins in the eugenics movement, standardized testing provided the technological apparatus for the functioning of the production model of education for four reasons: They allow for the efficient categorizing and sorting of human populations; in the process they commodify human beings, thus allowing learners to be viewed and treated as products; they increase the capacity of authorities to surveil and control processes of educational production; through the perpetuation of the myth of meritocracy, they provide ideological cover for the social, economic, and educational inequalities the tests themselves help maintain. Finally, I conclude this chapter with a more contemporary look at how inequality is deeply embedded in the structure of standardized tests themselves through an analysis of the contemporary college entrance exam, the Scholastic Achievement Test, and its historical and structural links to the racist eugenics movement.

SCIENTIFICALLY MANAGED EDUCATION

In the early 1900s there were strong pulls for a more radically democratic, working-class centered vision of both the workplace and society. During this time, the interests of capital engaged in a protracted fight with an insurgent, popular labor organizing movement (Boyer & Morais, 1975; Zinn, 1995). Public schools, rapidly increasing in size and social influence, proved to be a site where aspects of this fight played out and where curricular leaders struggled over competing visions of the aims and purposes of, as well as approaches to, education. An examination of this period, particularly of the work of John Franklin Bobbitt, serves here to illustrate how systems of standardization in education created conditions for increasing control over the process of education and lay the groundwork for the rise of standardized testing.

According to Kliebard (1979), no one "exemplified [the] spirit of scientific curriculum making more than John Franklin Bobbitt" (p. 74), because he was "the man who gave shape and direction to the curriculum field" (Kliebard, 1975, p. 55). Bobbitt was first brought to the University of Chicago's Department of Education as a lecturer in 1909. By 1910 he was promoted to the position of Instructor of School Administration, and by 1912 Bobbitt published his first article, "The Elimination of Waste in Education" (Bobbitt, 1912) which started his career as a leader in the field of curriculum (Kliebard, 2004). Bobbitt's importance in the history of curriculum studies lays in his application of Frederick Taylor's concepts of scientific management in factory production to systems of education. For Taylor, efficient production relied upon the factory managers' ability to gather all the information possible about the work which they oversaw, systematically analyze it according to "scientific" methods, figure out the most efficient ways for workers to complete individual tasks, and then tell the worker exactly how to produce their products in an ordered manner. As Noble (1977) argues, this most significant aspect of scientific management secured "managerial control over the production process and lay the foundation for the systematic reorganization of work....(p. 264)." Scientific management[3] also became the backbone for what has been termed the "social efficiency movement." This movement, with the "scientific" backing offered by Taylorism, promoted the idea that social and governmental waste could be identified and cut, and that social order would spring from carefully studied systems of "scientific" planning (Kliebard, 2004).

Bobbitt's vision of socially efficiency in education embodied a constellation of concepts that reflect Taylor's vision of scientific management in industry. According to Bobbitt (1920), efficiency in education is built upon the predetermination of objectives that fundamentally drive the entire process of education:

> It is the objectives and the objectives alone...that dictate the pupil-experiences that make up the curriculum. It is then these in their turn that dictate the specific methods to be employed by the teachers and specific material helps and appliances and opportunities to be provided. These in their turn dictate the supervision, the nature of the supervisory organization, the quantity of finance, and the various other functions involved in attaining the desired results. And finally, it is the specific objectives that

provide standards to be employed in the measurement of results. We are trying to introduce scientific methods into every aspect of the field; but, quite clearly, the interrelationships of these factors are such that we can never develop scientific procedure throughout the field until we have laid a secure foundation in the careful determination of the objectives. (p. 142)

In Bobbitt' model, the objectives for students are based on their predicted future social and economic lives "according to their social and vocational destiny" (Bobbitt, 1913, p. 26), and whether or not students are meeting these objectives would be measured through the establishment of standards (Bobbitt, 1913, 1920).

Within Bobbitt's educational vision—as in Taylor's vision of workers—it is the job of the administrator to gather all possible information about the educational process to develop the best methods for teachers to get students to meet the standards. He explains:

The new and revolutionary doctrine of scientific management states in no uncertain terms that the management, the supervisory staff, has the largest share of the work in the determination of proper methods...Under scientific management, the supervisory staff, whose primary duty is direction and guidance, must therefore specialize in those matters that have most to do with direction and guidance, namely, the science relating to the processes. (Bobbitt, 1913, pp. 52–53)

Teachers must be required to follow the methods determined by their administrators because, according to Bobbitt, they are not capable of determining such methods themselves:

The burden of finding the best methods is too large and too complicated to be laid on the shoulders of the teachers... The ultimate worker, the teacher in our case, must be a specialist in the performance of the labor that will produce the product. (Bobbitt, 1913, pp. 52–53)

And finally, principals and other administrators should use tests to determine "weak" and "strong" teachers as well as rates of teacher pay or access to other privileges (Bobbitt, 1913).

Bobbitt maps the industrial metaphor on to schools in a very simple and neat way. Students are the "raw materials" to be shaped into finished products according to their future social positions. Teachers are the workers who employ the most efficient methods to get students to meet the predetermined standards and objectives. Administrators are the managers who determine and dictate to teachers the most efficient methods in the production process. The school is the factory assembly line where this process takes place.

MEANS-ENDS RATIONALITY IN EDUCATION

The application of the principles of scientific management, however, included more than a change in style of school organization and management. It also provided the logic of technical control that would define the core of the curriculum. As Kliebard (2004) explains:

> [T]he use of scientific management techniques went far beyond the application of Taylor's ideas to the administration of schools; it ultimately provided the language and hence the conceptual apparatus by which a new and powerful approach to curriculum development would be wrought...Those educational leaders who forged the new doctrine made no secret of the source of their ideas, self-consciously and conspicuously following the principles of Taylorism in an effort to make curriculum a direct and potent force in the lives of future citizens... (pp. 82–83)

This logic, that of the "scientific," socially efficient education, asserts that the endpoints of predetermined objectives and/or standards alone drive the educational process (the production of educated students). All other aspects of education therefore must serve the ends of the education process. To do otherwise would be inefficient or wasteful. Students thus acquire content learning purely based on predetermination. Teachers then deliver this content via the administratively predetermined "scientific" methods. Subsequently, tests measure whether or not the goals of the predetermined content are met. The ends determine the means. This type of logic is termed "means-ends rationality," and assumes that, "it is a *technical* matter to decide such issues as instructional method and content, a matter best reserved for people with technical expertise about the methods and content optimally suited for particular objective" (Posner, 1988, p. 80).

Means-ends rationality has had tremendous impact on the shape of curricular content and student learning in the United States. Kliebard (1979) explains that:

> The implications of the application of scientific precision to the curriculum planning process by Bobbitt and his contemporaries were enormous. First, a standard procedure for stating the

> objectives of the curriculum was instituted....Second, the subjects of study would no longer be the central feature of the curriculum; they became relegated to the status of the *means* by which objectives...would be achieved. (p. 76, original emphasis)

Such precision allowed the curriculum to be broken down into minute units of work that could be determined in advance, taught in a linear manner, and easily assessed (Apple, 2000; M. L. Smith, 2004). Thus, "Curriculum development became an effort to standardize the means by which predetermined specific outcomes might be achieved" (Kliebard, 1979, p. 75). Moving toward a means-ends rationalized curriculum also greatly affected the relationships of teachers and students in the process of education: It dehumanized them both by alienating them from their own creativity and intellectual curiosity. Thus, according to Kliebard (1975):

> In education, as in industry, the standardization of the product also means the standardization of work. Educational activity which may have an organic wholeness and vital meaning takes on a significance only in terms of its contribution to the efficient production of the finished product. As in industry, the price of worship at the altar of efficiency is the alienation of the worker from his work—where continuity and wholeness of the enterprise are destroyed for those who engage in it. (pp. 65–66)

Additionally, as will be discussed in more detail later in this chapter, the application of the principles of scientific management to education allowed for continued administrative control over the process of teaching itself because it usurped substantial amounts of power from teachers-as-workers and allowed for increased surveillance over their teaching (Apple, 1979/2004, 1986; Apple & Beyer, 1988; Braverman, 1974; Carlson, 1988b; Noble, 1977).

Curricular means-ends rationality also maintained and justified socioeconomic hierarchies. With an unapologetic eye toward social engineering, the socially efficient curriculum would only teach learners information that they would use in their future roles in life. The development of the socially efficient curriculum included the "scientific" measurement and prediction of a student's future and the prescribing of appropriate content to match that prediction because it was considered wasteful for a student to learn anything beyond their predetermined life roles (Bobbitt, 1912; Kliebard, 1975, 2004). Kliebard (1988) remarks that:

...[A]n important concomitant of scientific curriculum-making became curriculum differentiation in which different curricula were prescribed for different groups depending on certain characteristics. These criteria included some measure of native intelligence, probable destination (particularly whether one was destined to go to college or not), and even social class. In this way, the curriculum could be geared directly to the activities one needed to perform in one's adult life. (p. 25)

The socially efficient curriculum entrenched the inequality of the status quo. The work you or your family do is merely the work you or your family is intended to do within the existing socioeconomic relations. Within this logic, society achieves progress if everyone plays their proper roles, therefore allowing society to develop along the most efficient lines (Kliebard, 2004). Backed by this new "science," it was thought that the curriculum could create social stability where there was instability, and could also be more cost efficient in terms of student output (Kliebard, 1975, 1988, 2004).

It is important to recognize at least two things. First, Bobbitt's educational vision was far from singular. Other educational leaders such as Snedden, Cubberley, Thorndike, and Spaulding also openly advocated the same capitalist production-minded educational reforms (Callahan, 1964; Cuban, 2004; Hursh & Ross, 2000). Second, even though this issue will be dealt with more thoroughly later in this chapter and Chapter 3, now almost 100 years later, it is not too far of a stretch to see the influence of social efficiency and forms of industrial capitalist production present in the organization of schools today. For instance, simply look at the structure of our high schools where students are typically housed in large, centralized facilities, moved from teacher to teacher and subject to subject at an evenly defined pace (periods and semesters), adding credits to their transcripts, until they are declared completed products at the end of their journey along the educational assembly line, receive their diplomas and graduate.

THE INSTITUTIONALIZATION OF THE PRODUCTION MODEL IN EDUCATION

As Timar and Tyack (1999) explain, private industry played a significant role in shaping the structure of the system of education in the early 1900s:

Accrediting agencies gave the stamp of approval to schools that were up to date. Some private companies created tests of "intelligence" and "achievement," while others cobbled together student textbooks. Foundations subsidized surveys and financed pilot projects...They were agents of private, not public, government. Everyday decision making in education remained officially with the public, which elected officials at the state and local levels. Informally, though, reformers determined much policy within their new, and buffered, hierarchies. (p. 10)

Considering the fact that during the late 1800s and early 1900s public education was largely a decentralized endeavor left up to local school boards (Counts, 1927/1969; Howell, 2005; Timar & Tyack, 1999), a significant question remains: How did the business model associated with capitalist production take hold in public education in the United States in the early 1900s? Cuban (2004) asserts that there are three central reasons why schools adopted business-like reforms: 1) A popular American belief that more education means more individual prosperity, and by extension national prosperity, in the economy (local and global); 2) civic and business leaders have continually looked to schools as a means of addressing national concerns; 3) school boards, which hold significant power in determining policy at the local level, are elected. As elected leaders, school board members are responsive to well financed and organized members of the community, the business community in particular (pp. 69–70).

Clearly, there is some merit to Cuban's (2004) argument. For instance, many people in the United Stats hold the long-standing commonsense belief that more education automatically equals more prosperity. This belief hinges, in part, on the idea of the American meritocracy—that individuals freely compete against each other, in part through education, and those that work the hardest make the most personal and economic gains (Lemann, 1999). Further, as I discuss in Chapter 3, it is also true that over the last 120 years business leaders and elected officials have constantly asserted that the education system operates as a mechanism of social reform. While Cuban's third reason does hold more merit, these first two reasons for the institutionalization of business models in education fall somewhat short because they remain largely in the realm of ideology and forego any substantive discussion of social conditions and economic tensions that shaped education according to the logics of capitalist production. I would argue that there are four central social and economic processes that lead to the institutionalization of the industrial capitalist production model of education, one of which coincides with aspects of Cuban's analysis, and three others that his analysis glosses.

Efficiency in Education and Society

One reason for the dominance of the production metaphor in education that is noticeably absent from Cuban's (2004) explanation is the social and educational context of the late nineteenth and early 20th century. For instance, as an extension of the social efficiency movement, the public placed tremendous pressure on schools and other large institutions to be less wasteful in times of fiscal restraint and economic instability (Callahan, 1964; Kliebard, 1988, 2004). Another related reason for the institutionalization of the model of capitalist production in education was the development of economies of scale in education during this time period. In the 1880s, for instance, public education had grown enough so that enrollment in free public high schools in the northern states surpassed those of private schools (Reese, 1998). Fourteen million immigrants entered the United States between 1865 and 1900 and one million a year more came for several years after 1900 (Callahan, 1964). It has been estimated that between 1890 and 1917, the U.S. population nearly doubled, with nine million immigrants entering the country in the first decade of the 1900s alone. Between 1920 and 1930, student enrollment in public schools rose by 22%, from 23.3 million to 28.3 million students (Chapman, 1988). The arrival of new immigrants and a general rise in the school bound population created schools of increasing sizes. Thus, as early as 1910, public high schools generally adopted the policy of moving students through five or six class periods of 45 to 60 minutes a day, making the experience similar to movement along a factory process line in the interest of efficiency. Increases in school size also meant increases in teaching loads as well, where high school teachers commonly taught between 150 and 200 different students a day (Callahan, 1964).[4] From a purely pragmatic perspective, a factory-like production approach is one way to efficiently address the institutional capacity demands created by mass education.

Social Control

There is, however, also an argument to be made that the adoption of measures of social efficiency in public education can be attributed to aspects of social control. The period between the 1880s and the 1920s, where industrial capitalists established increasing control of both production and society, was marked by massive struggles regarding the rights of workers. A brief survey of the amount of labor organizing and unrest during this time illustrates my point. During the 1870s and 1880s, the American Federation of Labor and railroad brotherhoods grew out of fights between labor and capital. During the Haymarket Riot of 1886, police brutalized workers, furthering the resolve of labor to organize against state repression. Several massive strikes also took place in the 1890s, including the Pullman and Homestead strikes, where many workers were killed. At the turn of the century, worker strikes only increased. The United Mine workers struck in 1900, 1902, and 1912, and the Western Federation of Miners struck in 1907. In 1909 workers struck against the Pressed Steel Car Company; the International Ladies Garment Workers struck as well. GE workers struck the Schenectady plant in 1913, and Westinghouse workers struck plants in Pittsburgh in 1915. Workers were also involved in free-speech struggles in Spokane, Washington, Fresno and San Diego, California in 1909 and 1912. Additionally, the Boston police strike, Seattle general strike, and United States Steel Strike all happened in 1919. In the midst of this domestic organizing, the Bolshevik Revolution in Russia happened in 1917, further advancing the power of workers around the world (Noble, 1977; Zinn, 1995).[5]

Between the increased influx of immigrants and the increased assertion by workers' to control the processes and products of their labor, industrial capitalists, in an attempt to increase their control over the workers themselves, promoted to the model of "scientific management" as a means of asserting control over the labor process (Braverman, 1974; Noble, 1977). Likewise, the growing influence of public schools in the socialization of working people during times of social upheaval and unrest meant that they were positioned to play a central role in shaping the new, socially efficient, and hence, more stable, society (Karier, 1967; Kliebard, 1988, 2004).[6]

Rise of Curricular Professionals

The class of professionals in the curriculum field like Bobbitt, who built their careers on technical expertise as educational "engineers," also provides another reason for the adoption and implementation of capitalist production models in education (Noble, 1977). In a process mirroring what took place with Taylorism and the rise of industrial capitalism generally, engineers (both curricular and industrial) struggled to establish themselves as necessary parts of the production process. Meiksins (1984) explains that the advent of large-scale capitalist production posed a dilemma for the once semi-independent, technically skilled, small shop engineer of the 19th century. As small shops disappeared under the growing shadow of industrial capitalism, these engineers began losing their autonomy and were increasingly employed by large production facilities in need of their technical expertise. This change transformed the role of the engineer, who,

> ...was shifted from his old role as proprietor of a small machine-shop to the role of employee of a large capitalist organization. He had become part of the complex, collective labor process created by the dynamics of modern capitalism. (Meiksins, 1984, p. 188)

Scientific management can thus be understood more generally as a response of this class fraction of engineers to their new, now less autonomous position within the production process. Taylorism was thus in reality,

> ...a kind of engineering ideology; a response to changing circumstances which offered, at once, to solve the problem of organizing the workplace and the labor of conception *and* the problem of how engineers could retain some of their traditional autonomy. (Meiksins, 1984, p. 189, original emphasis)

Curriculum experts like Bobbitt, Charters, Thorndike, Spaulding, Cubberley, Snedden, and others justified their own existence in the process of education by asserting the need for their expertise in order run the schools efficiently. Consequently, another explanation for the adoption of the capitalist production model in education appears within the field of education itself, as an ascendant class fraction of educational engineers doing "scientific" curriculum-making established its power base within the developing social/educational hierarchy. As I will argue later on in my discussion of high-stakes testing and No Child Left Behind, descendents of this class fraction, in the form of the professional and managerial new middle class, still hold significant power within contemporary educational structures.

School Board Demographics

The final, related, explanation of how the industrial capitalist model of education became hegemonic lies in the composition of school boards. Until the most recent era of educational policy, schools in the United States have been largely decentralized—at least in relation to the federal and state levels, as most educational decisions were left to local school boards (Cuban, 2004; Timar & Tyack, 1999). Reflecting on this time period, Counts (1927/1969) observed that:

> The fundamental character of public education in the United States is...determined by the board that controls the school. To be sure, back of the board stands the state, but to the board the state has delegated the practical control of public education. Within the wide limits created by legislative enactment, the broad outlines of policy are shaped by the members of this body...To a degree and in a fashion seldom grasped, the content, spirit, and purpose of public education must reflect the bias, the limitations, and the experience of the membership of this board. (p. 1)

Given the historical lack of a centralized, federal body in control of public education in the United States, Counts' explanation of the power of school boards to shape the direction of public education at the local level is an ultimately reasonable, if not a patently correct, assertion (Howell, 2005; Timar & Tyack, 1999). "As new state charters altered the form of governance of city schools," Timar and Tyack (1999) explain, "school boards increasingly were composed of business and professional elites elected at large rather than by districts" (p. 8).

Several studies of the composition of school boards during the early 1900s offer further evidence. For instance, in his study of 104 school boards from cities with populations over forty thousand, Nearing (1917) found that of the 967 total board members studied, 588 (60.8%) were either merchants, manufacturers, bankers, brokers, "real estate men," doctors or lawyers. Other board members were also either retired businessmen or wives of businessmen, and only 87 of the 967 were laborers (Callahan, 1964). Another study of school-board members from 169 cities with populations ranging from 2,500 to 250,000 found that, of the 761 total male board members, 455 (60%) were merchants, bankers, lawyers, physicians and business executives. Only 58 (7.6%) were classified as "manual labor" (Struble, 1922). In 1926 Counts (1927/1969) collected data from 532 city school boards,[7] with findings consistent to the two previous studies. Of the 2,934 male city school board members in Counts' study, 31% were "proprietors" (business owners), 31% were professionals, and 14% were managers. Only 6% and 8% of the male board members were clerical workers or manual laborers respectively, causing Counts to conclude that:

> [O]n the whole, the boards are very much alike all over the United States. Everywhere the boards are composed almost entirely of persons drawn from favored social and economic classes. (p. 58)

Thus, during the early 1900s, people who collectively benefited from capitalist production and economics predominated local school boards.

These boards not only influenced local school district policies, but also oversaw the hiring and firing of the district superintendents as well, giving them substantial control over the scope and direction of public education in the United States (Callahan, 1964; M. L. Smith, 2004).

While the research of Nearing, Struble, and Counts does an excellent job of highlighting the class interests at play in the composition of school boards of this time period, it is worth noting that the power wielded by these boards undoubtedly had gendered and racial dimensions as well. As Counts' (1927/1969) research confirms, school boards during the 1920s consisted of only 10% women. Likewise, the reporting of occupations of board members only included men. Based on Counts' work, we would have to presume that either the female board members were unemployed or that their employment was not officially recognized as an occupation (e.g., domestic work), thus reflecting a patriarchal bias both in the research and the times. Further, in terms of district hierarchies, the predominantly male school boards oversaw the work of a predominantly female teacher workforce. The percentage of women teaching elementary school increased from an estimated 59% in 1870 to nearly 89.5% by 1930, a number that has since remained relatively stable. This "feminization" of teaching coincided with patriarchal norms around women's work and the care of children, teaching and education being related to domestic training, as well as an economic push for women (and children) to work in factories as very cheap, highly exploitable labor (Apple, 1986; Blount, 1999). By the time the social efficiency movement was in full swing in the early 1900s, elementary teaching was largely a woman's profession.

It is also important to note that, while there are many reasons for this shift in the teaching force,[8] we must recognize a contradictory impulse here. On the one hand, the regulation of teaching by male-dominated school boards must be viewed as the assertion male authority over female labor. On the other hand, women were in fact actively asserting their power and opening up teaching, as well as other professions, as a space for increased female independence, where middle-class White women coincidentally initiated the first wave of feminism in the United States (Ferguson, 1984). Further, we must also presume that there were racial dimensions to board compositions as well, especially given the substantial number of racist laws and policies officially recognized and sanctioned all over the United States in this era. These, of course, stood along side the countless unofficial racist policies maintained by individuals and groups throughout the nation as well.

Schools boards, then, because of their social positioning, had a vested interest in maintaining their social and cultural power, via their institutional positions. Thus, the class, gender, and race implications of school board composition were also a concern for Counts (1927/1969) who declared that:

> A dominant class is a privileged class, a class that is favored by existing social arrangement. It therefore tends to be conservative, to exaggerate the merits of the prevailing order, and to fear any agitation favoring fundamental changes in the social structure. (p. 91)

Because of the social positioning of school board members and because of the amount of control that local school boards held over actual educational policy, school board composition provides one part of a plausible explanation for the hegemony of the model of capitalist production in education in the United States: These businessmen, and I use "men" here consciously, sought to shape school organization in ways that either reflected the practices of capitalist enterprise and/or reflected what they felt would be the best education to train future workers. In terms of hegemonic, commonsense consciousness, it is likely they thought capitalist forms of organization were simply the best way to run schools.

To a certain degree, it is here that I find merit in Cuban's (2004) third explanation that elected school board members "respond to well-organized, well-financed constituencies such as business leaders" (p. 70) in the adoption of business-minded, capitalist structured school reforms. True to Cuban's analysis, the elected school boards did in fact respond to the business community: They elected school board members mostly from their own ranks. Cuban, however, goes on to assert that regarding the manipulation of education by these businessmen, were unwarranted:

> Instead of being manipulated by interest groups, school board members drawn from business, managerial, and professional positions, more often than not, performed the civic roles for which they were elected. As elected officials they were expected to listen the public, sift data provided by administrators, and make decisions to serve the public good, not private interests....On the whole...board members drawn from business occupations met their civic expectations. (p. 83)

Cuban's analysis quite problematically misses the point. While certainly a possibility, the corruption of school board businessmen was not Counts' expressed concern, nor is it the concern of my overall argument here. The institutionalization of the industrial capitalist model does not require deviousness on the part of school board members, nor does it require that these business leaders shirk their civic duties as elected officials. Rather, the adoption of the business model in education simply requires that these school board members see the capitalist production model of school organization as the commonsense model for education reform.

Political and Curricular Resistance

Many individuals and organizations did resist the importation of the logics of capitalist production and scientific management into education. For instance, one of the loudest voices of protest at the time came from the official journal of the American Federation of Teachers (AFT), *American Teacher*, as the applications of the principles of social efficiency in education, both anti-union and anti-teacher, surely raised the ire of the AFT. Ironically, William C. Bagley, credited with being one of the first individuals to introduce the language of business into education, was a critic as well. According to Callahan (1964), both he and John Dewey "opposed the inappropriate application of business and industrial values and procedures to the schools and both criticized the oversimplified and superficial activity being engaged in, often in the name of science" (p. 124). However, Bagley did think that the application of science to schools was promising, but he did not expect it to solve all the problems at once. Likewise, Dewey approved of using testing, but was not in favor of how the test results were being used. He preferred them used for general diagnostic purposes, not to categorize or standardize individual students. Further, Dewey also questioned the "science" associated with social efficiency in schools, and argued that it was just typical teacher-centered education dressed in scientific terminology (Callahan, 1964).[9] Curriculum scholars such as George S. Counts, Harold Rugg, and others also fought against this trend and worked toward a more just, humanistic society during this time period (Callahan, 1964; Giordano, 2005; Hursh & Ross, 2000). Further, examples of curricular resistance to the inculcations of capitalist discourse, such as the Socialist community schools (Teitelbaum, 1993), manifested in many places both during this period and after (see also, Apple & Au, in press).

THE HEGEMONY OF SCIENTIFIC MANAGEMENT IN EDUCATION

However, even though there existed some choice between the education reforms offered by progressivists like John Dewey and that of the social efficiency of John Franklin Bobbitt, as Kliebard (1979) explains:

> [T]he emerging curriculum field clearly preferred the scientific precision and utilitarian payoff that social efficiency promised, and the impact of an ideological position drawing its modes of operation and criteria of success from the management industry has had a lasting...impact on curriculum thinking in the United States. (p. 80)

In part due to the make-up of school boards, in part due to the implementation of mass schooling in the United States, and in part due to a particularly heated struggle between capital and labor, scientific management and social efficiency in education became the dominant model. As Cuban (2004) writes:

> By the 1920s, business leaders were no longer in the forefront of school reform, but they could see the triumph of these core assumptions across the nation in new public school goals, reshaped governance, efficient organization, and differentiated curricula.... Occasionally challenged in subsequent decades, these assumptions about the relationships between education, the economy, and a stable society, and between business and schools, were generally unquestioned beliefs that shaped the thinking of business leaders, public officials, journalists, educators, and parents for the remainder of the twentieth century. (p. 50)

Consequently, the organizational structures, curriculum, and language of schooling and education in the United States came to be increasingly dominated by the logic and guiding principles of capitalist industry (Apple, 1979/2004; Callahan, 1964). Standardized testing played a prominent role in this process, largely because it proved to be the perfect technology for the efficient categorizing, sorting, and ranking of human populations. The origins of using these tests for sorting can be found within I.Q. testing and the eugenics movement.

I.Q. TESTING, EUGENICS, AND SOCIALLY EFFICIENCY

Standardized testing has its origins in the social efficiency movement and the institutionalization of the capitalist production model of education. These origins can be found in I.Q. testing and eugenics—the belief that intelligence is genetic and that certain races or ethnic groups are biologically inferior to Whites (Selden, 1999). Psychologist Alfred Binet, who had been commissioned by the French government to develop a way to assess if young children were mildly developmentally disabled, first developed the I.Q. test in France in 1904. His work in France established the "Binet Scale" of intelligence based on a measurement of a child's level of intellectual development in comparison to their chronological age. By dividing the first (mental age) by the second (chronological age), the idea of "intelligence quotient," or I.Q., was born (Gould, 1996). To be clear, Binet's use of testing was very specific:

- It was to be used on young children.
- It was purely a practical tool that in Binet's conception was not connected to any sense of hereditary or innate intelligence.
- It was considered to be a general empirical tool for making general decisions (as opposed to being a precise measurement for precise decisions).
- It was never intended to be used to measure children who were developing "normally."
- It was used with the intent of signaling that a child may need more help in their intellectual development (Gould, 1996).

However, when cognitive psychologists in the United States took up Binet's testing and measurement of I.Q., they distorted the fundamental use of the tests and their underlying presumptions about humans and human ability. Through the work of psychologists like Goddard, Terman, and Yerkes, I.Q. became thought of as hereditary and fixed, thus laying the groundwork for testing to be used to sort and rank different people by race, ethnicity, gender, and class according to supposedly inborn, innate intelligence (Gould, 1996).

In the United States, Yerkes played a particularly important role in this process. In 1917, as a psychologist and Army Colonel in charge of the mental testing of 1.75 million recruits during World War I, Yerkes worked with Goddard, Terman, and others to develop the Alpha and Beta Army tests. These tests were used to sort incoming soldiers and to determine their "mental fitness." Yerkes drew several dubious conclusions using this incredibly large pool of data. The first was that, according to his interpretation of the Army test results, the average White adult in the United States had an average mental age of 13. The second conclusion Yerkes arrived at was that the intelligence of European immigrants could be judged according to their country of origin: The darker peoples of eastern and southern Europe were less intelligent than their fairer-skinned, western and northern European counterparts. Yerkes' third conclusion was that African Americans were the least intelligent of all peoples. Not surprisingly, these findings were used by eugenicists of the time to rally around the idea that average American intelligence was declining due to the unregulated breeding of the poor and stupid, as well as the idea race mixing that was spreading the supposedly inferior intelligence of African Americans and immigrants (Giordano, 2005; Gould, 1996; Popham, 2001).

Thus, as Sacks (1999) explains, intelligence testing, with its penchant for sorting human populations, went hand in hand with the social efficiency movement:

> Ideology...under the guises of...managerial and social efficiency, drove these grand social experiments in the testing of army recruits, schoolchildren, and people aspiring to a college education. Testing became an early tool to try to weed out the intellectually weak from the cognitively strong. (p. 73)

The push to measure intelligence and compare different people is part and parcel with the social efficiency movement generally, and in education particularly. Literally echoing Bobbitt's calls for efficiency, schools needed a way to sort and rank their students according to their supposedly innate, native intelligence, thus preparing them for their "proper" future social roles. That poor people, African Americans, and darker southern and eastern Europeans were determined to have less intelligence just proved to these researchers that the tests were accurately measuring where each group fit within existing social and economic hierarchies (Selden, 1983, 1999). Thus, standardized testing, at its very root in intelligence testing and the eugenics movement, provided the technology to sort groups of people along race and class socioeconomic hierarchies (Apple, 1979/2004; Clarke, Madaus, Horn, & Ramos, 2000; Ellis, 2008; Selden, 1999; Stoskopf, 1999).

Like the principles of Taylorism, standardized I.Q. testing soon found its way into the institution of education. As Tyack (1974) explains:

> Intelligence testing and other forms of measurement provided the technology for classifying children. Nature-nurture controversies might pepper the scientific periodicals and magazines of the intelligentsia, but schoolmen found IQ tests invaluable means of channeling children; by the very act of channeling pupils, they helped to make IQ prophecies self-fulfilling. (p. 180)

Horace Mann, as secretary of the Massachusetts Board of Education in 1845, oversaw some of the first standardized testing of children in public schools. For Mann, these tests promised the development of a more efficient, standardized, and accountable way of assessing student learning (Chapman, 1988; Madaus & Kelleghan, 1993; Sacks, 1999). The trend of developing tests to measure efficiency in schools continued to grow into the early 1900s, where by 1911 the National Education Association had appointed the "Committee on Tests and Standards of

Efficiency in Schools and School Systems" and by 1913 several hand-writing and arithmetic tests had been created and were being used in some schools (Callahan, 1964).

Stanford University professor of psychology, Lewis M. Terman, under the sponsorship of the National Academy of Sciences, played a key role in adapting the above mentioned army tests into the National Intelligence Tests for schoolchildren in 1919, and by 1920 over 400,000 copies of these tests had been sold nationwide. Terman and others also created the Stanford Achievement Test in 1922, and by late 1925, he reported sales of this test to be near 1.5 million copies. Further, A 1925 survey of 215 cities with populations over 10,000 found that 64% of these cities used intelligence tests to classify and sort elementary students, 56% used the tests to classify and sort junior high school students, and 41 did the same for high school students. Another survey of superintendents of school districts in cities with populations over 10,000 people, completed in 1926, produced similar results. Marketing Terman's own later-developed intelligence test, the Terman Group Test, the World Book Company reported annual sales of over 775,000 tests by 1928 (Chapman, 1988). By 1932, 112 of 150 large city school systems in the United States had begun to use intelligence testing to place students into ability groups, and colleges had also begun to use these tests to justify admissions as well (Haney, 1984).

To be sure, it is no coincidence that I.Q. testing, eugenics, and standardized testing all became prominent during the same period that Bobbitt and others imported scientific management into education.[10] In terms of the political economy of the origins of testing, Bisseret (1979) argues that the shift toward genetically-based aptitude and the use of tests to measure such aptitude correspond with the ascendancy of bourgeoisie as the dominant class within capitalist production. According to Bisseret,

> The ideology of natural inequalities conceived and promoted by a social class at a time when it took economic, and later on political, power gradually turned into a scientific truth, borrowing from craniometry, then from anthropometry, biology, genetics, psychology, and sociology,...the elements enabling it to substantiate its assertions. And by this very means, it was able to impose itself upon all the social groups which believed in the values presiding over the birth of aptitude as an ideology: namely Progress and Science. (p. 26)

Thus, we can see how the rise of testing also fits with the rise of industrial capitalism in the United States and the establishment of race, class, and gender hierarchies (Karier, 1967). Further, in terms of prominent curriculum theorists, Bobbitt (1913) himself asserts that educational standards are to be based on the "native ability" of students, and their curriculum should reflect this "native ability." Bobbitt also was active in the eugenics movement. In addition to his belief in "native ability," in his article, "Practical Eugenics" (Bobbitt, 1909), he laments that not much could be done to help children of what he considered low or poor genetic stock. Bobbitt and others like him saw their work in education and curriculum as being directly linked to the more racist, classist, and nativist social engineering of the eugenics movement in the United States (Ellis, 2008; Selden, 1999).

It is important to note that, among others, African American educators were acutely aware of the racism inherent in both the eugenics and I.Q. testing movements. For instance, in 1940, W.E.B. DuBois recalled:

> It was not until I was long out of school and indeed after the (first) World War that there came the hurried use of the new technique of psychological tests, which were quickly adjusted so as to put black folk absolutely beyond the possibility of civilization. (as quoted in Guthrie, 1998, p. 55)

Indeed, as Stoskopf (1999) explains, the lower scores of African Americans were regularly used to track Black students into vocational education or for White teachers to explain away any difficulties these students might be having in their classrooms. One of the earliest African American educators to publicly challenge the findings of prominent psychologists involved in the I.Q. testing and eugenics movements was Horace Mann Bond—the Director of the School of Education at Langston University in Oklahoma. In 1924 Bond critiqued I.Q. testing and eugenics in *Crisis*, the magazine of the National Association for the Advancement of Colored People (NAACP). Martin Jenkins, the first African American to receive a PhD in psychology from Northwestern University, also completed research in the 1930s in the area of intelligence testing and found high test scores to be mainly linked to economic and educational privilege whether amongst Blacks or Whites (Stoskopf, 1999). Unfortunately, despite the work of these and other pioneering resisters to the racism embedded in standardized I.Q. tests (see also, Chapman, 1988; Giordano, 2005, for further discussion of resistance in the psychology community), the tests and their inherent inequalities became hegemonic, in part because the tests met the practical, political, and ideological needs of those working to fashion schools along the lines of industry.

STANDARDIZED TESTING AS A TECHNOLOGICAL, CONCEPTUAL, AND IDEOLOGICAL APPARATUS

So far, this chapter has largely been historical, as I've attempted to briefly explain the rise of the production model of education and the relationship of standardized testing to I.Q. testing, eugenics, and the social efficiency movement in education. It is important to recognize, however, that the technology of standardized testing, beyond its role in I.Q. and eugenics, proved to be a pivotal technical, conceptual, and ideological apparatus in the ascendancy of the application of scientific management and models of capitalist production to education. In essence, the tests, as a technology (Ellis, 2008; Madaus, 1994), enabled this form and vision of education to operate in several key ways. They establish universalized norms or standards through which to categorize, make comparisons, mark deviance and, hence, sort human populations under the guise of scientific objectivity; based on the establishment of objectivity, standardized tests also commodify those being measured by the tests, thereby allowing learners to be viewed and treated as products; commodification consequently allows learners to be categorized and sorted as "things," and creating conditions for systems of production to be monitored, surveiled, and ultimately disciplined; finally, standardized tests, resting on the foundational concepts of scientific objectivity and students-as-individual-commodities, ultimately uphold the ideology of meritocracy, which posits that all individuals have the opportunity to work hard and compete freely to achieve educational and social success in the United States. In what follows, I take up each of these points in more detail.

Standardization, Objectivity, and Objectification

Standardized test results are validated based on the assumption that they can be universally applied to different populations, thus enabling the fair and objective comparison of individuals across different contexts. This assumption, for instance, is what allows policy makers to assert that student X in Massachusetts has met a tested standard, but that student Y in California has not. The validity of such comparisons is only possible by assuming the universal objectivity of the test itself. In order for such comparisons to be meaningful, however, standardized tests have to deny certain amounts of local context, local variability, or local difference, thus establishing a common measurement that can reach across localities. Otherwise it would be impossible to compare student A to student B, school C to school D, district E to district F, state G to state H, and country I to country J. Hence, standardization, in order to maintain a claim to objectivity, has to assume that local, individual conditions and local, individual factors make no difference in either student performance or test-based measurement. Indeed, the assumed validity of objective measurement provided by standardized tests rests upon this denial of individual differences: The tests are considered objective because they supposedly measure all individuals equally and outside of any potential extenuating circumstances. Thus when students (and teachers, schools, districts, states, and countries) are measured by standardized testing and compared to other students, they are necessarily decontextualized in order to make such comparisons possible. Indeed, it is through such decontextualization that claims to objective measurement are maintained. In the process, students are literally "objectified."

In her study of the impact of high-stakes testing policies in Chicago schools, Lipman (2004) observes that:

> Students, as well as teachers, with all their varied talents and challenges, were reduced to a test score. And schools, as well as their communities, in all their complexity—their failings, inadequacies, strong points, superb and weak teachers, ethical commitments to collective uplift, their energy, demoralization, courage, potential, and setbacks—were blended, homogenized, and reduced to a stanine score... (p. 172)

The reduction to a numerical score is a key requirement of systems of standardized testing, because it enables the perpetuation of the means-ends rationality associated with social efficiency. In the process of the quantification of student knowledge and understanding, students themselves are necessarily quantified as a number. This quantification lies at the heart of the measurement itself, which turns real people and real social conditions into easily measurable and comparable numbers and categories. As De Lissovoy and McLaren (2003) state:

> The key principle at work in the use of standardized tests, which is also what allows them to serve as the mechanism for accountability initiatives, is the reduction of learning and knowledge to a number, i.e. a score. Once this takes place, scores can be compared, statistically analysed and variously manipulated....In reducing learning to a test score, policy makers seek to make the knowledge of disparate individuals commensurable. (p. 133)

Further, the process of reducing students to tests scores, essentially abstracting a number with which to define them in relation to other students, requires that their individuality be omitted, that their variability be disregarded and reduced "to one or two characteristics common to the larger universe of objects" (McNeil, 2005, p. 103). Standardized tests thus, by definition, literally objectify students by reducing them into decontextualized numerical objects for comparison. This objectification is the key link to understanding the fundamental connections between systems of standardized testing and the application of logics of capitalist production and social efficiency to education. By reducing students to numbers, standardized testing creates the capacity to view students as things, as quantities apart from their human qualities. Indeed, as Apple (2006a) argues, such standardization is a requirement for the marketization of education because comparison of educational commodities within systems of school "choice" requires a standard from which comparisons may arise.

Standardized Testing, Commodification, and Commodity Fetishism

The objectification-through-quantification of students by standardized testing consequently creates the capacity for students to be seen as products, and for education to be conceived of within the paradigm of production. In this way, standardized testing essentially *commodifies* students, that is, the tests turn students into commodities to be produced, inspected, and compared (Berlak, 2000; Sleeter, 2005). Consequently, standardized tests, through the commodification of students and education, enable systems of education to be framed as akin to systems of commerce, even if central assumptions guiding this framing are fundamentally flawed (Cuban, 2004), because the logics of capitalist production require products (commodities) to be made, assessed, compared, and exchanged on the market (Brosio, 1994; Marx, 1967). Thus, we see how standardized testing enables schools to be viewed as factories, where teachers-as-laborers work on an educational assembly line "producing" students-as-commodities, and whose value is measured and compared vis-à-vis the tests.[11]

Such a view of the production of commodities (whether students or material goods) is problematic, however, because it evacuates the actual human relations that exist in the process of their production. As Marx (1967) explains, in the process of production and exchange of commodities under capitalism, something "mysterious" happens:

> A commodity is therefore a mysterious thing, simply because in it the social character of [human] labour appears...as an objective character stamped upon the product of that labour: because the relation of the producers to the sum total of their own labour is

presented to them as a social relation, existing not between themselves, but between the products of their labour. This is the reason
why the products of labour become commodities, social things
whose qualities are at the same time perceptible and impercep-
tible by the senses. (p. 72)

Here Marx explains that, under capitalism, when we deal with commodities, we see them as having characteristics that exist separately
from the social relations that went into their production. Put differently, when the average U.S. consumer purchases a Nike soccer ball, for
instance, they rarely see or take account the Pakistani child labor that
might have gone into the production of that soccer ball. Thus, the labor
that goes into a commodity is masked because we see commodities as
things and not as the manifestation of labor that went into the production of that thing. As Marx (1967) explains, labor thus appears to exist
as relationships between things, "between the products of...labour," as
opposed to relationships between people, "as a social relation...between
themselves." This disconnection of labor from commodities, this mysterious relationship between labor itself and the products of labor under
capitalism, is what Marx calls a fetish of commodities, "which attaches
itself to the products of labour, so soon as they are produced as commodities..." (p. 72).

Although the comparison is not exact, Marx's concept of commodity fetishism provides a window into how students are viewed within
the capitalist logics of standardized testing. As soon as a commitment
to the assumptions of standardized tests is made, students are viewed
as commodities. This is evident in the reduction of students (or teachers or schools) to mere test scores, discussed above, where their value
in the educational marketplace is measured by their testing achieve-
ments. This value is determined through the measurement, categorization, and comparison of students-as-commodities, for they gain or
lose their value only in relation to other students (other commodities):
Those with higher test scores are more highly valued and can gain more
highly valued credentials and diplomas, thus further increasing their
value within the educational and employment marketplaces. Likewise,
those with lower test scores are similarly commodified with lower value
and for lower level work (Lapayese, 2007).

Within systems of standardized testing, then, the value of students is therefore not to be found in their humanity. Rather, students'
value is found in their test scores—reified, objectified, commodified,
one-dimensional, and highly abstracted versions of the human beings
sitting in a classroom. What is lost in this vision of students-as-com-

modities, what is fetishized in this process, are the social relations that exist "behind" these test scores. Hence, students' lives, home cultures, histories, educational differences, and socioeconomic conditions mean nothing within the logics of high-stakes, standardized testing. The realities of local conditions or specific contexts that impact, affect, and shape student performance are denied by standardized testing regimes. Instead, a universalized norm is imposed from above regarding what the products (student-commodities) need to be like, in the same stroke alienating students from the process of education. Consequently, distancing test scores from the realities of students' lives and school conditions, systems of high-stakes testing effectively mask the existence of social relations and structural inequalities exploitation that persist in their lives, resulting in what some have called the "new eugenics" (B. Baker, 2002; Ellis, 2008).

Students and learning, however, are not the only things commodified in systems of high-stakes, standardized testing. The tests themselves are also alienated and distanced from the very real processes and social relations that exist in their production. The idea that standardized tests neutrally and objectively measure students, masks the economic, historical, and social factors that contribute to test design and test result interpretation. The task of de-fetishizing high-stakes testing is thus important because it strips away the aura of objectivity that surrounds the tests. As De Lissovoy and McLaren (2003) observe:

> [O]nce it is recognized that this 'objectivity' is rather contingency and bias, then it follows that the success and failure that the tests pretend to report are actually manufactured by the instruments themselves. (p. 135)

Consequently, it is through such manufacturing of success and failure that standardized tests allow systems of education to be monitored and controlled.

Standardized Testing, Control, and Surveillance

Standardized tests, however, do more than just commodify students and learning, enabling them to fit into the production model of education. As part of the process of *standardization* of education, the tests are also linked to *control* over the process of education. Just as standardization of factory production allowed for increased control over the process of production itself that in many ways also allowed for control over both producers (labor) and products (Braverman, 1974; Carlson, 1988b;

Noble, 1977), the standardization of education vis-à-vis testing allows for increased control over teachers (labor) and students (products) in the process of education (Apple, 1986; Apple & Beyer, 1988). Consequently, as Berlak (2000) notes, within systems of standardized testing:

> It becomes possible to instill more discipline into the "delivery system". Authorities can identify the teachers, schools and local districts that fail to produce, and institute marketplace remedies, privatization, vouchers, charter schools and other policies that encourage schools to compete for students and resources.... (p 190)

Systems of high-stakes, standardized testing are therefore aimed at *discipline* in addition to control and standardization (Vinson & Ross, 2003). Sorting human populations serves no point if there is no *purpose* for the sorting, no framework within which the sorting takes meaning. Thus disciplinary categories of test-determined "winners" and "losers" are created to distinguish some students from others.

Essentially, to make sense of standardized test scores—to understand the meaning of sorting functions of the tests—policies using high-stakes testing must set cut scores, must determine who is passing and who is failing, in order to determine who needs punishment (Lipman, 2004; M. L. Smith, 2004). However, as M. L. Smith (2004) observes:

> [C]ounting the number of children depends on first constructing categories, the meaning and boundaries of which are ambiguous. The process of "counting as" depends on a dynamic of interests, ideologies, and political tactics of the persons involved. The accountability movement teeters on a fragile system of categories such as pass and failed, or "exceeds the standard," or "approaches but does not reach the standard." Typically political entities perform this task and make such categorizations—not by technical or statistical procedures, but by political processes....Even when political entities use statistical procedures to establish levels, categories, and cutoff scores, results are problematic and the application of those levels is political. (p. 154)

Hence, standardized testing must be seen as a technology that marks deviance from the norm (Berlak, 2000; Hanson, 2000; Lipman, 2004; M. L. Smith, 2004) that also operates as a form of surveillance. Through the very political and ideological process of setting up the categories of interpretation of standardized test results, authorities are able to monitor educational production and highlight those who do not fit within the regulated boundaries. Systems of standardized testing consequently place individuals within an ever increasing web of control and surveillance (Hanson, 2000) that works, in part, because the categorical defined "deficiencies" are made "visible, individual, easily measured, and highly stigmatized within a hierarchical system of authority and supervision" (Lipman, 2004, p. 176). The irony is that, because of the assumed objectivity of standardized tests in measuring individuals, an ideology of equality ultimately masks the aspects of standardization, commodification, control, and surveillance operating through systems of high-stakes, standardized testing.

Standardized Testing and the Ideology of Meritocracy

As discussed above, one of the key tenets of standardized tests is that they purportedly measure humans objectively as individuals. As such, they are supposed to provide a common baseline, a common measurement, that can be used to accurately compare individuals regardless of context or local experiences and conditions. This objectivity also lends the tests a sense of fairness and equality, that everyone is being measured for what they are individually and not based on other factors. This is one of the ideological underpinnings of standardized tests in that objectivity lends "scientific" accuracy, and is part of the legacy of the social efficiency movement and scientific management. As Sacks (1999) explains, this believed objectivity of the tests was seen by some as a way of challenging caste-like social and economic inequalities:

> Standardized testing, rendered with complete objectivity and couched in terms of an empirical 'science,' would be the death knell to the insidious influences of class privilege perpetuated by the blueness of one's blood. (p. 264)

Because the tests supposedly offer individual fairness, transparency, and objectivity in educational measurement, many envisioned standardized testing as a way to challenge nepotism and the elite aristocracies that have existed historically in the United States (Lemann, 1999). Due to the assumed fair and objective measurement of individuals, standardized tests have thus been characterized as one of the means to challenge race-, class-, and gender-based hierarchies by promising that every individual who takes a test gets a fair and equal shot at educational, social, and economic success. Problems like institutionalized racism and class privilege are thus supposedly ameliorated through testing. This characterization of standardized testing as a means of challenging social, economic, and educational hierarchies is rooted in the ideal that the United States operates as a meritocracy; that is, regardless of social position, economic class, gender, or culture (or any other form of difference), based on merit and hard work, any one individual competes freely and equally with other individuals in order to become "successful" (Lemann, 1999; Sacks, 1999).

Such an ideology does show some good sense in that, faced with a highly stratified social and economic structure, systems of education and assessment that treat individuals equally and fairly should be developed, and people should have equal and equitable access to educational and economic opportunities. Thus it is not unreasonable that many saw (and still do see) standardized testing, with its pretenses to transparent, objective measurement, as an advance over inherited privileges. However, as I have argued in this chapter, the idea of individuals freely competing in the realm of education has not been born out by the realty of standardized testing. Clearly, the outcomes of early standardized tests reflected race-, ethnic-, gender-, and class-based differences and provided supporting evidence for the racist eugenics movement (Selden, 1999). Standardized tests, however, with their focus on individual, meritocratic achievement, serve a particular ideological purpose within the (re)production of socioeconomic inequalities. As Bisseret (1979) writes, the ideology of meritocracy masks structural inequalities under the guise of "naturally" occurring, yet variable aptitude amongst individuals:

> Generally speaking, the idea of a just and equitable selection ensured by institutions offering everybody equal opportunities to establish his or her 'true' aptitudes constitutes the bedrock of a conception which seeks to legitimize social order, founded on the value attributed to individuals who are ultimately regarded as fundamentally unequal. (p. 26)

Bisseret thus explains how the ideological orientation toward individual merit allows dominant elites to justify their powerful social and economic positions as earned through individual hard work as opposed to as gained through systemic privilege.[12] Indeed, meritocracy might be best viewed as the ideological extension of the logics of capitalist production, where individual products and individual producers "freely" compete in the educational and social market places, where only the "best" products and the most hardworking producers succeed, and where those that fail merely didn't work hard enough. Such an ideology epitomizes the invisible hand of capitalist markets in practice (Brosio, 1994) and ultimately denies any role that socioeconomic systems might play in the maintenance of inequalities. Schools, then, "may claim that they adhere to meritocratic principles when in fact they sort children into slots that reflect the place of each in a class system" (M. L. Smith, 2004, p. 38). The low achievement on standardized tests of working-class people and non-White populations can then be attributed to the failure of individual students or individual groups (or cultures), and not attributed to existing structural inequalities (see, e.g., McWhorter, 2005; Rushton & Jensen, 2005).

Even though popular notions of meritocracy and individual equality are part of the commonsense understandings and rhetorical arguments revolving around standardized testing, the tests have not broken from the legacies of racism, the eugenics movement, and social efficiency in education. Given that research finds that high-stakes, standardized tests consistently (re)produces educational and social inequalities (Darling-Hammond, 2007; Lomax, West, Harmon, Viator, & Madaus, 1995; Madaus & Clarke, 2001; McNeil, 2005; McNeil & Valenzuela, 2001; Nichols, Glass, & Berliner, 2005; Orfield & Wald, 2000), and based on my analysis in this chapter, I would argue that these tests cannot be divorced from such (re)production and are, in fact, a *mechanism* in the process. As we shall see in the next section, even the contemporary Scholastic Assessment Test (SAT) has difficulties shaking off the racist legacy of eugenics because such inequalities are structured into the very foundations of standardized test construction itself.

The SAT and Educational Inequality

The SAT provides a good example for analysis because it is a high-stakes test that is one of the contemporary gatekeepers to higher education.[13] In 2001, 1.3 million high school students out of 2.85 million high school graduates took the SAT. Over half took the test two or more times in attempts to improve their scores, and hence improve their chances at getting into the college of their choice (Kidder & Rosner, 2002–2003). The SAT was developed by the racist eugenicist, Carl Brigham (Sacks, 1999). Brigham was a Princeton University professor who left Princeton to work as an Army psychologist under the supervision of Yerkes. Using the same World War I Army test data as Yerkes, Brigham arrived at similar racist and classist conclusions: Immigrants were genetically less intelligent than people born in the United States. Further, like other eugenicists of his time, he found that Whites born in the United States were the most intelligent of all peoples. After leaving his position as an Army psychologist, Brigham returned to Princeton to work in the admissions office, where he continued his work on testing and intelligence by developing an exam that would sort through the young men applying for entrance into the elite halls of Princeton. To do so,

Brigham created the "Scholastic Aptitude Test." This test was the first mass-based college entrance exam. Today it is known as the "Scholastic Assessment Test" or the SAT; the name was changed as a result of public distaste for "aptitude" tests during the 1970s and 1980s (Sacks, 1999).

In addition to its origins in racist (and classist) I.Q. testing, a contemporary study of SAT questions finds significant racial bias buried deep within the structure of the test construction itself. Kidder and Rosner (2002–2003) performed a study of 100,000 SAT test-takers in October of 1989 and included a second database of 209,000 test-takers in New York state as well. These researchers also analyzed a collection of 580 SAT test questions from four SATs given between 1988 and 1989.[14] In their study, Kidder and Rosner examined the percentages of questions that Black, White, and Chicano (Mexican American) students answered correctly. Using calculations of average scores on each question by racial group, Kidder and Rosner then determined what they termed the "racial impact" of each test score. For instance, if 50% of Whites and 30% of African Americans answered a particular SAT question correctly, the question was given a 20% Black-White racial impact.

In their study, Kidder and Rosner found that, "African Americans and Chicanos did not outperform Whites on any of the seventy-eight Verbal and sixty Math questions" (p. 148). Whites correctly answered 59.8% of the verbal questions on average and African Americans correctly answered 46.4% of the verbal on average, resulting in an overall 13.4% Black-White impact. Additionally Chicanos correctly answered Verbal test items at an average of 48.7%, giving an 11.1% Chicano-White impact. The story was much the same in Math. Whites had an overall 58.4% correct answer rate, and African Americans had a 42% correct answer rate, giving an average disparate impact of 16.4%. Almost three out of ten Math questions averaged a 20% disparate impact. The average Chicano correct answer rate for Math questions was 46.5%, establishing an 11.9% Chicano-White impact.

Kidder and Rosner find an explanation for these disparate test scores within the structure of the test design itself. The Educational Testing Service (ETS), who traditionally administers the SAT, establishes statistically valid questions by using one of the six sections of the test as an experimental section, essentially trying out questions to potentially use on future SATs. Based on the responses the experimental test items receive, psychometricians make decisions to either keep a question and use it in the regular sections of future tests or discard it as an unusable, "invalid" test item. Kidder and Rosner compared some of the regular test items with the experimental ones and arrived at some interesting conclusions. For example, on one Verbal test item of medium difficulty,

62% of Whites and 38% of African Americans answered it correctly (for a 24% disparate impact). This question was a test item from one of the regular, non-experimental test sections. By comparison, an item of similar difficulty used in the experimental test section resulted in African Americans outperforming White students by 8% (that is, 8% more African American students answered the question correctly than White students). Additionally, 9% of women outperformed men on this same question.

Test designers determined that this question, where African Americans scored higher than Whites (and, women higher than men), was psychometrically invalid and was not included in future SATs. The reason for this was that ETS bases its test question selection on statistics established by performance averages on previous tests: The students who statistically on average score higher on the SAT did not answer this question correctly enough of the time, while those who statistically on average score lower on the SAT answered this question correctly too often. By psychometric standards this means that this question was an anomaly and therefore was not considerd a "valid" or "reliable" test question for a standardized test such as the SAT. At issue is the fact that statistically, on average, White students outperform Black students on the SAT. Higher-scoring students, who tend to be White, correctly answer SAT experimental test questions at higher rates than typically lower scoring students, who tend to be non-White, ensuring that the test question selection process itself has a self-reinforcing, built-in racial bias (Kidder & Rosner, 2002–2003). Rosner (2003) explains this process of psychometrically reinforced racism thusly:

> Each individual SAT question ETS chooses is required to parallel outcomes of the test overall. So, if high-scoring test takers—who are more likely to be white—tend to answer the question correctly in [experimental] pretesting, it's a worthy SAT question; if not, it's thrown out. Race and ethnicity are not considered explicitly, but racially disparate scores drive question selection, which in turn reproduces racially disparate test results in an internally reinforcing cycle. (p. 24)

This is the general process with which ETS makes decisions regarding which questions to include on the SAT.

Couched in the language of statistical reliability and validity, the supposedly race-neutral process of test question selection ultimately structures in very race-biased results into test questions themselves (Kidder & Rosner, 2002–2003). Based on his study, Rosner (2003) hypothesizes that:

[E]very SAT in the past ten years has favored whites over blacks…
Skewed test question selection certainly contributes to the large
test score disparities between blacks and whites. (p. 24)

The encoding of racial bias in the very structure and definition of what
makes a "valid" SAT question speaks to how deeply the race implications of high-stakes standardized testing extend into contemporary
institutions and society. In the end, the issue is all about how "objective"
validity of test items is determined, and within such determination, we
can still see the legacies of I.Q. testing and beliefs in eugenics at play.

HAUNTED BY INEQUALITY

In one respect, such findings regarding the SAT and other equity-based
research of other forms of mass, standardized testing should come as
no surprise. Given the historical origins of standardized testing in the
social efficiency movement, I.Q. testing, and the eugenics movement,
there is no reason to believe that these testing systems could shake off
their racist and classist legacies so easily. For instance, in the mid-1990s,
the authors of *The Bell Curve* (Herrnstein & Murray, 1996) claimed that
there was an hierarchical ordering of races where African Americans
were the least intelligent of all races, followed by Latinos, Whites, and
Asian Americans, who, according to the authors, were purported to be
the most intelligent. Like Yerkes and Brigham before them, Hernstein
and Murray based their conclusions on an analysis of standardized test
scores. Despite the substantive, critical responses rejecting the arguments put forth in *The Bell Curve* (see, e.g., S. Fraser, 1995), the racist, eugenicist position is still popularly upheld by some scholars. For
instance, Rushton and Jensen (2005) in their analysis of "Thirty years of
research on race and cognitive ability," assert that there are genetically
based racial differences in I.Q. (Jensen is professor emeritus of educational psychology at University of California, Berkeley). Others, such
as Barrow and Rouse (2006), a senior economist at the Federal Reserve
Bank of Chicago and a professor of economics and public affairs at
Princeton respectively, examined the relationship between education,
race, and pay. In their study, they explicitly rely on the work of Hernstein and Murray as a baseline for their analysis. It appears that the
ghosts of eugenicists like Carl Brigham, Yerkes, and other standardized
intelligence test-makers from the early 20th century still linger via the
very racialized and class-disparate outcomes of the modern day, high-stakes, standardized testing movement.

3

THE EDUCATIONAL ENTERPRISE
NCLB, Neoliberalism, and the Politics of Equality

Henry Ford created a world-class company, a leader in its industry. More important, Ford would not have survived the competition had it not been for an emphasis on results. We must view education the same way. Good schools do operate like a business. They care about outcomes, routinely assess quality, and measure the needs of the children they serve.

Former U.S. Secretary of Education Rod Paige (2003, p. 12)

Clearly, based on the arguments and evidence I've presented thus far, the roots of inequality and control run very deep within systems of high-stakes, standardized testing. However, the relationships between the production model of education, high-stakes testing, and inequality are not just historical. They also manifest within contemporary education policy design and rhetoric. In this chapter I take up an analysis of the modern-day high-stakes testing movement as well as the links between contemporary education policy, the continued influence of business community on policy structure, and neoliberalism in education reform. I begin here with *A Nation At Risk* because this report set the trajectory of the modern-day high-stakes, standardized testing movement. From there, I discuss the overt relationships between current federal education policy and the interests of capital, linking these relationships to ideologies of inequality, social efficiency, and neoliberalism. After that, I move to an analysis of the contradictory impulses that exist within federal education policy, particularly the ways in which, on one hand this policy orients itself toward control over the process of education, while on the other hand it relies on a rhetoric of individual equality to hegemonically garner the support of as many people as possible. Finally, I conclude this chapter with an explanation of the ways in which contemporary social and economic conditions do not match the standardized, factory-like models that generally structure our educational system.

A NATION AT RISK AND THE BIRTH OF CONTEMPORARY HIGH-STAKES TESTING

By most accounts, the publication of *A Nation At Risk: The Imperative for Education Reform* (National Commission on Excellence in Education, 1983) signaled the beginnings of the modern day high-stakes, standardized testing movement (Amrein & Berliner, 2002b; G. M. Jones, Jones, & Hargrove, 2003; Kornhaber & Orfield, 2001; Nichols & Berliner, 2007; Nichols, Glass, & Berliner, 2005; Paris & Urdan, 2000). The Reagan administration produced this report, which attacked many of the equity-minded reforms associated with the Elementary and Secondary Education Act of 1965 (Jennings, 2000). Echoing the social efficiency reformers of at the turn of the 20th century, *A Nation At Risk* (National Commission on Excellence in Education, 1983) painted a particularly distressing picture public education in the United States at the time. In its opening sentences, the report asserts:

> [T]he educational foundations of our society are presently being eroded by a rising tide of mediocrity that threatens our very future as a Nation and a people. What was unimaginable a generation ago has begun to occur—others are matching and surpassing our educational attainments. (p. 5)

Thus, *A Nation At Risk* labeled the entire system of education as mediocre and substandard, and simultaneously asserted that other countries have passed the U.S. in "educational attainments."[1] According to *A Nation At Risk*, the educational crisis of falling educational attainment constituted a national security threat, the specter of which looms large:

> If an unfriendly foreign power had attempted to impose on America the mediocre educational performance that exists today, we might well have viewed it as an act of war. As it stands, we have allowed this to happen to ourselves. We have even squandered the

gains in student achievement made in the wake of the Sputnik challenge. Moreover, we have dismantled essential support systems which helped make those gains possible. We have, in effect, been committing an act of unthinking, unilateral educational disarmament. (p. 5)

This "manufactured crisis" in education (Berliner & Biddle, 1995) was equated with "unilateral educational disarmament" and "an act of war," even with the supposed gains made "in the wake of the Sputnik challenge." While it never mentions the Soviet Union or the Cold War specifically, it creates an image of global thermo-nuclear war over the horizon. *A Nation At Risk* calls reformers to arms, and essentially blames the impending war on the failures of public education. An impeccably crafted argument, *A Nation At Risk* managed to position any opposition as being unpatriotic at best and as threatening the economic and national security of the whole country at worst.

Not surprisingly, *A Nation At Risk* makes several recommendations for school reform in the United States, among them an increase in graduation requirements, specific content recommendations for graduation requirements, higher standards and expectations for all students, increased requirements for admission into four-year colleges, a longer and more efficiently used school day and year, the establishment of core knowledge requirements (which the report called "New Basics"), higher educational standards for teachers, and that teacher salaries be based on student performance on tests (National Commission on Excellence in Education, 1983). Thus, as Sacks (1999) writes, *A Nation At Risk* both "galvanized the fledgling accountability movement, transforming it into a national project with purported national security implications" (p. 77) and ushered in the contemporary standards and high-stakes testing movements.[2]

A Nation At Risk had a tremendous impact on U.S. educational policy, one that can be measured by the avalanche of policies designed and implemented almost immediately after the report was published. Fifty-four state level commissions on education were created, and 26 states raised graduation requirements within a year of the report. Three years after publication, 35 states instituted comprehensive state education reforms that revolved around testing and increased course loads for students (Kornhaber & Orfield, 2001). *A Nation At Risk* thus set the trajectory of education reforms into the 1990's, where 43 states implemented statewide assessments for K-5 by 1994, and by the year 2000 every state but Iowa administered a state mandated test (G. M. Jones, Jones, & Hargrove, 2003).

The march toward high-stakes, standardized testing continued through then Vice President George H. Bush's campaign for the presidency, as he announced he would be the "education president," endorsing minimum competency testing for grade promotion and graduation. G.H. Bush carried this agenda forward into his Summit on Education, which he held with the U.S. governors, and which became the groundwork for Bush's America 2000 plan—focusing on testing and establishing "world class standards" in schools. President Bill Clinton and Vice-President Al Gore committed themselves to following through on the goals established by the America 2000 plan, maintaining the rhetoric of the necessity of "tough standards" in our schools and pursuing a national examination system to meet those standards. The standards, testing, and accountability movement carried into the 21st century as well, where Gore, in his 2000 presidential campaign, called for all states to establish high-stakes high school graduation tests, and within the first week of taking office in 2001, President G.W. Bush pushed for federal Title I funding to be tied to student test scores (Kornhaber & Orfield, 2001).[3]

In 2002, the federal government passed the No Child Left Behind Act (NCLB) into law (U.S. Department of Education, 2002). As a policy, NCLB uses high-stakes testing as the central mechanism for school reform. In its original configuration, NCLB mandates that by 2006, all students be tested in Grades 3–8 and once in high school, in reading and math. By 2008, NCLB also mandates that students be tested at least once at the elementary, middle, and high school levels in science. If schools do not show consistent improvement on these tests, meeting "Adequate Yearly Progress" (AYP), in subgroups related to race, economic class, special education, and English language proficiency, among others, they face sanctions such as a loss of federal funding or the diversion of federal monies to pay for private tutoring, transportation costs, and other "supplemental services." Under NCLB, all students in all subgroups are also expected to be testing at 100% proficiency by the year 2014 or face the above-mentioned sanctions. In the current era, NCLB dominates the educational landscape as students, teachers, administrators, schools, districts, states, and the federal government struggle with the complexities of implementing the 670-page law (Karp, 2006b).

By 2004, in addition to the NCLB federally mandated tests, 24 states required high school exit exams, with all but six withholding diplomas based on the test scores (Emery & Ohanian, 2004). Politically, based on the historical record, Kornhaber and Orfield (2001) conclude that:

[T]here has been an unbroken line of rhetoric, extending across six presidential terms, fostering high-stakes testing. For almost two decades, all the national leaders of both parties have embraced the theory that our schools have deteriorated and that they can be saved by high-stakes tests. So have the state leaders in almost all of our states. (p. 4)

Including President Bush's re-election to office in 2004, the rhetoric and policy focused on high-stakes testing now stretches across seven presidential terms (and will likely continue into an eighth). Thus, high-stakes, standardized testing is now entrenched as *the* policy tool for enforcing educational reform.

CORPORATE BACKED EDUCATION POLICY

The relationship between corporate interests and public education has been a long one that has included, but has not been limited to, the design of policies such as NCLB. NCLB is significant, however, because as Smith (2004) explains, it codifies the application of the capitalist production model in federal education policy:

Major policy events of the 1990s (culminating in the No Child Left Behind legislation) represent the triumph of the business metaphor. Those policies treat instruction, academic standards, testing, and accountability as business practices. (p. 197)

As I demonstrated in previous chapters, private industry has had an interest in public education for over 100 years. Earlier relations, such as those embodied by Bobbitt, were characterized by the application of the logics of industrial capitalist production to education. While this trend still generally holds true today, the relationship between capital and education seems to have grown even tighter in recent decades. During George H. Bush's and Bill Clinton's presidential terms, when high-stakes testing was first being built into state and federal educational policy, the business community maintained continued influence (Sacks, 1999). Cuban (2004) recounts that:

Lamar Alexander, secretary of education under the first President Bush, hired David Kearns, former chair of the Xerox Corporation, to develop national academic standards…Federal officials also created a privately funded initiative, the New American Schools Development Corporation, to design extraordinary schools that would be twenty-first century models of whole school reform for the nation. Business leaders drawn from all segments of the private sector and political leaders of both parties endorsed the creation of a National Skills Standards Board as part of the Goals

2000 legislation and later, during the Clinton administration, the School-to-Work Opportunities Act. (p. 55)

As another example, a joint statement from the Business Roundtable Education Task Force, the National Alliance of Business, and the U.S. Chamber of Commerce from 1996 asserts:

> As organizations representing American business and employing 34 million people, we are concerned that the graduates of America's schools are not prepared to meet the challenges posed by global economic competition. Our nation's future economic security, and our ability to flourish as a democratic society, demand a generation of high school graduates with solid academic knowledge, world-class technical skills, conscientious work habits, and eager, creative, and analytical minds. Despite some encouraging recent gains, business continues to have trouble finding qualified workers. The time has come for business to participate far more actively in generating high achievement. (Augustine, Lupberger, & Orr III, 1996, n.p.)

Clearly, the business community and the interests of capital have maintained substantial interest in the overall shape and direction of public education in this country.

Groups like the Business Roundtable (BRT) also illustrate the increased influence of the interests of capital on federal education policy. The BRT was founded in 1972 as an association of corporate Chief Executive Officers (CEOs) who took up the mission of analyzing and offering input on issues that effect the U.S. economy. In 1989 a group of Roundtable CEOs from the largest 218 corporations met and decided how to best implement the National Education Goals developed by the governors of the United States, and by 1995, the BRT had established what they termed the "Nine Essential Components of a Successful Education System" (Emery & Ohanian, 2004). As might be expected the BRT explicitly advocated for high-stakes testing and national standards (Altwerger & Strauss, 2002) and, a careful look at the BRTs "Nine Essential Components" leads to a notable coincidence: All their components are included in the design of No Child Left Behind. Further, it is interesting to note that the BRT provided a thirty-three page handbook advising business leaders in how to overcome resistance to high-stakes testing (Emery & Ohanian, 2004).

Similar to the Business Roundtable, many corporate leaders are connected with elaborate networks that place them in very powerful positions in relation to education policy. Edward Rust, CEO of State Farm

Insurance, is an excellent example because he sits (or has sat) on many committees and boards, including: the Business Coalition for Excellence in Education (co-chair), the Business Roundtable (chair, Education Task Force), the National Alliance of Businesses (former chair, member of the board), the Committee for Economic Development (co-chair, Subcommittee on Education Policy), Achieve (board member), McGraw-Hill publishing company (board member), the American Enterprise Institute (board of trustees), and President Bush's Transition Advisory Team Committee on Education (Emery & Ohanian, 2004). Similar webs of CEOs and advocates of free market education reforms can be found among the advocates of the privatization of teacher education and certification (Au, 2004) and the textbook and educational testing and products industries as well.

Another way to track the interests and influence in education that corporate capitalists have maintained is to look at the powerful web of foundations and the projects they choose to fund. Take, for instance, the John M. Olin Foundation, which was established in 1953. This foundation has contributed to educational policy debates in the following ways: It financed Hernstein and Murray's (1996) book *The Bell Curve*, the book discussed in the previous chapter that links intelligence to race; granted $110,000 to Chubb and Moe for *Politics, Markets, and America's Schools* which promoted vouchers and school choice in the free market; awarded neoconservative Diane Ravitch a total of 17 grants worth over $2,100,000; given nine grants totaling $950,000 to former secretary of education under Ronald Reagan, William Bennett; and given Chester Finn, another free market educational reform conservative, ten grants totaling $961,000. Similarly, John Walton of Wal-Mart has given over $50 million to CEO America, a conservative group that promotes school voucher programs. Walton and Ted Forstman (a Wall Street venture capitalist) together contributed $100 million to found the Children's Scholarship Fund, an organization which is closely affiliated with CEO America (M. L. Smith, 2004). The Bradley Foundation, another notable conservative granting agency, in addition to financially supporting *The Bell Curve*, mentioned above, also gives money to organizations that promote the privatization of public education through school voucher programs (Apple, 2006a).

High-Stakes Testing and the New Middle Class

Thus far I have focused on the power of business leaders on educational policy in the United States. However, in doing so, I have neglected the role of another powerful set of conservative interests involved in educational reform that also seeks to use high-stakes, standardized testing as part of business-like assessment: the professional and new managerial middle class (Apple, 2006a; Ball, 2003a; Bernstein, 1977). In his analysis, Apple (2006a) explains that,

> [I]t is important to realize that a good deal of the current emphasis on audits and more rigorous forms of accountability, on tighter control, and a vision that competition will lead to greater efficiency is not totally reducible to the needs of neoliberals and neoconservatives. Rather, part of the pressure for these policies comes from educational managers and bureaucratic officers who fully believe that such control is warranted and "good."...[T]ighter control, high-stakes testing, and (reductive) accountability methods provide more dynamic roles for such managers. (pp. 105–106)

It is this class fraction of professionals and managers that builds its identity around technical proficiency and the idea that efficiency and accountability in education can solve existing problems (Apple, 2006a). Indeed, this class fraction can be viewed as the progeny of the insurgent class of engineers that appeared during the rise of social efficiency and Taylorism in industrial capitalist production I discussed in Chapter 2. In the past, this class justified its own existence by asserting control through their technical expertise in the labor process (Meiksins, 1984). In modern times the technical abilities of the professional and new managerial middle class help maintain the capitalist production model of education, for they provide the technical expertise to build and interpret the results of psychometric tools like high-stakes, standardized tests, as well as hold positions of power within the bureaucracies that develop, interpret, and implement policies that use these tools. Additionally, following Bourdieu (1984), Apple (2006a) notes:

> The increasing power of mechanisms of restratification such as the return of high levels of mandatory standardization, more testing more often, and constant auditing of results also provides mechanisms—and an insistent logic—that enhance the chances that the children of the professional and managerial new middle class will have *less competition* from other students. Thus, the introduction of devices to restratify a population...enhances the value of credentials that the new middle class is more likely given to accumulate, given the stock of cultural capital it already possesses. (pp. 106–107, original emphasis)

In these ways the professional and managerial new middle class not only justify their own existence within educational processes and policies and maintain their own social and economic upward mobility, but they also create the room to align themselves with the interests of neo-liberals and others.[4]

From Symbolic to Economic Control

Given the increasingly tightly knit relationship between big business and governmental appointments, as well as the role of middle-class professionals in upholding systems of testing, we can see how education policy has come to be increasingly influenced by corporate interests advancing specific ideological and organizational forms associated with capitalist production. Further, we can see how these changes result in a policy narrative that trickles down into the language and structures of school life, for as Cuban (2004) observes:

> Other business influences also have become obvious. School boards renamed superintendents CEOs and their deputies "chief operating officers" and "chief academic officers." Many urban school boards have inserted performance clauses in their superintendents' contracts that pay bonuses when students' test scores rise. Many districts have "outsourced" to private firms transportation, building maintenance, food services, security, purchasing, and, in some instances, entire schools. School policymakers and administrators (but rarely teachers) salt their vocabulary with such terms as "satisfying the customer," "benchmarking," and "marketing our services." District administrators have imported from the private sector such business mainstays as marketing studies, strategic planning and "total quality management."(p. 63)

Thus, the field of education, which historically has been associated with the field of cultural or symbolic control, is increasingly coming under the sway of agents and agencies within the field of economic control. As Bernstein (2001) explains:

> Perhaps one of the most significant changes taking place in the agencies within the field of symbolic control is a change in the field membership of its dominant managerial agents. The extension of market rationality to these agencies by the State has led to the gradual replacement of managerial agents drawn from the field of symbolic control by dominant managerial agents from the economic field. Further, management training of agents indigenous to the field of symbolic control draws on the rationality of the economic field's mode of management. The changes have the consequence of economizing the culture of symbolic control agencies of the State as those agencies and agents become subject to market criteria of effectiveness and rationality. (pp. 30–31)

Hence, under policies like NCLB, as agencies and agents of symbolic control both schools and teachers experience the economizing of their organizational/work culture as agents of economic control (e.g., business leaders) are increasingly granted sway over educational policy at the federal, state, and local levels. One of the markers of this increased sway over educational policy is the standard assumption that humans exist as forms of capital to which value may be added through education and therefore contribute positively to the U. S. position in the global economy.

NCLB AND HUMAN CAPITAL THEORY

Undergirding much of the rhetorics surrounding contemporary education policy structures, such as AYP, and one of the ways that we see the logics of capitalist production running through systems of high-stakes testing, is the explicit advancement of the concept of human capital theory. As an extension of the commodification of students, this theory posits that the United States cannot compete within global capitalism if the workers that its schools are producing are "inferior" to those from other countries (M. L. Smith, 2004). Within this ideological framework, then, humans are constructed as discrete pieces of capital to which value may be added through increased education and measured through testing. Education reformers from both major U.S. political parties as well as business leaders argue that national economies depend on education in order to remain competitive in the global economy, and standardized testing further provides them with "objective" and "reliable" data in order to determine which populations to invest their capital in internationally. These arguments rely on human capital theory as their central platform: The logic being that our U.S. national economy has slumped or grown relative to the quality of educational "products" (students) our schools produce.

There are several ways in which this logic, and human capital theory generally, prove inconsistent and incorrect. For instance, over the last 30 years the economies of both the United States and Japan have experience tremendous highs and lows. During this same period, however, research finds that the overall academic achievement of students in the United States has remained relatively consistent (Berliner & Biddle, 1995; Krueger, 1998; Orlich, 2004).[5] This would seem to belie the idea that a fluctuating economy correlates with fluctuating test scores. As Cuban (2004) observes:

> [A]fter the early 1980s, when the media magnified perceptions that Japan and Germany were outperforming the United States in

world markets, the mid-1990s found these previously successful foreign competitors in a prolonged slump, precisely when the U.S. economy enjoyed an eight-year stretch of prosperity. Few pundits or business leaders pointed out that the highly productive employees contributing to the U.S. boom were the very same cohorts who supposedly who had been poorly schooled in the 1980s. (p. 137)

Thus we see a basic fallacy underlying human capital theory. Historically, test scores have had little to do with the overall performance of the U.S. economy generally (K. Baker, 2007), even if what goes on in schools plays an important role in (re)producing particular ideologies associated with production and economic distribution. It seems a commonsense argument to make, but it points to a logical fallacy upon which most mainstream and conservative educational reforms have been built upon for 100 years (Cuban, 2004; M. L. Smith, 2004).

As another challenge to human capital theory, research has also found that more education—that is, increased investment in human capital—does not necessarily correlate with increased economic advancement. As Brown and Lauder (2006) point out in their analysis of economic globalization, more education in the United States has not necessarily meant higher earnings for college graduates. Indeed, increases in college education have only helped a very small minority of higher wage earners increase their earnings, leaving the earnings of most college graduates stagnant since 1973 (adjusting for inflation). According to Brown and Lauder, while getting a college degree does generally get one a higher paying job, the jobs themselves are only higher paying relative to the wages of workers without degrees, which have fallen precipitously over the last 30 years. Further, from a common sense perspective, the upper echelons of our current capitalist economy cannot employ everyone. Economically, the reality of employment opportunity for most people is just the opposite: The majority of jobs in the United States lay in lower echelons of the service, healthcare, and temporary work industries—many of which are low paying. Additionally, decreased state funding and subsequent rising tuitions at college are making higher education even less accessible, taking away even more opportunities for individual advancement (Sleeter, 2005). The advancement of human capital theory, so often offered by corporate interests in regard to public education—particularly in our current era of neoliberalism and increased globalization—serves to propagate the American Dream of individual opportunity and meritocracy while denying the very real structural inequalities that are increasingly being imposed on more and more people in this country and around the world. Despite these problems, the logics of neoliberal economics to are still built into policy structure, resulting in the increased privatization of public education and the garnering of huge profits for private industry.

THE INVISIBLE HAND OF EDUCATION REFORM

Fundamentally, NCLB creates conditions where schools compete with each other in the "free market" of education. Failing schools will be shut down or reorganized under new management, and successful schools will attract more customers/students. As George W. Bush (1999), asserts in a presidential campaign speech delivered to the conservative think-tank, the Manhattan Institute:

> Federal funds will not longer flow to failure. Schools that do not teach and will not change must have some final point of accountability. A moment of truth, when their Title 1 funds are divided up and given to parents, for tutoring or a charter school or some other hopeful option. In the best case, schools that are failing will rise to the challenge and regain the confidence of parents. In the worst case, we will offer scholarships to America's neediest children. (n.p.)

Thus, schools become like any other business enterprise where the rules of efficiency and free-market competition apply (Sacks, 1999). In this neoliberal model, Adam Smith's invisible hand of capitalism will ensure that "bad" educational producers will go out of business and be removed from the market while "superior" educational producers will survive the private competition (Brosio, 1994). It is plainly an expression of the capitalist notion of "free," individual choice and production in the competitive market place—one that, as I pointed out in the previous chapter, works well with the notion of the American meritocracy. This neoliberal, free market logic can also be observed in the way that NCLB creates opportunities for private industry to gain access to the public education market through school restructuring, the public funding of privately offered "supplemental services" like tutoring, and other education-related industries, thus promoting the privatization and deregulation of public education as a whole (Apple, 2006a; Apple & Pedroni, 2005; Burch, 2006; Emery & Ohanian, 2004; Hinchey & Cadiero-Kaplan, 2005; Hursh, 2005; Karp, 2006b; Kohn, 2004; Lipman, 2000; McNeil, 2000; Miner, 2003; Pedroni, 2007; M. L. Smith, 2004).

One of the most profound examples of structuring educational policy to create private markets that draw from public monies can be found in the testing industry. Much like the testing market that boomed surrounding intelligence testing in the earlier 1900s (Giordano, 2005), the contemporary high-stakes testing movement creates markets that capture the interests of capital as well (Burch, 2006). Writing in 1999, before the No Child Left Behind Act was passed and state testing became mandatory in order to receive federal funding, Sacks (1999) notes how the nation's penchant for testing reaps big financial returns for private enterprise. He estimates that in education alone, anywhere from 143 to 400 million tests were taken a year. Outside of education he also estimates that 50 to 200 million tests are taken for jobs, and he did not include the several million tests that are taken in the military. All in all, as of 1999, this means that people in the United States could have taken as many as 600 million standardized tests every year. Although determining the exact numbers of standardized tests being taken is a tricky, often inexact endeavor, Sack's estimation shows a tremendous increase from the previous decade (the 1980s) where Haney, Madaus, and Lyons (1993) estimate that between 143 and 395 million tests were administered annually. In 1997, standardized test sales in public education alone were more than $191 million—a 21% increase from 1992. When then California Governor Pete Wilson decided to move the state to a multiple choice test, Harcourt Brace received a four year contract for its Stanford 9 achievement tests to be delivered to over four million children in public schools. Harcourt Brace made $30 million on this deal in 1998 alone (Sacks, 1999).

Compliance with the testing provisions of NCLB only means that more states will offer more tests, with increased profits for select firms. As Burch (2006) observes:

> Test development firms have sought to use NCLB mandates to attract new business. Major suppliers of test development and preparation firms explicitly reference the No Child Left Behind Act on their Web pages, and several named the law as spurring revenue in their recent financial statements. In addition, they all have links to the Department of Education's Web site on No Child Left Behind, and include in their marketing materials references to how their products can help districts comply with NCLB. (p. 2590)

The Education Sector, an independent education think tank, reports that during the 2005–2006 school year alone, the 23 states that had not fully implemented NCLB's testing requirements will administer 11.4 million new tests in reading and math to meet the federal mandate.

Additionally, by the 2007–2008 school year when states will be required to test in science as well, another 11 million new tests will also be needed. This will be in addition to the estimated 45 million tests required under NCLB generally (Toch, 2006). The testing market, likewise, has reached incredible heights. Sales of test-related printed materials rose from $211 million in 1992 to $592 million in 2003 (Burch, 2006). Edventures Inc. estimates the total value of the tests, test-prep materials, and testing services in 2006 in the United States to be $2.3 billion. This total includes $517 million for all NCLB related test development, publishing, administering, analyzing, and reporting during the 2005–2006 school year alone. Eduventures also estimates that 90% of the revenues generated by statewide testing is collected by only a few companies including, Pearson Educational Measurement, CTB/McGraw-Hill, Harcourt Assessment Inc., Riverside Publishing (a subsidiary of Houghton Mifflin Co.), and ETS (J. M. Jackson & Bassett, 2005).

In addition to test development, the high-stakes testing associated with policies like NCLB has in essence created other test-related ancillary markets (Burch, 2006). For instance, National Computer Systems Incorporated (NCS) received $12 million a year from Harcourt Brace to handle and process the massive amounts of test data that would be produced by their contract with California. In their niche of the testing industry—processing data from the standardized testing of schoolchildren—NCS grew into a $400 million business, and they estimate that the test administration and processing market was worth more than $1 billion during the 1990s. NCS sales rose almost 60% between 1994 and 1998 (Sacks, 1999). In direct response to NCLB, one leading firm in the area of test-based technological solutions for districts and states grew by nearly 300% (Burch, 2006). Other periphery businesses, like the test-prep industry, also cash in. For instance, the Princeton Review, most famous for its SAT preparation programs, had sales of $60 million in 1996 (Sacks, 1999). In addition to the opening the test preparation and data analysis markets, regimes of high-stakes testing associated with NCLB have also increased profits for remediation and professional development programs (both content and services) aimed at increases in test scores. For-profit tutoring companies did $4 billion dollars in business in 2003 and expected this number to rise to $5 billion by 2005. Further, even though the market is nearly equally shared with non-profit companies, for profit companies offering NCLB related content and services to school districts saw revenues of nearly $1.62 billion in 2003 (Burch, 2006).

CTB/McGraw-Hill, a subsidiary of the McGraw-Hill companies, also illustrates the market potential behind standardized testing. As Sacks

(1999) reports, CTB employs 600 people and publishes sixty-five different tests, including the Comprehensive Test of Basic Skills and the California Achievement Test. Although McGraw-Hill doesn't break down its profits by sub-division, its Educational and Professional Publishing Group (where CTB is housed) had revenues of $1.6 billion in 1997. A large portion of these revenues were generated from the testing industry (Altwerger & Strauss, 2002; Sacks, 1999; M. L. Smith, 2004). Suspiciously, the Bush family has very close personal ties to the McGraw family of McGraw-Hill companies (Hinchey & Cadiero-Kaplan, 2005; Metcalf, 2002), who not only produce textbooks and tests but also publish both the Open Court and Reading Mastery programs—two of the phonics driven, direct instruction reading programs that the government has sanctioned as "scientifically" based under NCLB's Reading First initiative. In 1999 McGraw-Hill's educational sales were over $4 billion (M. L. Smith, 2004).[6] Amidst the mountain of dollar signs and profits, a simple reality is sometimes lost: Most of these monies are public tax dollars being funneled directly into the coffers of private industry.

HEGEMONY AND HIGH-STAKES TESTING

A real question remains as to how powerful elites can maintain their legitimacy, especially given how policies such as NCLB are so clearly constructed to serve their interests. Part of the way in which dominant groups maintain hegemonic power is to work to establish what passes as commonsense (Gramsci, 1971). This broad framing of production-minded, educational accountability based on the quantification provided by high-stakes testing, represents the political legacy of school accountability systems (Dorn, 1998). This political legacy, operating through high-stakes testing policies, determines the contours and often defines the limits of the political debate. In this regard, any discussion taken seriously within "acceptable" educational policy has to at least recognize, and perhaps cater to, the common sense discourses surrounding test-score productivity. That the schooling process should be equated with the process of economic production has merely become a common sense "umbrella under which many groups can stand but which basically still is under the guiding principles of dominant groups" (Apple, 2000, p. 64).

However, as Apple (1995) observes, "The need for *economic* and ideological efficiency and stable production tends to be in conflict with other *political* needs" (p. 53, original emphasis). The construction of NCLB aptly illustrates Apple's point. NCLB is actually the 2002 reauthorization and renaming of the equity-minded Elementary and Secondary Education Act, an act that has its origins in the popular reform movements of the 1960s and 1970s to challenge both poverty and racism in the United States (Jennings, 2000). As an expression of its political legacy, there are thus two contradictory (and at times competing) tendencies running through this federal education policy. On the one hand, as discussed above, NCLB manifests many aspects of neoliberal, free market reforms as well as ideological remnants that can be associated with the social efficiency movement and inequality. On the other hand, NCLB also makes appeals to social equality through its language and certain aspects of its structure (Gay, 2007), demonstrating the political needs of those in power to maintain legitimacy in the face of such socioeconomic disparity. If we look closely at contemporary education policy, we can see how dominant elites work within the commonsense boundaries of the capitalist model of production in their discussions of education reform, as well as the way in which they draw on peoples' "good sense" to gain as much support as possible for policies that, in the end, may serve to increase educational inequality (Hursh, 2007).

An example of this hegemonic commonsense can be found in a column written by Major Owens in *The Nation*, ranking Democrat on the Workforce Protection Subcommittee of the House Committee on Education and the Workforce (Owens, 2006). In this article, Owens comments on education policy in the United States as an "alternative" to the State of the Union address delivered by President George W. Bush in January, 2006. While Owens' call for increased federal spending must be lauded, his column is peppered with language that is reminiscent of social efficiency. In his view, we need to develop our "skilled workforce" to compete in the global economy, noting that:

> While some parts of the country already have schools capable of achieving maximum student outputs, a critical percentage of the school-age population resides in densely populated urban areas where education productivity is either stagnant or accelerating downward. (p. 24)

The above example demonstrates how, even in the party that is supposed to be oppositional to the Bush administration and even in a politically progressive magazine such as *The Nation*, critics frame their discourse of education reform within the logics of capitalist production as the only acceptable, even reasonable discourse. In fact, as this example illustrates, it may be useful to view the relationship between contemporary corporate interests and public education in another way: That the neoliberal logic of global capitalism seeks to maintain the social conditions (both domestically and internationally) necessary to increase profits and access to markets so that capitalist profit-making can thrive (Altwerger & Strauss, 2002). These social conditions include preparing students for their role as consumers (McLaren & Farahmandpur, 2005) and promoting "a culture of private accumulation of wealth and individualistic choice" (Weil, 2001, p. 509).

However, as I highlighted in the text from *A Nation At Risk* and Major Owens' article, some contradictory tendencies do exist within this discourse. These tendencies speak back to the earlier discussion of the role of schools in social reproduction. As Carnoy, Castells, Cohen, and Cardoso (1993) explain:

> Politics can and does go beyond creating an environment for capital accumulation. There is an inherent tension between democratic visions of society and the vision held up by national or multinational enterprises. The democratic nation-state has historically had to develop institutions and pursue policies which reflect that democratic vision at the same time it tries to create a suitable environment for capital accumulation. (p. 4)

Schools and education play a role in this tension because, as we have seen with NCLB, a "suitable environment for capital accumulation" has indeed been created and capitalist discourse in education has been taken on as hegemonic commonsense. Hegemony, however, while working on the level of setting these parameters, also draws on aspects of good sense in order to gain the support of as many people as possible (Apple, 1979/2004; Apple & Buras, 2006a). As an expression of the tensions between maintaining the conditions for capital accumulation while simultaneously promoting the existence of a democratic ideal (whether real or imagined), No Child Left Behind both embraces forms of free market neoliberalism and models of capitalist production, discussed above, while rhetorically advocating principals of social and educational equality.

A brief analysis of the introduction to *No Child Left Behind: A Desktop Reference* (U.S. Department of Education, 2002) proves particularly illustrative of this process. For instance, the *Desktop Reference* asserts that:

> Federal policy has had a significant impact on America's schools and children ever since ESEA was enacted in 1965. Yet, despite hundreds of programs and hundreds of billions of dollars invested during the last generation, American students still lag behind many of their fellow foreign students and the academic achievement gap

in this country between rich and poor, white and minority students, remains wide. Indeed, President Bush expressed concern that "too many of our neediest children are being left behind."

Since the *Nation at Risk* report was issued nearly 20 years ago, there has been a vigorous national debate over how to improve our nation's schools and our children's achievement. Out of these years of debate, a general consensus has emerged that schools and districts work best when they have greater control and flexibility, when scientifically proven teaching methods are employed, and when schools are held accountable for results. These are the guiding ideas behind the NCLB Act. (p. 9)

There are a number of discourses operating through this quotation, all of which attempt to speak to peoples' good sense regarding education and society. The clause, "Yet, despite hundreds of programs and hundreds of billions of dollars invested during the last generation" (p. 9), first sets a tone both consistent with the social efficiency movement of the early 1900s and *A Nation At Risk* from the 1980s: Public money and time has been wasted on education programs that have not worked. This argument draws on people's good sense that the public deserves to "get their moneys worth" from public institutions.

The *Desktop Reference* also draws up good sense in the adjoining statement, "…the academic achievement gap in this country between rich and poor, white and minority students, remains wide" (p. 9). This point in particular has been very key for the rhetorics surrounding No Child Left Behind. Here the federal government evokes the current (and very real) crisis in education: Poor students and students of color are not being served adequately by our educational system. This recognition serves double duty. It allows the public schools to be targeted for a widespread, blanket attack that is flat and empty of the complexity that actually exists in schools today, and it allows a very conservative presidential administration to rhetorically assert its care and compassion for social, economic and racial equality in this country. Indeed, this point is reinforced by the very next sentence, which explains that the Bush administration is "concerned" that "our neediest children are being left behind" (p. 9).

With the foreground now painted, the problem defined, and the "good" intentions of the federal government clearly communicated, the next paragraph explains how NCLB will solve these problems—including ending educational inequality. After recalling the legacy of *A Nation At Risk*, the *Desktop Reference* admits that there has been a "debate" about how to fix education. It then asserts that from this "debate" a "consensus" has emerged. This language is powerful because it creates the impression that all sides and perspectives have made their cases, and through this process "a general consensus" has been reached about what works in education, positioning the reader in specific ways. If you agree with the Bush administration and its education policies, then you are embraced as part of the "general consensus" that has been reasonably arrived at over these years. If you disagree, then you are obviously out of step with the commonsense understanding of what is good for schools and education.

The *Desktop Reference* then lays out its plan, where it states:

> ...schools and districts work best when they have greater control and flexibility, when scientifically proven teaching methods are employed, and when schools are held accountable for results. (p. 9)

Using the terminology of "flexibility" for schools and districts alleviates fears the reader might have that the federal government is going to assume a strong hand in controlling what is happening locally. This can be seen as a nod to the good sense of peoples' desire for local control over schools and as an appeal to the Right's populist constituents (Apple, 2006a). In a linguistic reminder of social efficiency, the document then tells us that schools work best when "scientifically proven teaching methods" are used. This point draws on peoples' good sense about the need for research and study when it comes to teaching and policy intervention. Finally, we are left with the idea that schools need to be held "accountable for results." This statement takes for granted the idea that schools have been unaccountable up to this point, and that the federal government will be stepping in to remedy this problem. All of which, in the context of those two paragraphs, is couched as working in the best interests of the country.

AYP and Inequality

The nod toward individual and racial equity embedded in NCLB is more than just discursive, however. As mentioned earlier, structured into the policy is the idea of "Adequate Yearly Progress," which requires that all of the test score data be disaggregated—that is, broken down—by race, class, (dis)ability, and English language proficiency among others. If a school fails to raise test scores in any single one of ten possible groups, and therefore fails to meet the state determined goals for AYP, then these failing schools are put on watch lists. If a school does not meet AYP for three years, then sanctions are triggered (U.S. Department of Education, 2002).

AYP represents the contradictory impulses within NCLB. From a very pragmatic perspective, disaggregating test scores for the purposes of demonstrating improvement appeals to those concerned with educational equality because it provides empirical proof that yes, indeed, educational inequality does exist. Many interested in education reform in this country, myself included, have made serious and substantive critiques of the ways that many working-class students and students of color are being underserved in order to define the shapes of equality-minded reforms. On a most basic level, then, disaggregating test scores provides a tool to address this issue.

However, policies like AYP also present many problems. As Linn (2003) and Darling-Hammond (2007) argue, the expectation to achieve 100% proficiency on high-stakes, standardized tests by 2014 is a statistical impossibility. This is because standardized tests are constructed so that a certain percentage of students perform poorly so that comparisons can be made, and because, in real life applications, test scores consistently level out after three years of improvement after teachers begin teaching to the tests. As I discussed in Chapter 2, standardized tests are, at their core, constructed to sort through populations in order to make comparisons. Within this logic, comparisons become invalid if there is no demarcation of difference, no way to distinguish who passes and who fails. It simply goes against the logical assumptions of standardized tests. If all students performed well on a test, then the test would be considered psychometrically invalid because test are designed so that test score achievement exists on a spectrum of varying success similar to a "bell curve."

Additionally, it has been found that, from a purely economic perspective, it will be impossible for schools to get all students to 100% proficiency by 2014. Applying microeconomic theory to AYP, Haas, Wilson, Cobb, and Rallis (2005) find that there is a simple mathematical curve in the relationship between increased test score achievement and the resources necessary to support such an increase. The closer a school comes to 100% proficiency, the more financial resources it takes to show improvement. For instance, it takes substantially more resources to move a student from 99% to 100% proficiency than it does to move a student from 60% to 61% proficiency. Consequently, AYP is a good example of how, drawing on people's good sense regarding the need to empirically demonstrate educational equality, a policy can be constructed which ultimately sets up schools and students to fail (Apple, 2006a).

Reading First and Scientific Management

The combination of a rhetoric of equality and the hegemonic logics of scientific management are equally apparent in the "Reading First" initiative in NCLB. As discussed above, in an appeal to good sense, the federal government has promised to fund only those reading programs that are grounded in what NCLB calls "scientifically-based" or "evidence-based" research, i.e., those reading programs based on direct instruction and phonics that the Bush administration claims have been "scientifically" proven to be effective (Altwerger, 2005; Berlak, 2003; Eisenhart & Town, 2003), despite the fact that the "science" behind this research is suspect and refutable (Coles, 2000, 2003; Garan, 2005; Land & Moustafa, 2005). Additionally, because of the federal definition, by and large only those programs that apply completely scripted, direct phonics instruction can receive federal monies. While this is not a universal occurrence, teachers in many low performing districts have been required to use commercially packaged reading instruction programs such as Open Court and Reading Mastery, which tell teachers exactly what page to be on for each day as well as every word and line they are allowed to say while teaching reading (Berlak, 2003; Gerstl-Pepin & Woodside-Jiron, 2005; Land & Moustafa, 2005; M. L. Smith, 2004). It is a prime example of outside experts conceiving the "best," most efficient methods of teaching reading and of teachers being coerced to use these methods under threat of policy-designed sanctions—a process that Coles (2003) calls the end of "wiggle room" in reading instruction. The Reading First initiative in many ways epitomizes the logics of scientific management found within NCLB. Teachers' skills and knowledge are devalued while they are required to provide scripted, direct instruction, and school districts are "encouraged" by the federal government's definition of acceptable, "scientifically-based" instruction provided by commercially packaged reading curriculum—all under the guise of providing sound, scientifically proven, successful methods of reading instruction.[7]

As the above discussion of AYP and "scientifically-based" reading research demonstrates, NCLB draws on peoples' good sense regarding the efficient use of resources, local control of schools, the use of effective teaching methods, holding schools responsible to their communities, and, as the title of the No Child Left Behind Act suggest, the use of education to ameliorate social inequalities of class and race. Within this discourse, to challenge NCLB is to challenge these sensibilities. Conversely, to uphold NCLB is to embrace these sensibilities. Thus, even though we can see the structural logics of capitalist inequality at play within the policy design itself, this fact is deflected through the discursive compromises toward individual equality and social responsibility.

Consequently, while it is true that some communities consciously take advantage of the discursive and policy spaces created through the rhetorics of progressive politics, even actively using regressive aspects of policies such as NCLB to their own advantage (see, e.g., Pedroni, 2007), policy makers' reliance on the discourse of meritocracy ultimately serves to obfuscate the very real race and class inequality that does indeed exist in our society and our schools (Bisseret, 1979; Freeman, 2005; Sacks, 1999) while simultaneously allowing the responsibility for socially produced inequality to be exported from the state onto the individual (Lipman, 2004). In this way, NCLB can be seen as part of the "political spectacle" that hides structural inequality behind the language of individual equality (M. L. Smith, 2004). I make this point to illustrate "the ways in which the right has had some success in its attempt to bring groups who would normally find little support in its agenda under the ideological leadership of the conservative alliance" (Apple, 2006a, p. 116). As evidence of this strategy in action, several prominent groups representing people of color have thrown their support behind the promises made by NCLB (Chenoweth, 2004; The Education Trust, 2003; see also, Apple, 2006, Ch. 4; Apple & Pedroni, 2005 for analyses of this process), and it has been pointed out by many that this legislation was written by, and passed with the support of liberal Democrats (Giordano, 2005; Karp, 2006b; Kornhaber & Orfield, 2001).

HIGH-STAKES TESTING AND SCHOOL REFORM IN THE ERA OF GLOBALIZATION

While in this chapter I have attempted to draw a strong ideological trajectory from the social efficiency movement to the contemporary high-stakes testing movement, it is important to recognize that there are some distinct differences between the two. For instance, contrary to the rhetorics of social inequality surrounding the social efficiency movement, as I have demonstrated here, today's high-stakes testing policies are cloaked in rhetorics of social equality. While there was some belief in meritocratic equality embedded in the origins of standardized tests, there was also a strong rhetoric of social sorting and assumed inequality associated with social efficiency. Another marked difference, however, can be found in the structure of the economy. The structure of today's capitalist economy is dramatically different than the industrial capitalism that existed 100 years ago. The increased global integration of the capitalist economy in recent years has created networks and circuits of capital that reach across international boundaries with new intensity and speed (Carnoy et al., 1993; Greider, 1997; Hardt & Negri, 2000). Information and technology's increased importance in the process of production is paramount, where nations with more developed capitalist economies export their factory production operations to poorer countries while simultaneously developing a reliance on the production, exchange, and use of knowledge (Castells, 1993). Further, as Collin and Apple (2007) explain, this economic transformation has also called upon service workers to be reskilled to increasingly rely on the processing of information. Thus, as Castells (1993) observes, in nations with more developed capitalist economies, these changes result in,

> ...a profound transformation in the *organization* of production and of economic activity in general. This change can be described as shift from standardized mass production to flexible customized production and from vertically integrated, large-scale organizations to vertical disintegration and horizontal networks between economic units....[T]he matter at hand is not so much the decline of the large corporation (still the dominant agent of the world economy) as it is the organizational transformation of all economic activity, emphasizing flexibility and adaptability in response to a changing, diversified market. (p. 18, original emphasis)

In these economies, instead of the old-style corporations with large numbers of permanent workers organized in strict hierarchies of control, we now see businesses with increasingly flattened hierarchies that distribute their production into smaller, faster, more flexible and more adaptable units—resulting in what has been called "fast" capitalism by some (Gee, 2000).[8] Even though "fast" capitalism still operates on profit motive, economic power, and the exploitation of labor globally (Brown & Lauder, 2006), this economic transformation raises interesting issues for policies like No Child Left Behind that are built upon strict vertical hierarchies of power and rigid policy tools such as standardized testing.

As I explained in detail in Chapter 2, by and large, our current educational structures grew out of the period of capitalist expansion in the United States associated with mass production and factory assembly lines, and thus there are aspects of our current system of education that manifest this logic. These aspects include the factory-like organization of schools (large populations being moved at regular intervals through an assembly line of teachers), the vertical hierarchies between administrators, teachers, and students, and the linear means-ends rationality embedded in standardized testing. Indeed, these rigid and inflexible attributes reflect the "old" industrial capitalist economy rather than the "newer," more flexible, formations that capitalism has taken in recent decades (Kalantzis & Cope, 2000). Thus, individuals like Robert B. Reich (2001), former U.S. secretary of labor under former U.S. President Clinton, have critiqued the standards and standardized testing movements by observing that:

> Many of the new jobs depend on creativity—on out-of-the-box thinking, originality, and flair. Almost by definition, standardized tests can't measure these sorts of things. They're best measuring the ability to regurgitate facts and apply standard modes of analysis....[O]ur new obsession with standardized tests runs exactly counter to the new demands of the modern economy. It is training a generation of young people to become exquisitely competent at taking standardized tests, and a generation of teachers to become exceedingly good at teaching how to take them. Neither of these competencies has much to do with preparing young people for what they will encounter when they leave our schools. (p. 65)

Reich is no radical. As a former presidential cabinet member, his perspective represents one voice in the chorus of both Democrats and Republicans who are concerned that our current factory-like, test dominated system will not adequately prepare students for much beyond schools, work and social life included. Others in education, who do not necessarily share Reich's politics, have also made similar critiques in regards to schooling generally (Nordgren, 2002), literacy (Lankshear, 1997), and school leadership (Blackmore, 2002).

Reich's perspective, however, does raise an important point. Although I have made a particularly strong argument regarding the undue influence of business interests on the overall direction and content of education in the United States, I do not intend to be overly simplistic in my analysis. The reality is that the interests of capitalists are not completely unitary and monolithic, and that there are class fractions amongst big capital (see, e.g., Sklair, 2002) that disagree and struggle over the "best" direction for institutions like education to take in relation to the economy. Thus, Reich (2007) represents at least one fraction of capitalist interests clearly displeased with the tensions created between standardized testing and the educational and social demands created by the "new" economy. Additionally, the demands of the "new" globalized economy also place particular strains on the professional and new managerial middle class, discussed above, because even as systems of high-stakes, standardized testing increase the likelihood of their children gaining academic success, such testing also structures the educational experiences of their children in ways that limit their abilities to develop the kinds of flexible literacies they will need to be successful and upwardly mobile within fast capitalism (Collin & Apple, 2007).

Some particularly politically powerful voices have attempted to assert themselves at the forefront of this particular debate surrounding the outdated structure of today's education system in the United States (Grubb & Oakes, 2007). For instance, the *New* Commission on the Skills of the American Workforce, a commission made up of CEOs past and present, professors from prominent colleges of education, current and former union leadership, school district leadership, former politicians and high level cabinet members (including former U.S. Secretary of Education, Rod Paige), and university and school district chancellors, published a report entitled *Tough Choices or Tough Times* (National Center On Education and the Economy, 2006). This report has been called "*A Nation At Risk* for the next generation..." (National Center On Education and the Economy, 2006, p. 2) by noted conservative Chester Finn.

Tough Choices or Tough Times is indeed similar to *A Nation At Risk* (Grubb & Oakes, 2007). It critiques the public school system for being outdated, inefficient, and insufficient in its training of a new generation of "innovative" workers necessary to keep the United States competitive in the global economy. Instead of recommending a series of reforms, however, this report recommends a complete overhaul of the U.S. system of public education and teacher preparation. It suggests current teacher education policy be "scrapped," and that each state needs to set up a "Teacher Development Agency" to centralize and coordinate the recruiting, training, certification, and eventual placement of new teachers. Other teacher-focused changes suggested by the report include the dismantling of current structures of teacher retirement and benefit programs and reshaping them along the lines of corporations. This shift would be accompanied by a pay-for-performance salary structure. Further, the report recommends the establishment of new "Board Exams" based on standards that are competitive with other countries internationally. The report also advocates for schools to be run by "independent operators," with local school boards taking up the role of quality monitors. Additionally, the report proposes that "regional economic development authorities" made up of key economic leaders be established for,

> ...coordinating the work of the region's education and training institutions to make sure that each region's workers develop

the skills and knowledge needed to be successful in that labor market. (National Center On Education and the Economy, 2006, pp. 19–20)

Clearly, the logics of capitalist production and free market competition run through many recommendations of this report.

I must note, however, that *Tough Choices or Tough Times* does attempt to draw on peoples' good sense. For instance, it does recognize that the current global economy is leading to increased middle-class unemployment in the United States ("Survey: more pain than gain," 2006), and attempts to offer a solution to such increased unemployment vis-à-vis public education. Additionally, the report critiques standardized tests as assessments that do not serve the needs of the global economy and as assessments that do not support innovative and creative students, thus making appeals to the growing anti-standardized testing movement (Karp, 2006b). Further, *Tough Choices* advocates for universal early childhood education and a shift away from public education funding being determined largely by local tax bases. Disparities in both of these areas contribute to disparities in educational achievement, and by addressing these concerns, *Tough Choices* positions itself as a reasonable plan that addresses educational inequality.

There are some immediate contradictions present in *Tough Choices*, however. On one hand, the report claims that our current corps of teachers is drawn from the lower third of high school graduates that go on to college, essentially arguing that today's teachers do not represent the best and the brightest minds. Further, the report claims that "Many of our teachers are superb" (National Center On Education and the Economy, 2006, p. 12), or "The problem is not with our educators. It is with the system in which they work" (p. 9) while simultaneously recommending that the current teacher education system be overhauled.

The policy recommendations of *Tough Choices or Tough Times*, while making appeals to some good sense reforms, ultimately represent the evolving influence of capitalism in education. It suggests an increased centralization and control over the education of both students and teachers as well as increased influence of corporate interests in the shape and direction of public education in the United States. The contradictions within the report, as well the ways in which it draws on peoples' good sense, however, do point to the realities of hegemonic control of education. In the most basic sense, the *Tough Choices* report demonstrates how attempts to shift educational policy, and therefore, shifts in educational power, are oftentimes contradictory in and of themselves: In the same stroke that, in this case, the entire system of teacher education is targeted for explicit attack as being both dysfunctional and out of the direct control of the "proper" authorities (e.g., state government), other, more egalitarian educational concessions are offered that may appease critics.[9] Further, *Tough Choices* illustrates the existing contradictory tensions between schools and capitalist production in two ways. First, as I noted earlier, it symbolizes disagreement amongst the varying interests of capital about whether or not the current system of education meets the needs of the global economy: Some forms of capital require more symbolic analysts and are more likely to reject standardized testing, while other forms of capital still rely on more traditional labor and are more likely to support standardized systems of education. Second, it shows how the political needs of those in power can be at odds with the needs of the economy, particularly regarding the structure of school reform (Apple, 1995).

Finally, another important aspect to consider regarding the *Tough Choices* report is that the forces within the conservative modernization feel the need to attack the institution of public education. These attacks have appeared in the form of earlier reports like *A Nation At Risk* and in the form of detrimental policies like NCLB that set schools up for failure, punishment, and privatization (Apple, 2006a; Hursh, 2007). This fact again points to the contradictory space that education occupies, for there is a simple logic at work. If the institution of public education did not already exist as a site of cultural, political, and social resistance to the conservative modernization (Apple, 2006a; Shor, 1986) and to the production of inequality, then conservative forces would not be compelled to attack it so regularly and so vehemently. That, I would argue, is one central reason why the system of teacher education is a focus of attack in *Tough Choices* (as well as a focus of attack by the conservative right generally, see Maher, 2002 for further discussion) because teacher education programs, although imperfect and varied, often promote more progressive pedagogies and content in their credentialing curricula (Baltodano, 2006; Weiler & Maher, 2002).

Similar arguments can be made regarding the American Diploma Project (ADP) as well. The ADP started as a partnership between the Education Trust, Achieve, Inc., the Thomas B. Fordham Foundation, and the National Alliance of Business. Essentially recycling the same human capital arguments as *A Nation At Risk* and *Tough Choices or Tough Times*, this group has advocated for national standards, national testing, and the withholding of high school diplomas if students do not pass exit exams (Grubb & Oakes, 2007). As Grubb and Oakes (2007) observe:

The answer from the American Diploma Project is in effect a simple faith in the behaviorist power of tests to force teachers and students to comply with new requirements. That is, the ADP proposal simply assumes that the threat of withholding a diploma will make students and teachers work harder.... The basic assumptions of the American Diploma Project violate much of what we know about student behavior. (pp. 9–10)

Further, both the New Skills Commission and the ADP are vague and lackluster regarding their proposals: Neither organization offers tangible strategies for actual school reform. Both of their arguments essentially rely upon a "carrot-and-stick" vision of educational restructuring (e.g., more standards, more tests, and just work harder), with no detailed attention to what combination of school environment, funding, in-service teacher training, working/learning conditions, and community involvement might be necessary to be "successful" (Grubb & Oakes, 2007).

Regardless of whether or not *Tough Choices or Tough Times* becomes the new *A Nation At Risk*,[10] and regardless of whether or not the ADP is successful in its goal of national standards and national high-stakes testing, it will be important to track how the contradiction between the newer forms of capitalism and the less flexible forms of education play out in the coming decades,[11] particularly since our current capitalist economy can't support a fully educated workforce that is ready to be hired into an increasingly shrinking number of high-paying jobs (Brown & Lauder, 2006; Sleeter, 2005).

IDEOLOGY, CONTROL, AND THE EDUCATIONAL ENTERPRISE

Based on the evidence and analysis I have provided both in this chapter and in the previous two, there is a compelling argument—historical, political, economic, and ideological—to be made that the interests of capital, supporting free market, neoliberal ideology, in addition to the interests of the professional and managerial new middle class, substantially influence the over-arching logics, directions, and designs of education policy in the United States, and that this influence is done through a hegemonic narrative of individual equality. The problem is that the success of these types of business-like, neoliberal approaches to both economic and social programs remain unproven (Cuban, 2004) and in many cases have only lead to increasing inequality both domestically in the United States and internationally (Apple, 2006a; Hursh,

2005; Lauder et al., 1999; Lipman, 2004; Miner, 2006). Further still, as I have argued throughout this chapter, there is a contradiction present in the struggles over the configuration of contemporary education policy. While the logics of capitalist production—particularly factory-like, industrial capitalism—are still present, our system of education may not be meeting the needs of varying and contentious fractions of capital that continually call for education reforms that are not standardized (or at least not as standardized as the current system). Such a contradiction points to the role of the state (with its own varying interests) as a mediating force for the varying interests of capital (Apple, 1995; Fritzell, 1987).

In making this point, however, I do not intend to offer a purely economic determinist argument regarding the relationship between capitalist interests and public education, nor do I intend to suggest any neat, mechanical, or linear correspondence between the needs of capital and the structure of education (e.g., Bowles & Gintis, 1976). Instead, I want to concur with Apple's (1995) point that:

> As an aspect of the state, the school mediates and transforms an array of economic, political, and cultural pressures from competing classes and class segments...[T]his does not mean that the logics, discourses, or modes of control of capital will not have an increasing impact on everyday life in our educational institutions... (p. 127)

As such, I hope my arguments in this chapter have made clear that the "logics, discourses, or modes of control of capital" deeply impact public education in the United States, without my argument falling prey to the idea that a cabal of corporate capitalists directly controls and consciously manipulates of every aspect of education. Rather, as I argue in the next chapter, a conspiracy of controlling capitalists is not necessary. Instead, increased control over the education simply requires the implementation of systems of high-stakes, standardized testing—as an extension of the presumed wisdom of the logics of capitalist industry—within existing political and educational hierarchies, allowing classroom practices and identities to be regulated from a distance.

4

STEERAGE AT A DISTANCE
High-Stakes Testing and Classroom Control

I use the entire academic year preparing my students for the United States history subject area exam. My choice of instructional delivery and materials is completely dependent on preparation for this test. Therefore, I do not use current events, long-term projects, or creative group/cooperative work because this is not tested and the delivery format is not used. All my tests reflect the testing format of the subject area tests...

A Mississippi Social Studies teacher
(as quoted in, Vogler, 2005, p. 19)

Having now provided historical, conceptual, ideological, economic, and political analyses of high-stakes, standardized testing, the issue still remains as to how control, regulation, and (re)production manifest in the classroom. In order to address this issue, I begin this chapter with a clarification of the conception of "curriculum" I use here, as well as elaborate on Apple's (1995) application of the political economy of production to education. I then follow with a summary review of research on the effects of high-stakes testing on the curriculum, arguing that these effects illustrate five different types of classroom control. In order to fully understand how these controls operate hegemonically, I continue with an analysis of the unevenness and resistance that exists in local contexts and conclude this chapter by arguing that the controls outlined here represent a form of steerage at a distance, where policy makers and those with power attempt to steer what happens at the classroom level.

TEACHING UNDER THE YOKE OF TESTING

To assert that teachers are teaching to the tests probably seems commonsensical to most public school teachers and education activists. The research base surrounding high-stakes testing and classroom practice is fairly conclusive in supporting this point (Au, 2007b; Perreault, 2000). In some districts teachers are being bombarded by test data generated from test scores and are regularly confronted with warnings from administrators about the seriousness of the stakes involved in their students' performance (Johnson & Johnson, 2006; Sloan, 2005). Study after study shows that teachers respond to these pressures by teaching to the tests in varying ways (see, e.g., Bebray, Parson, & Avila, 2003; Clarke et al., 2003; Gayler, 2005; Hillocks Jr., 2002; McNeil & Valenzuela, 2001; Paris & Urdan, 2000; Pedulla et al., 2003; Sleeter, 2005). For instance 40% of the respondents of a survey of almost 4,200 teachers nationwide said that the results of high-stakes tests influenced their daily practices (Pedulla et al., 2003). A nationwide study conducted by the Center on Education Policy found that 71% of the school districts surveyed reduced the number of elementary school curricular offerings in order to increase teaching time in the tested subjects (Renter et al., 2006, see also CEP, 2007). Studies of individual states such as Colorado (Taylor, Shepard, Kinner, & Rosenthal, 2001), Florida (B. D. Jones & Egley, 2004), Illinois (Lipman, 2004), North Carolina (Groves, 2002; Murillo Jr. & Flores, 2002), Texas (McNeil, 2000; McNeil & Valenzuela, 2001), New York (Costigan III, 2002; Grant et al., 2002), Massachusetts (Luna & Turner, 2001), Mississippi (Vogler, 2005), Kansas, Michigan (Clarke et al., 2003), Virgina and Maryland (Gayler, 2005) among others, are finding the same thing: When punitive consequences are attached to test scores, teachers do indeed match their pedagogy and content to the test norms (Au, 2007b; Madaus, 1988). There are a flurry of smaller, more individualized case studies and focus groups where this finding holds true as well (see, e.g., Agee, 2004; Brimijoin, 2005; Gerwin, 2004).

The pressures that teachers are feeling, however, are not universally the same across all contexts. Comparative studies of differing states find that the higher the stakes, the more teachers focus their teaching on the tests (Clarke et al., 2003; Debray, Parson, & Avila, 2003; Hampton, 2005; Pedulla et al., 2003), which means that lower performing states are feeling the most intense pressure due to high-stakes testing and accountability systems (Nichols, Glass, & Berliner, 2005). While some scholars have argued that research has been inconclusive and that we cannot really tell if teachers are changing their curriculum or are in fact teaching to the test (see, Gradwell, 2006; Grant, 2003; van Hover, 2006), the above studies make a strong case for the argument that teachers' practice has indeed been affected by high-stakes testing.

While the above summary communicates the general effect of high-stakes testing, we don't get a clear picture of what this effect means in terms of actual classroom practice—what it concretely means to "teach to the test." What I intend to develop in this chapter is a more nuanced mapping of how test-induced curricular control operates; to explore how the policy structures and the structures of the tests themselves interact to create a powerful system of control over pedagogy and the structure of knowledge in the classroom. Such an analysis will, hopefully, allow for a deeper conception of the mechanisms of social control at play within high-stakes tests while also opening a path to examine how issues of power and inequality become embedded in the structure of knowledge itself. However, in order to begin to understand how curricular control is exerted via high-stakes testing, it is important to clarify what I mean by "curriculum" as well as the analytical distinctions between the types of control I discuss here. Thus, in the next section I draw on both curriculum theory and the political economy of education.

CURRICULUM AND CONTROL

"Curriculum" is a word that is widely used, yet is defined in multiple ways. In this way "curriculum," like many other words, is a sliding signifier, the actual definition of which changes depending on who is speaking, with whom they are speaking, in what context they are speaking, and for what purposes the concept is being used (Gee, 1996). It would follow, then, that within education generally, and within the field of curriculum studies specifically, definitions of "curriculum" range widely (Beauchamp, 1982; P. W. Jackson, 1996; Kliebard, 1989). Historically, the term "curriculum" has its roots in the Latin word *currere*, which means a-course-to-be-run (Eisner, 1994) and was first used at the University of Glasgow in the 17th century to describe "a formal course of study that the students completed" (Harden, 2001, p. 335). This definition is perhaps the most recognizable because it is evident in the way so many schools are organized around a course of predetermined required subject matter classes that students must pass to graduate. Granted, discussions of definitions are laborious and at times tedious, particularly in relation to such broad concepts as "curriculum." However, as Jackson (1996) points out:

> ...[A]ll definitions are parts of arguments. The rhetorical structures in which definitions are lodged and play an important part are attempts to persuade us of the value of looking at something in a particular way and of later using a word or phrase to stand for that perception. We may disagree with that way of looking, but we nonetheless cannot avoid making use of the definition even while expressing our disagreement...All we can do in the final analysis is to proffer reasoned arguments in support of one definition over the other. (p. 12)

My intent here is to offer *a* definition of curriculum that I think is theoretically robust enough to carry through my analysis.

Clearly, subject matter content—content that is deemed worth knowing—is an important aspect of the curriculum. Most in the field at least recognize that curriculum encompasses a body of knowledge to be learned in some way, shape, or form. To stop at the level of content, as most conservative, traditional, or commonsense conceptions of curriculum do, however, obscures other important aspects. For instance, subject matter content within schools and classrooms implies not only *selection* of contents deemed important, valued, or "official" (Apple, 2000; Bernstein, 1999), but also the *transmission* of content as well, in that:

> Subject matter is always an expression of a desire to communicate ideas to others...Differences within the form and content of various expressions of subject matter reflect an understanding of differences in the backgrounds of potential audiences and the circumstances of the subject matter's formulation. (McEwan & Bull, 1991, p. 331)

Indeed, all content selection for the classroom is simultaneously pedagogic because such selection is presupposed by a need or want to communicate ideas to an audience of students (Segall, 2004a, 2004b). Further still, the selection of contents with the intent to pedagogize these selections for classroom or educational dissemination also implicates the structure of knowledge itself, because the process of selecting and teaching content also requires attention to the intended form in which the content will be communicated (Apple, 1995). Thus, the concept of curriculum also implicates the structure of knowledge embedded in curricular form[1] as well as pedagogy. The trilogy of 1) subject matter content knowledge, 2) structure or form of curricular knowledge (as well as the implications of this structure), and 3) pedagogy—how content knowledge is taught, are thus three defining aspects of the concept of "curriculum" (Au, 2007b).[2] This conception of curriculum is the one I use here.

In addition to the above discussion of the concept of curriculum, I also want to attend to Apple's (1995) discussion of three types of educational control commonly associated with capitalist production. The first is "simple" control, where someone else decides what is best and simply directs others to follow their instructions or face consequences. The second is "technical" control, where control is "embedded in the physical structure of your job" (p. 128). The third is "bureaucratic" control which, according to Apple, is "embodied within the *hierarchal* social relations of the workplace" (p. 128, original emphasis). Building on Apple's distinctions and definitions, my analysis will make use of both technical and bureaucratic controls while also elaborating on and reaching for other types of controls that operate through high-stakes testing as well.

One significant departure from Apple's (1995) formulation is that my analysis disregards the idea of simple control. Apple's conception of simple control is too vague in that it is not clearly distinguishable from bureaucratic control—where others in the bureaucratic hierarchies have the institutional authority to simply demand those below to do as they are told or face consequences if those demands are not met.[3] This allows simple control to be folded into the concept of bureaucratic control, a concept of Apple's that remains intact for my analysis. Additionally, as Apple explains, technical control is a type of control that is rooted within the organization and arrangement of one's work. In industry, technical control manifests in many ways and can be illustrated by an assembly line, where the tasks of the assembly-line workers' jobs are determined by the structure of the assembly line itself: Certain stations require specific tasks, the overall order and form of which have been determined by engineers or managers. Indeed, as I argue here, "teaching to the test" is in fact technical control in operation. However, while Apple's formulation is useful, analyzing the impact that high-stakes tests are having on teaching and learning requires a more nuanced conception of technical control. In the following I maintain Apple's technical control as a broad categorical lens but, using the conception of curriculum discussed above, I explain how high-stakes testing manifests into the classroom control vis-à-vis content control, formal control, and pedagogic control (see also, Au, 2007b).

TEACHING TO THE TEST 1: CONTENT CONTROL

The most prevalent and consistent finding in the empirical research is that high-stakes testing narrows the instructional curriculum because, to varying degrees, teachers shape the content norms of their curriculum to match that of the tests (see, e.g., Abrams, Pedulla, & Madaus, 2003; CEP, 2007; Hill & Lake, 2002; B. D. Jones & Egley, 2004; Pedulla et al., 2003; Renter et al., 2006; Rosenbusch, 2005; Taylor et al., 2001; von Zastrow, 2004). For instance, in a nationwide survey of almost 4,200 teachers, 43% of the respondents from states where high-stakes were attached to the tests, reported that a "great deal of increased time" was being spent on tested areas (Abrams et al., 2003). Another nationwide survey found that 71% of the districts reported cutting at least one subject to increase time spent on reading and math as a direct response to the high-stakes testing mandated under No Child Left Behind (Renter et al., 2006). These findings are bolstered by another nationwide survey of 349 school districts, where it was reported that 62% of districts reported increased instructional time devoted to math and English/language arts in elementary school since 2002, including a 37% increase in time spent on math and a 46% increase in time spent on English/language arts education (CEP, 2007). Kentucky, which tests both science and social studies in the fourth and fifth grades respectively, is another case in point. A two year study of 152 schools that included a survey of 479 teachers found that there was a 49% increase in time spent teaching science in the fourth grade and a 60% increase in time spent teaching social studies in the fifth grade, when those subjects are tested (Stecher & Barron, 2001).[4] In cases where social studies are included in the high-stakes tests, such as Virginia and Mississippi, teachers find themselves scrambling to add content, reduce non-tested social studies knowledge and cover the test required content in very compressed amounts of time (Salinas, 2006; Segall, 2006; A. M. Smith, 2006; van Hover, 2006; Vogler, 2005). Similar findings arise in the body of qualitative research as well (see, e.g., Agee, 2004; Au, 2007b; Clarke et al., 2003; Gayler, 2005; Hill & Lake, 2002; Johnson & Johnson, 2006; Lipman, 2004; McNeil & Valenzuela, 2001; Murillo Jr. & Flores, 2002; Sleeter, 2005; Sloan, 2005; Wright & Choi, 2005).

Because of the limited and finite nature of school time and resources, it is becoming increasingly clear that the curriculum is essentially a zero sum game. Subjects considered to be nonessential to the high-stakes, standardized tests are being reduced or cut altogether. Several studies found that instruction in subject areas such as science, social studies, foreign language, art, music, and physical education is being reduced as a direct result of the tests (Abrams et al., 2003; Au, 2007b; Groves, 2002; Lapayese, 2007; Pedulla et al., 2003; Renter et al., 2006; Siskin, 2003; Taylor et al., 2001; Vogler, 2005; von Zastrow, 2004; Wright & Choi, 2005). For instance, a survey of almost 1,000 principals across four high-stakes testing states found that 25% reported decreased time for the arts, with 33% predicting additional cuts to the arts in the future due to high-stakes testing (von Zastrow, 2004). Another survey also found that test-induced increases in math and English/language arts instruction came at the cost of reductions in other subjects, where 44% of schools surveyed reported that they reduced the amount of instruction in subjects such as social studies, science, art, physical education, music as well as time spent at lunch or recess by over 30% (CEP, 2007). In some districts in California, the lowest performing students have had to take extra classes in reading and math, which has meant that these students have had to cut science and social studies from their course load completely (Renter et al., 2006). Other studies have found that foreign language classes are also disappearing from school offerings. For instance, of 165 districts surveyed in the northeastern United States, 22% have reported district level cuts to the teaching of foreign languages, 24% reported the elimination of foreign language teaching positions, and 22% reported that one or more foreign languages were cut from district programs completely (Rosenbusch, 2005). High-stakes testing is, in essence, creating a "zero sum curriculum."

Thus, as Groves (2002) remarks, "For schools struggling for basic survival, the natural reaction it to teach only those subjects tested. In this way, assessment (the test) actually drives curriculum and instruction in schools" (p. 25). This process is the on-the-ground manifestation of the means-ends logic of Bobbitt's "scientific" curriculum development discussed in Chapter 2. The ends of instruction are determining the means: The tests are determining what is taught. Thus, high-stakes testing is exerting *content control* over the curriculum.

TEACHING TO THE TEST 2: FORMAL CONTROL

In addition to content control, we can see control over curricular form, or *formal control*, operating through high-stakes testing as well. Curricular form refers to the organization of meaning and action, including the order in which we are introduced to content and the very form that knowledge itself takes, in the curriculum (Apple, 1995). As the content of the curriculum moves to match what the tests require (content control), the structure of curricular content knowledge shifts toward the fragmentation demanded by the tests. In this way, knowledge learned for the tests is transformed into a collection of facts, operations, or data mainly needed for rote memorization in preparation for the tests (McGuire, 2007). Thus, students are increasingly learning knowledge associated with lower level thinking, and they are often learning this knowledge within the context of the tests alone (Bigelow, 1999; Clarke et al., 2003; Grant, 2001; Luna & Turner, 2001; McNeil, 2000; Pahl, 2003; Pedulla et al., 2003; M. L. Smith, 1991; Toch, 2006; Vogler, 2005). This means learning information outside of the context of students' lives and outside of the context of the world. Knowledge learned for the tests thus represents disconnected, fragmented, and isolated knowledge (Au, 2007b). Therefore, in addition to content control, we see high-stakes testing also exerting control over the very form and structure that knowledge takes in the curriculum. It is this *formal control* that leads directly to control over teachers' instructional practices.

TEACHING TO THE TEST 3: PEDAGOGIC CONTROL

In teaching to the tests, teachers end up adopting pedagogical strategies in their classrooms that correlate to the forms of knowledge and content contained on the high-stakes tests. In the classroom this translates into teachers adopting more teacher-centered pedagogies, such as lectures, to meet the content and form demands of the tests (Au, 2007b; Gayler, 2005; Grant, 2001; Grant et al., 2002; G. M. Jones, Jones, & Hargrove, 2003; Luna & Turner, 2001; McNeil, 2000; McNeil & Valenzuela, 2001; Stecher & Barron, 2001; Taylor et al., 2001; van Hover & Heinecke, 2005; Vogler, 2005). Pedagogy is thus reduced to figuring out how to dispense "packaged fragments of information sent from an upper level of the bureaucracy" (McNeil, 2000, p. 5). This pedagogical trend toward "multiple choice teaching" (M. L. Smith, 1991, p. 10) also manifests in increased time doing test drills and practicing for the types of information, questions, and test-taking skills that the tests require (Au, 2007b; CEP, 2007; Hillocks Jr., 2002; Luna & Turner, 2001; Perreault, 2000). As was recounted in Chapter 3 regarding scripted reading programs, many districts are becoming "more prescriptive about how and what teachers should teach" (Renter et al., 2006, p. 99) in response to high-stakes testing, and, as Fickel (2006) notes in a case study concerning the teaching of social studies in Kentucky:

> The growing sense of pressure within a high-stakes climate affected [the teachers'] decisions around content as they focused on chronological coverage. The test also led [the teachers] to make changes in their assessment practices. Over time the teachers in

the department began slowly shifting the writing tasks, especially in required history courses, to match the testing format...[T]hey began to highlight test-taking strategies, rather than the real-life, authentic application of knowledge... (p. 99)

In Virginia, teachers have been found to both reduce inquiry learning and critical analyses in favor of teacher-centered lectures in order to meet the content and time demands of the state social studies tests (A. M. Smith, 2006). Nationally, the Center on Education Policy found that 84% of districts reported changing their curricula to emphasize test content and skills (CEP, 2007). While never absolute, the pedagogic control exerted by high-stakes testing creates the conditions where teachers are increasingly compelled to be "alienated executors of someone else's plans" (Apple, 2000, p. 118), and where, as in a Michigan study, "...teachers see the test as a restricting force, as something that prevents them from doing certain things in their classrooms" (Segall, 2006, p. 116).[5]

Teachers, however, are acutely cognizant that their pedagogy is being changed by the pedagogic norms established by the high-stakes testing. In response to this pedagogic control, teachers feel that they are teaching in ways that are contradictory to best practice (Abrams et al., 2003; Agee, 2004; Brimijoin, 2005; Clarke et al., 2003; Costigan III, 2002; Pedulla et al., 2003; van Hover & Heinecke, 2005). In their nationwide survey, Abrams and colleagues (2003) found that 76% of the teachers in states with "high" stakes testing and 63% of the teachers in their study from states with "low" stakes testing reported that their state testing programs were contributing to unsound educational practices.

There is also evidence that new teachers specifically are feeling the pedagogical constraints established by the tests. Costigan III (2002), in a study of newly credentialed teachers and their experiences in high-stakes testing environments, found that the tests became the focus of the new teacher's first year of instruction, that this type of teaching was having an adverse effect on their students and their practice, and that teachers developed a sense of powerlessness in the face of the amount of testing and the pressures involved. Many of the teachers in Costigan's study felt that "a very real culture of testing has been created in the schools and districts in which they teach..." and that they were "unable successfully to negotiate between a testing curriculum and personal best practice" (p. 33). Agee (2004) found similar evidence in a case study of a new teacher in her first three years of teaching in a high-stakes environment, and pre-service teachers have also reported feeling tensions due to the pedagogical demands of the tests, which they feel operate in contradiction to the pedagogies they are learning in their credentialing programs (Gerwin, 2004). Consequently, as much of the available research has found, this shift, which emphasizes test score achievement rather than good teaching, has created substantial dips in teacher morale and motivation (Agee, 2004; B. D. Jones & Egley, 2004; Nichols & Berliner, 2005; Perreault, 2000; Taylor et al., 2001). In these most basic ways, in addition to the content and formal controls, we see high-stakes testing operating as a *pedagogic control* over teachers' practice.

TEACHING TO THE TEST 4: BUREAUCRATIC CONTROL

Schools exist within institutional hierarchies that extend from the extreme local contexts of students and teachers, through the school, district, and state levels, on up to the federal level. The fact that high-stakes testing, as a part of a policy design (Schneider & Ingram, 1997) developed and implemented through these hierarchies, exerts so much control over the curriculum is evidence of the existence of hierarchies of institutional power. Indeed, high-stakes tests hold so much power because their results are tied to rewards or sanctions that can deeply affect the lives of students, teachers, principals, and communities (negatively for low performers, and positively for high performers). This is a condition of any test that is considered "high-stakes." Therefore, in addition to the other types of control outlined above, the curricular control exhibited by high-stakes testing also manifests *bureaucratic control,* or control "embodied within the *hierarchal* social relations of the workplace" (Apple, 1995, p. 128, original emphasis). I employ "bureaucracy" here in a Weberian (1964) sense, which is defined as an organization that relies upon,

> ...a complex rational division of labor, with fixed duties and jurisdictions; stable, rule-governed authority channels and universally applied performance guidelines; a horizontal division of graded authority, or hierarchy, entailing supervision from above; a complex system of written record-keeping, based on scientific procedures that standardize communications and increase control;... predictable, standardized management procedures following general rules; and a tendency to require total loyalty from its members toward the way of life an organization requires. (Ferguson, 1984, p. 7)

Bureaucratic control is evident in relation to regimes of high-stakes testing. Research consistently finds that systems of high-stakes, standardized testing centralize authority at the top of federal, state, and district bureaucracies, and generally take control away from local decision makers and local contexts (Apple, 2000; Gibson, 2001; Hanson, 2000; Madaus, 1988; McNeil, 2000; Natriello & Pallas, 2001; Sloan, 2005; Sunderman & Kim, 2005). The relocation of power up the bureaucratic ladder is a function of policy design itself, where those "on the bottom" are to be held accountable to those "on top" in administrative hierarchies (McNeil, 2005; Natriello & Pallas, 2001). As McNeil (2005), in her discussion of the accountability system in Texas schools, explains:

> The accountability system is an extreme form of centralization. The controls hinge on a standardized test. Through a simple set of linkages, the centralized educational bureaucracy of the state has established a test that must be taken by all children, in key subjects in key grades. The state then rates each school according to the test scores of the children in the school. School districts are rated by the scores of all their schools. Set up as a hierarchical system, each layer of the bureaucracy is held accountable to the one above it. The rules are set at the top and there can be no variations in their implementation, nor can schools or districts opt out if they prefer a different method of evaluating children's learning or assessing the quality of their schools. (p. 59)

Within the bureaucratic control of high-stakes testing, state or federal government authorities determine standards and tests. Student test scores are publicly reported, and state authorities use those scores to hold districts, schools, administrators, teachers, and students "accountable" for increases in those scores—handing out sanctions or rewards depending on student performance. Within these systems:

> The decisions are made centrally, and at the top of the bureaucracy. The lower levels of the bureaucracy, where teachers and children reside, are not invited to create variations or improvements on this system or to offer alternatives to it. They are, rather, intended to merely comply. They are to be accountable to those above them. (McNeil, 2005, p. 60)

The structure of such systems of accountability based on high-stakes standardized tests pull decision-making away from the professional teachers and the students and puts it into the hands of technical experts and bureaucrats who operate with their own political agendas far away from local contexts (Apple, 1995; G. M. Jones et al., 2003; McNeil, 2000). The power in this model, then, is located in the bureaucracies that have the authority to both determine the assessment and determine the criteria for what counts as passing or failing. Additionally, as part of their policy designs, these bureaucracies also have the power to determine the sanctions and punishments for those that do not meet their criteria for passing—thus putting the "high-stakes" into high-stakes testing. In these ways, high-stakes testing programs are an extremely effective tool for government agencies, which have regulatory power, to influence what happens at the classroom level (Goodson & Foote, 2001; Natriello & Pallas, 2001).

Bureaucratic control also has profoundly gendered implications: We still have a body of mostly male governmental and administrative authorities overseeing and managing the work of a predominantly female workforce. In the year 2000, 75% of the total teaching workforce was female (National Center for Education Statistics, 2004). In elementary and middle school education specifically, where the bulk of high-stakes testing is required by No Child Left Behind, 91% and 73% of the teachers, respectively, are women (Provasnik & Dorfman, 2005). Hence, a particular dynamic within high-stakes testing, particularly in regards to No Child Left Behind, exists. The male super-majority legislative and executive branches of the federal government assert very strong institutional authority over a teacher workforce that is a female super-majority. This gendered trend is less prevalent in secondary education, but it still exists. The teachers at the high school level are 55% female, where as the principals at the same level were 78% male (Wirt, Choy, Rooney, Provasnik, & Tobin, 2004). These skewed numbers still support the existence of patriarchy within the educational bureaucracies as well as the increased masculinization of administrative power over a feminized teaching profession (Blount, 1999).

Further still, the bureaucratic *form* itself is gendered. As Arnot, David, and Weiner (1999) argue, managerial forms associated with bureaucracies that support cut-throat competition and individualism, such as regimes of high-stakes testing, are ultimately masculinist. Additionally, the reliance of high-stakes testing systems on positivist forms of rational "objective" measurement, also reflect gendered norms in that objectivity is defined by being value-free, detached, unemotional, and public (that is, nondomestic), all of which are associated with masculinity (Franzway, Court, & Connell, 1989). In the case of bureaucratic control, the hierarchical power structure itself also establishes a system of dominants and subordinates, a system that mirrors the gendered norms of male subordination of women that exists generally in patriarchal societies (Ferguson, 1984). Thus, high-stakes, standardized testing policies such as NCLB and the bureaucratic control embedded in their structures should very much be viewed both as an assertion by male authorities over the labor of women and the assertion of administrative masculinity over teacher femininity in ways themselves that are masculinized.

TEACHING TO THE TEST 5: DISCURSIVE CONTROL

While I have elaborated and expanded upon Apple's (1995) basic categories of bureaucratic and technical control, I have not departed significantly from the foundation of his theoretical framework. I would argue, however, that the implications of these controls go deeper than Apple addresses, and as such, in order to understand how these controls operate, we need to look at one other broad form of control unaccounted for in Apple's formulation: *Discursive control*. It is through the curricular content, the standardization of knowledge around particular norms, the acceptance and rejection of particular identities in the classroom, and the embodiment of socially defined categories within policy structure itself that high-stakes testing exerts a form of *Discursive control* over the process of education. This form of control does not contradict Apple's conceptualization. Indeed, it is complimentary and is used here to deepen our understanding of the processes that are taking place.

In terms of the bureaucratic, pedagogic, content, and formal controls exerted by the tests, high-stakes testing represents a tool of what Gee (1996) would call a "dominant Discourse." For Gee, a Discourse (with a capitol "D") represents more than just language. It encompasses ways-of-being that express certain norms through a variety of signals, including language, dress, rituals, movement, culture, and identity. Within this framework, high-stakes tests may be understood as hegemonic devices that are used by dominant elites to determine who is and who is not a part of their dominant Discourse. As Gee (1996) remarks:

> Very often dominant groups in a society apply rather constant tests of the fluency of the dominant Discourses in which their power is symbolized; these tests become both tests of natives or, at least, fluent users of the Discourse, and *gates* to exclude non-natives…(p. 146, original emphasis)

While within the context of his work in sociolinguistics and literacy, Gee is clearly referring to the types of social testing that happens in day-to-day interactions; it is clear that the analogy is more than appropriate as high-stakes tests seem to select for specific identities and Discourses.

Although Gee's conception of Discourse is more expansive than traditional conceptions of discourse, which tend to focus on language, it is true that Discursive control does operate at the level of policy language (and therefore, policy structure). Ultimately, bureaucracies have the power to define the categories and set the limits determining who is "passing" and "failing." In order to be able to interpret what the results of high-stakes tests mean, categories must be constructed around the test scores. Policies erect a series of categories to define various groups (in this case students and schools) as "good" or "bad," "passing" or "failing," "meets the standard" or "approaches but does not meet the standard," "functionality" and "dysfunctionality" (Lipman, 2004; M. L. Smith, 2004). In this sense, as Hanson (2000) points out, "The individual in contemporary society is not so much described by tests as constructed by them" (p. 68) because the "tests transform people by assigning them to various categories...and then they are treated, act and come to think of themselves according to the expectations associated with those categories..." (p. 74). These linguistic/social categories represent a form of control over the classroom Discourse that is built through high-stakes testing, one that essentially operates and extends through the bureaucratic control. As such, these categories are defined and established through very political and ideological processes and do not represent an expression of "objective" goals and research. Further, as M.L. Smith (2004) explains:

> ...[C]ounting the number of children depends on first constructing categories, the meaning and boundaries of which are ambiguous. The process of "counting as" depends on a dynamic of interests, ideologies, and political tactics of the persons involved...Typically political entities perform this task and make such categorizations—not by technical or statistical procedures, but by political processes...Even when political entities use statistical procedures to establish levels, categories, and cutoff scores, results are problematic and the application of those levels is political. (p. 154)

Under the current regime of NCLB, the power of such definitions can be seen in the language of "scientifically based" reading programs (M. L. Smith, 2004) and "proficiency" under AYP (Au, 2005b; Kim & Sunderman, 2005). Such categorization and naming provides a framework for selecting specific pedagogic identities of teachers as well as learner identities of students.

Discursive Control and Pedagogic Identities

On one level, the Discursive control of high-stakes testing defines the acceptable *pedagogic identities* of teachers. High-stakes testing creates norms surrounding what types of teaching and what types of teacher are considered "good" or "bad." As Nichols and Berliner (2005) note:

The overall result of high-stakes testing, for many teachers and school districts, seems to be a restricted vision of what should be taught and how it should be taught. Less obvious but of equal concern is that there also exists a restricted vision of the kind of person who should be teaching. Implied is that a good deal of teaching in high-stakes testing environments is of a technical rather than a professional nature. (p. 109)

The "restricted vision of the kind of person who should be teaching" is that of a de-skilled and a re-skilled teacher, who, because of the high-stakes attached to the tests, sees their best (or pragmatically, their most immediate) interest served by focusing on the technical delivery of information to students in preparation for the tests (Apple, 1995, 2000; Kincheloe, 2001; Lipman, 2004; McNeil, 2000). Both "good" teaching and the "good" teacher become defined by the test scores themselves (Booher-Jennings, 2005) or through policy definitions of a "highly qualified teacher" (see Au, 2004). Indeed, in one case a new teacher gave up her goal of being an anti-racist catalyst for change in her school under the weight of the testing regime (Agee, 2004). Her identity as a teacher was in fact limited by the control functions of high-stakes testing.

Discursive control over teachers' identities provides some insight into why so many teachers, as actors within bureaucratic structures, do change their pedagogies to match that of the high-stakes tests. This control operationalizes what Bernstein (1999) refers to "mechanisms of projection" where teacher identity is a "reflection of external contingencies" and the "maintenance of this identity depends upon the facility of *projecting* discursive organization/practices themselves driven by external contingencies" (p. 251, original emphasis). This Discursive control of pedagogic identities also relates to pedagogic control, for as Ball (2003b) explains:

Teachers are no longer encouraged to have a rationale for practice, account for themselves in terms of a relationship to the meaningfulness of what they do, but are required to produce measurable 'improving' outputs and performances, what is important is *what works* (p. 222, original emphasis)

Further, when low test scores come to mean that you, as an individual, are a "bad" teacher (and by extension maybe even a "bad" person), then the social and cultural pressures to teach to the tests are piled on top of the political, professional, and economic pressures as well. This phenomenon is a condition of the "performativity" of teaching within the context of high-stakes testing education policies, where Ball (2003b) writes that teachers have "an emotional status dimension…Thus, our responses to the flow of performance information can engender individual feelings of pride, guilt, shame and envy" (p. 221).[6]

Discursive Control and Learner Identities

Discursive control also has a profound impact on students. This impact manifests itself in the tacit and explicit accepting and rejecting of specific *learner identities*, where certain student identities are effectively locked out of the curriculum by the test-established controls. In particular, research finds high-stakes tests systematically push out multicultural subject matter content because the tests do not assess such content (Agee, 2004; Berlak, 2000; Bigelow, 1999, 2001; Darder & Torres, 2004; Karp, 2006b; Lapayese, 2007; McNeil, 2000; McNeil & Valenzuela, 2001; Themba-Nixon, 2000). For instance, in a study of the New York state world history and geography tests, Grant (2001) found that Western nations dominate the test content. As another example, also discussed above, Agee (2004) studied the experience of an African American teacher who gave up her original goal of teaching multicultural content because of the pressures created by the tests. As yet another example, Toussaint (2000/2001) tells a personal story of how, as an employee of a private firm grading state exams from four states, he was required to use a scoring rubric that mandated students validate a Eurocentric view of manifest destiny in order to achieve a high score. This trend points to the standardization of knowledge that is considered to be acceptable for children to learn, where the high-stakes tests operating as one of the central controls over determining that acceptability.

Because high-stakes tests function to force schools to adopt a generic, standardized, non-multicultural curriculum, this curriculum ultimately silences the "voices, the cultures, and the experiences of children" (McNeil, 2000, p. 232), particularly if those voices, cultures, and experiences fall outside the norms of the tests. In this way, students' lives, in all their variation, are effectively locked out of the curriculum by high-stakes tests, as schools press to structure learning to fit the test-based curricular norms (Goodson & Foote, 2001; McNeil, 2000, 2005; Rex, 2003). High-stakes testing systems thus *require* diversity to be subtracted because of their emphasis on standardization (Valenzuela, 1999). McNeil (2005) sums up the "subtractive" logic thusly:

> The illusion that if all children are being tested alike, then we must be teaching all children the same thing, has been very successfully misleading. From inside classrooms we know that the system has to de-personalize, has to exclude, has to structure out personal and

cultural identities to claim objectivity. It has to silence differences, whether cultural, developmental, or idiosyncratic, or it loses its potency. *The system has to be subtractive or it cannot function as a generic, standardized, system.* (pp. 93–94, original emphasis)

Subtraction is a function of systems of high-stakes testing because the standardization of knowledge constructs classrooms as spaces where only specific content and specific cultures and identities are recognized as legitimate. Thus, we also see that diversity itself—diversity of students, student performance, student ability, and student experience—being viewed negatively by teachers and schools with high-stakes testing environments. This is because the test scores of children who fall outside of the norms established by the tests may have a negative impact on schools' overall scores, which in turn may trigger sanctions against teachers, administrators, and the students themselves (Darling-Hammond, 2004; Kane & Staiger, 2002; McNeil, 2005). As such, student identity, in all of its many facets, is restricted and bracketed as existing outside of acceptable, worthwhile and valuable education. As the concrete manifestation of the hegemonic logics of standardized high-stakes testing I discussed in Chapter 2, diversity itself has become a threat to survival and success within the system because it is antithetical to the process of standardization.

This contradiction between diversity and high-stakes testing plays out in policy implementation as well. Research has found that the pressures of high-stakes standardized testing are greatest in states with high "minority"[7] populations (Nichols et al., 2005); at the school level, research has also found that the narrowing of the curriculum is most drastic in schools with large populations of students of color (Lomax, West, Harmon, Viator, & Madaus, 1995; von Zastrow, 2004). For instance, in von Zastrow's (2004) research of the decline of liberal arts education due to high-stakes testing, 25% of the respondents nationally reported a decrease of time spent on the arts. However, in schools with "high minority" populations, 36% of the principals reported decreases in the arts (an 11% increase in cuts). Additionally, 23% of the principals in schools von Zastrow labeled "high minority" reported cuts to foreign languages, and 47% of the principals surveyed from "high minority" K-5 schools reported decreases in time spent teaching social studies. Another study found that 97% of high-poverty school districts, which are largely populated by students of color, have instituted policies specifically aimed at increasing time spent on reading. This is compared to only 55% to 59% of wealthier, lower poverty districts (Renter et al., 2006). Groves (2002) points out that, as low performing schools narrow their curriculum and teaching practices, "large groups of students, largely low income and of color, no longer have access to the same knowledge as their middle class white peers" (p. 26).

The above findings demonstrate that districts with high concentrations of low-income and students of color are institutionalizing high-stakes testing pressures at greater rates than their high-income counterparts, thus creating more restrictive, less enriching educational environments for the very students that high-stakes, standardized test based educational reforms like NCLB are supposed to be helping. Compounding these findings with the increased drop-out rates of students of color and the continued educational inequality associated with high-stakes testing discussed here, it is not too bold to assert that high-stakes testing represents a form of "cultural imperialism" in the classroom (Berlak, 2000).

The Triple Bind for Non-Standard Identities

Taken on the whole, students whose identities fall outside of the norms established by standardization, face somewhat of a triple bind because of high-stakes testing. First, as the curriculum becomes increasingly adapted to the content expectations of high-stakes tests, content that recognizes the diversity of student history, culture, and experience becomes increasingly unacceptable in the classroom. These curricular content changes are further reinforced by pressures to perform well on high-stakes tests, as both teachers and students are compelled to match the standardized knowledge and knowledge forms the tests require. Second, this standardization of both pedagogy and content, then, not only prohibits a diverse curriculum in the classroom, it also works against a diversity of identities in the classroom. Finally, as a consequence of the disparate achievement in high-stakes testing environments, students of color ultimately feel more intense pressures to perform well—even as their curricular environments are becoming increasingly restricted and less rich.

Because identities are complexly interwoven (Gee, 1996), Discursive control thus constructs students in particular ways in relation to the classroom. For instance, research on working-class African American male students has concluded that these students *can* (but not always) come to associate the educational norms of schooling with being "soft," feminized, White, and middle class (Au, 2005a; Dance, 2002; Davis, 2006; Noguera, 2003b; Tatum, 1997). Such gender, class, and race constructions within schools have been noted to create particular resistances to education among working-class students generally (Shor, 1992; Willis, 1977, 2003). Because of its Discursive control, high-stakes testing plays a role in this process. On one hand, the poor performance of working-class African American males, both on the tests and in schools, plays into the broader sociopolitical process of the criminalization of Black male youth generally, where they are regularly depicted as gang members, criminals, and fearsome predators incapable of being productive in civil society (Titus, 2004). On the other hand, there is a lack of incentive to do well in school and on the tests that operates both within and without the classroom: Rising unemployment and wage disparities between the rich and the poor and between racial groups, as well as a lack of community-based employment that pays livable wages (Anyon, 2005), contribute to the feelings that, for many young people, school is not worth the effort. Inside of the classroom, working-class African American males are further alienated from their education through the Discursive controls of high-stakes testing, as local and/or culturally relevant knowledge and pedagogies (Ladson-Billings, 1995) are disregarded in the face of the tests. Thus, the responses of these students is simultaneously raced, masculinized, and classed, as they negotiate an unresponsive educational and social system.

This last point is crucial to the arguments presented here. The importance of acknowledging the "home" cultures and identities of the students we instruct, in order to make our teaching more effective and less alienating, has long been recognized by scholars in the field (see, e.g., Ladson-Billings, 1994, 1995; Noguera, 2003a; Valenzuela, 1999; Vavrus, 2002). These scholars maintain that students' lives, the curriculum, content, and educational achievement are often knitted together, and that if the cultures and experiences of children and their communities are not named, not included in the standards or the tests, then they are not deemed relevant to learning. The exclusion of knowledge through standardized testing is a technical reality associated with trying to measure knowledge generally: Some knowledge is included, some is not (Horn, 2006). By standardizing knowledge, effectively exerting curricular control and locking the home cultures of students out of the classroom, high-stakes testing directly contributes to the reproduction of social and educational inequality via the tests' roles as both gatekeepers to opportunity (grade promotion, diplomas, and credentials) and regulators of official knowledge (Apple, 2000).

CONTRADICTIONS OF CLASSROOM CONTROL

It is important to understand that some contradictions operate within the classroom controls outlined in this chapter. For one, the leverage of curricular control is not a completely predetermined occurrence.

Rather, it must be seen as a trend that exists among significant numbers of teachers, but not necessarily universally. For instance, in previous research (Au, 2007b), while my overwhelming finding was that high-stakes tests exert significant control over the curriculum, I did not find that such control was ubiquitous. Rather, I found that the extent of curricular control was often related to the test construction itself. Thus, there are several cases where teachers did not restrict their content, form, and pedagogy *as much* as others. These cases revolve around teachers whose test-based instruction involves the development of critical literacy skills (see, e.g., Clarke et al., 2003; Libresco, 2005 ; Rex & Nelson, 2004 ; Wolf & Wolf, 2002 ; Wollman-Bonilla, 2004; Yeh, 2005). For instance, New York State's history exam involves a mix of multiple-choice questions and a document-based essay question (DBQ; Grant, 2003). Social studies teachers, in preparing students for DBQs, have the charge of teaching a specific critical literacy skill set instead of being forced to focus solely on a rigidly imposed collection of historical facts (see, e.g., Bolgatz, 2006 ; Clarke et al., 2003; Grant, 2003; Libresco, 2005). It is likely that teachers in these studies thus find the potential for increased flexibility in the content and pedagogy they use to teach social studies in their respective high-stakes environments (Au, in press).

Such findings indicate a likely relationship between the construction of the high-stakes tests themselves and the curricular changes induced by the tests. Research supports the existence of such a relationship. As Yeh (2005) finds, teachers in Minnesota report that their pedagogy is not negatively affected by high-stakes tests because they feel the tests there are well designed and do not promote drill and rote memorization. It should be noted, however, that Minnesota recently changed their exams to be more like "traditional" restrictive, high-stakes, standardized tests (Yeh, 2007). Another example comes from Hillocks Jr. (2002), who analyzes the teaching of writing in relation to the writing examinations delivered in Texas, Illinois, New York, Oregon, and Kentucky. One of Hillocks's main findings is that states with poorly designed systems of writing assessment promote a technical, mechanical, five-paragraph essay form, and that teachers' pedagogy adapts to that form in those states. Conversely, states with tests that promote less mechanical forms of writing compel better writing pedagogies. The findings of these studies suggest that test construction matters in terms of teachers' curricular responses to high-stakes tests (see also Clarke et al., 2003).

Further, there is some fluidity in this curricular control due to the differing levels of performance of schools, as higher performing schools have been found to have an easier time adapting themselves to the norms established by the high-stakes tests. Teachers in these higher performing schools are feeling less pressure to conform because their students and educational programs are already meeting the test-established norms and policy expectations (Bebray et al., 2003). However, it is equally true that where schools are low performing and where the stakes are higher, teachers feel increased pressures to conform to the norms established by the tests (Abrams et al., 2003; Chabran, 2003; Clarke et al., 2003; Hampton, 2005; Taylor et al., 2001).

However, even where high-stakes pressures do exist, teachers are resisting the test-influenced pedagogic norms. For instance, Perreault (2000) finds that teachers often create space for what they consider to be "real teaching" in the face of the high-stakes testing pressures, but that this usually requires some sort of deception on the part of the teacher. Such resistance can be difficult, however, because those teachers who outright challenge the pedagogical norms established by the tests can face severe punishments, including the loss of their jobs—as was the case with one Oakland, California, teacher (see, e.g. Jaeger, 2006).

I do not intend to be overly romantic here. Given that teachers are capable of teaching in ways that are racist, sexist, classist, homophobic, ablest, etc., the act of regulating teacher practice, in and of itself, should not be viewed as inherently negative. Indeed, one could imagine situations where the enforcement of, for instance, a required curriculum based on equality and social justice might have to be enforced through outside monitoring (although, hopefully, the nature of the controls and the monitoring would be substantively different than what we currently have). Within the context of socioeconomic inequality in the United States, however, the types of controls currently asserted over education generally reinforce and (re)produce educational and social inequalities.

STEERAGE AT A DISTANCE

As the analysis done in this chapter shows, high-stakes testing is having a tangible impact on the educational experiences of students. Thus it is important to recognize that high-stakes testing is in fact changing the educational environments of schools: Not only do teachers lose control of curricular decisions, but any power the students might have had as contributors to their own educational process is also taken away. What results is that, in addition to having their lives, cultures, and histories structured out of the curriculum, student voice and power is increasingly structured out as well since they have reduced control over determining (or even co-determining) their own educational objectives

(Grundy, 1987). Not only do the tests sort students along particular epistemological, cultural, economic, and sociological lines, they also work to disempower students generally (and teachers too). Between the restricted course offerings, the pedagogies focusing on rote memorization and test-like drills, the increased time and energy devoted to taking tests, the increased pressures and anxieties associated with the stakes the tests are attached to, the diversity and multiculturalism that is being pushed out of the curriculum, and the overall reduction of resources (time and money) allowed to be spent on enriching but less structured learning experiences (i.e., field trips), schools are becoming increasingly alienating and disempowering spaces for all students, and students of color in particular, to exist.

However, I want to be clear that this body of negative outcomes does not simply represent "unintended" consequences of high-stakes testing, as some scholars assert (see, e.g., B. D. Jones, 2007; G. M. Jones et al., 2003; Stecher & Barron, 2001). In reality, systems of "accountability" built upon high-stakes, standardized tests are *intended* to control and regulate what happens in schools and classrooms (Madaus, 1994). Noted policy conservative and school "choice" advocate Terry M. Moe (2003) explains this rationale quite clearly when he states:

> The movement for school accountability is essentially a movement for more effective top-down control of the schools. The idea is that, if public authorities want to promote student achievement, they need to adopt organizational control mechanisms—tests, school report cards, rewards and sanctions, and the like—designed to get district officials, principals, teachers, and students to change their behavior in productive ways....Virtually all organizations need to engage in top-down control, because the people at the top have goals they want the people at the bottom to pursue, and something has to be done to bring about the desired behaviors.... The public school system is just like other organizations in this respect... (p. 81)

The intentions of promoters of regimes of test-based reforms are clear in the structures and outcomes of the policy designs, designs that require intent, and the intention is to negate "asymmetries" between classroom practice and the test score related goals of those with political and bureaucratic power (Wößmann, 2003)—hence the five types of control outlined in this chapter. It thus seems evident that test-based systems of high-stakes "accountability" are relatively successfully in increasing control of teachers' practices in that teachers have changed and adjusted to the norms established by the tests—thus tightening of the loose coupling between policy makers' intentions and the institutional environments created by their policies (Burch, 2007). Or, framed differently, high-stakes testing can be seen as increased control over teachers and their practices by policy makers and state authorities—control over the process of educational "production." Systems of high-stakes, standardized testing thus truly represent a form of "steerage from a distance" (Menter, Muschamp, Nicholl, Ozga, & Pollard, 1997; see also, Apple, 2006), where the state uses its regulatory power to guide the actions of local actors from afar.

As I explained in this chapter, however, the implications of this steerage are more than just technical. They are also Discursive, they are cultural. Thus, to assert relative control over the curriculum, in its various technical aspects, is also to assert relative control over classroom identities. This aspect of curricular control is important because it points to a relationship between the ways in which knowledge is communicated in the curriculum and the regulation of identities. I take up this relationship in detail in the next chapter.

5

DEVISING INEQUALITY
High-Stakes Testing and the Regulation of Consciousness

The pedagogic device acts as a symbolic regulator of consciousness; the question is, whose regulator; what consciousness and for whom? It is a condition for the production, reproduction and transformation of culture.

Basil Bernstein (1996, p. 53)

In a sense, the analysis I have presented thus far has only described the curricular outcomes that high-stakes testing produces in the classroom and has offered some theoretical tools through which to view the effects of a process. This is not to underemphasize the importance of such a description. Given the highly politicized climate surrounding education policy and research, my hope is that the work completed here serves to highlight the deleterious effects high-stakes tests are having on the educational experiences of children. However, if critical educators and critical educational researchers are to seek out solutions to inequality, then an analysis of the effects of high-stakes testing on classroom practice must move beyond description. It must undertake an analysis of the processes that produce the phenomena found in the research. Put differently, while it is important to understand "what" is happening, it is also important to understand "how" something happens as well.

This chapter is an attempt at such an analysis. Here I use work in the sociology of knowledge (Bernstein, 1971, 1975, 1977, 1990, 1996) to examine how linguistic and discursive codes are transmitted and acquired in classroom settings, thus providing a explanation of how social inequalities are (re)produced in and through education. In what follows, I begin by delineating Bernstein's (1990, 1996) sociological concepts of power and control as a way to clarify how the types of control outlined in Chapter 4 function in relation to high-stakes testing. This also provides theoretical grounding for my use of Bernstein's (1977, 1990, 1996) conceptualizations of "classification" and "framing" as well as my final analysis of high-stakes testing as a manifestation of what Bernstein (1990, 1996; Bernstein & Solomon, 1999) calls the "pedagogic device." In this way I intend to demonstrate how high-stakes, standardized testing inherently (re)produces inequality through the selective regulation and distribution of different forms of knowledge, and therefore through the selective regulation and distribution of different forms of consciousness.

HIGH-STAKES TESTING AND THE
SOCIOLOGY OF EDUCATION

At the root of Bernstein's (1996) conceptual framework lies his distinction between power and control. Power relations, he notes,

> ...create boundaries, legitimize boundaries, reproduce boundaries, between different categories of groups, gender, class, race, different categories of discourse, different categories of agents. Thus, power always operates to produce dislocations, to produce punctuations in social space. (p. 19)

Power thus manifests through establishing relations *between*: between subject areas, between categories of students, between students and teachers, between teachers and administrators, between schools and districts, between state and federal agencies. Power determines the borders of relations. Power is thus also cognitive because the categories and distinctions we use to make sense of the world, to understand how thing relate to each other, are defined socially (Vygotsky, 1987). For instance, the sanctions outlined by NCLB are a perfect example of Bernstein's distinction of power. In the case of NCLB, power is expressed through the federal government's determination that schools (and states) will lose federal monies if they do not meet federally defined standards expressed in a federally passed law. The power therefore lies in the distinction between local education agencies (public schools) and federal governing agencies and those agencies that either meet or do not meet standards. Through a policy like NCLB, the federal government exercises its power to set the terms of the relationship, a relationship that is obviously hierarchical, highly stratified, and top-down.

While power may be categorical, control, on the other hand, is essentially communicative: It conveys how boundary relations defined through power are communicated and operationalized. In this regard, Bernstein (1996) posits that, "Control…establishes legitimate forms of communication appropriate to different categories. Control carries the boundary relations of power and socializes individuals into these relationships" (p. 19). As an example, thinking again in terms of educational policy, *power* is expressed through policy structures that define relationships between agents, agencies, or policy actors, defines categories such as "passing" or "failing," and defines the boundary relations between these categories. This points to, as in the above case regarding federal authority to determine funding, schools that lose money as an NCLB sanction make decisions internally about how to best control their resources within the limits they are given. They operationalize the funding limits established through federal power. In terms of educational policy, then, *control* is how power is operationalized, realized, implemented, and communicated.

Situating Bernstein's conception of power and control more firmly within the context of this book, we can see high-stakes testing operating at the level of power. For instance, as I demonstrated in Chapter 4, high-stakes tests set particularly strong boundaries on what content knowledge is considered valid or worth knowing. There is test-included content and there is test-excluded content. This boundary is an expression of power. How teachers respond to this expression of power, by molding their curricular content and pedagogy to fit into the test-defined boundaries, is an expression of the process of control, an expression of socialization into the test-established boundaries. Teachers essentially communicate the power-defined boundaries through their practice. This communication is "control" because it is the operationalization of the boundaries. Even in cases where teachers feel they have more control over classroom content support this distinction. In these cases, the content demands required by the tests are more focused on critical literacy skills and less focused on specific contents. The high-stakes tests therefore manifest less power regarding the boundaries of "acceptable" knowledge content, and manifest less control over how teachers operate within those boundaries.

This same argument can be made for all of the other forms of control outlined in Chapter 4. Pedagogic control is an expression of how teachers operationalize test-defined curricular content and curricular forms in response to high-stakes tests. Teacher control over their pedagogy is related to the strength of the boundaries of knowledge content and form established through the power of the tests (or the test and policy makers), and teachers operationalize the pedagogies they feel they can within the strongly defined confines of the tests. Discursive control is also an extension of this expression of power, as identities are similarly defined in this process. Students and teachers feel pressures on their identities as learners and pedagogues. How they operationalize these identities within the constraints of the test-established classroom pressures illustrates the amount of control being exerted over both. Indeed, the type of control Bernstein outlines in his formulation matches well with the types of control I detailed in Chapter 4 because all five forms of control discussed there illustrate how power, in Bernstein's terms, is communicated in the classroom.

Bernstein's conception is essentially one of macro-micro relations (Morais, 2002). Power, or the ability to determine boundaries and limits of categories (and therefore determining the relations between those categories) in our consciousness and language, is an expression of macro-social relations (Vygotsky, 1987). This should be self-evident in that those with power in a hierarchical society manifest their power through their ability to define the categories, define the boundaries and their level of strength (Lipman, 2004; M. L. Smith, 2004). Thus, as Bernstein (1990) asserts, the relationships between categories have "...their origin in the social division of labour and its social relations of material production" (p. 47). Those without power, while never lacking the ability to define their own categories, lack the social and economic positioning for their definitions, their boundaries, to manifest with equal effect as those with power.

Power is rarely absolute, however, and at the micro level it often gets obscured, appropriated, reappropriated, interpreted, recontextualized, or redefined by individuals (Apple, 1995; Au, 2005a; Dance, 2002; Willis, 1977). Bernstein's conception allows for relatively subjective individual interpretations because it distinguishes power from control. Even if, as noted above, control "carries the boundary relations of power..." (Bernstein, 1996, p. 19), because control is analytically distinct from power, Bernstein's conception allows for an analysis that denies a one-to-one correspondence between the two. Power may imply control, and control operates within the limits of power, but power does not mean absolute control. This relationship is evident in the findings I reported in Chapter 4, where, even though it is evident that high-stakes tests generally exert control over classroom practice and educative environments, the exact manifestation of this control varies. Teachers communicate power relations in their classrooms to varying degrees, even as the vast majority of teachers communicate the relations in some way, shape, or form. The imposition of high-stakes testing through educational policy is an expression of power, but the control that extends from that expression of power is not simple, automatic, or linear. Thus, however limited, there is room for teacher resistance within the bounds of testing's power (e.g., Perreault, 2000), particularly where, as I found in Chapter 4, less rigid test forms related strongly to increases in teachers' pedagogic flexibility. Further, students may or may not acquire the transmission of power relations in the way that the teachers (or policy makers) intend, just as teachers may or may not succumb to the power relations communicated by high-stakes testing. While this distinction between power and control may seem minute and overly theoretical, it is highly relevant to how we conceptualize the process of education and the role of high-stakes testing within that process, because power and control are communicated in classroom practice and translated into educational outcomes.

CLASSIFICATION AND HIGH-STAKES TESTING

Classification is the translation of power at the level of cognition and individual consciousness. It explains how things relate to each other in our understanding of the world, in our consciousness, in social relations. Bernstein (1996) explains that classification "deals with relationships between boundaries and the category representations of these boundaries…whether these categories are between agencies, between agents, between discourses, between practices" (Bernstein, 1996, p. 20). Classification does not define the category itself, however. Rather, it refers to the relations *between* categories. As Bernstein explains:

> …[T]he crucial space which creates the specialization of the category—in this case the discourse—is not internal to that discourse but is the space between that discourse and another. In other words, A can only be A if it can effectively insulate itself from B. In this sense, there is no A if there is no relationship between A and something else. The meaning of A is only understandable in relation to other categories in the set…In other words, it is the insulation between the categories of discourse which maintains the principles of their social division of labour. In other words,

it is silence which carries the message of power; it is the full stop between one category of discourse and another; it is the dislocation in the potential flow of discourse which is crucial to the specialization of any category.

If that insulation is broken, then a category is in danger of losing its identity, because what it is, is the space between it and another category. Whatever maintains the strengths of the insulation, maintains the relations between the categories...Thus, the principle of the relations between categories, discourses—that is, the principles of their social division of labour—is a function of the degree of insulation between the categories... (pp. 20–21)

Thus, classification is ultimately about identity creation and maintenance of that identity in relation to others. Take, for instance, the education-related categories of "teacher" and "student." These two categories exist in relation to each other. To varying degrees, the category of "teacher" implies the existence of the category of "student," and vice versa. Indeed, under current social and educational arrangements, "teacher" and "student" only exist in relation to each other. In this case, classification refers to the boundary, limit, and even insulation between the categories of "teacher" and "student."

Classification, as a concept, is meant to convey flexibility and can thus be weaker or stronger depending on the level of insulation between categories. Consequently, within any given set of relations, boundaries between categories can be delineated as either weakly classified (more integrated) or strongly classified (highly stratified). Taking the above "teacher" and "student" example, the relationship between a teacher and a student may be considered to exhibit strong classification if we see strong separation, or insulation, between the two. This would be the case when teacher authority and power over students is strong, thus indicating a strong separation, a strong delineation, between teacher and student. In this case, direct instruction and teacher-centered pedagogy would be associated with strong classification because such pedagogy reinforces the distinction (the boundary relation) between teachers and students. In these forms of delivery, the teacher is *here*, and "delivers" the information to the students over *there*. In this example, strong classification means that teachers-are-teachers and students-are-students, and there can be no confusion or overlap between the two. A weakly classified relationship between teachers and students would be decidedly different, however. With weak classification, students may be placed more in the role of being teachers in the classroom, just as teachers may see themselves more as learners in relation to the students. Weaker classification exists in more student-centered, constructivist (see, e.g., Dewey, 1916), and critical pedagogies (see, e.g., Freire, 1974, 1982).

Classification is a translation of power at the individual level because power is required to be able to define, maintain, and enforce the categories and their boundaries. Thus, strong classification tends to point toward increased social stratification and inequality, because stronger boundaries (or increased insulation) imply power to maintain those boundaries—like in the strongly classified "teacher" and "student" example offered above. As Bernstein (1996) explains, "Attempts to change degrees of insulation reveal the power relations on which the classification is based and which it reproduces... [C]lassifications, strong or weak, always carry power relations" (p. 21). Finally, classification, as a translation of power, exhibits aspects of hegemony, for power relations are hidden through classification and appear as a natural ordering of the world, "...as real, as authentic, as integral, as the source of integrity" (p. 21).

I want to be careful in this explanation of classification, however. While strong classification tends to serve as a marker for social stratification and inequality, the opposite does not necessarily hold true: Weak classification does not necessarily mean the absence of social stratification and inequality, or the absence of power relations. For instance, Sharp and Green (1975) find that the open, progressive, child-centered classrooms of a primary school in their study were leading to increased social stratification of students. They assert that this process took place in part because teachers adopted a lassez-faire, hands off pedagogy as their interpretation of student freedom in the classroom. This pedagogy, in turn, led to some students gaining access to classroom opportunities while others did not, as an expression of increased alienation in these "progressive," child-centered classrooms (see also, Shor & Freire, 1987, for further critique of lassez-faire approaches to teaching).

Sharp and Green's (1975) findings do not negate Bernstein's conception of classification, however. Instead, their research points to the flexibility that, in my opinion, Bernstein strove for in his formulation. Even though strong classification might indicate strong social stratification, weak classification merely points to the *potential* for the realization of different, and perhaps more equal, social relations. The existence of this potential, however, does not guarantee its manifestation in pedagogic discourse, does not guarantee that this potential is activated and realized in the classroom. In fact, strong classification may even be understood as an attempt to limit the space for such potential to exist. Indeed, as I make clear in the following analysis, this potential for realization is one of the key concepts guiding Bernstein's formulation.

Classification explains how power is translated at the level of the individual and the classroom, particularly in relation to how high-stakes testing changes educational environments. In regard to curriculum, high-stakes testing exhibits strong classification of knowledge content. As I illustrated in Chapter 4, a significant majority of studies have found that high-stakes testing constricts or narrows the curricular content to those subjects and content areas that are tested. This demonstrates the strength of the classification of knowledge exerted through high-stakes testing. In a broad sense, the tests establish strong, highly insulated boundaries between valued knowledge and unvalued knowledge. Tested knowledge is valued; untested knowledge is not. Math and Reading/Language Arts are clearly marked as tested subjects, while other subject matter categories are clearly marked as non-tested subjects. These non-tested subjects take on an identity of "not-Math" and "not-Reading," and thus, not teachable within the high-stakes, standardized test-defined boundaries. This boundary is clearly delineated and maintained by the high-stakes nature of the tests, where the pressure to show gains or face severe consequences creates thick insulation against challenging those boundaries. Challenging the knowledge domains required by the tests can be a high-risk operation for those at the classroom level who may lose their jobs or be denied their diplomas/credentials.

High-stakes testing also leads to a strong classification of knowledge forms. As I discussed in Chapter 4, there has been an increase in the decontextualization and fragmentation of knowledge in response to high-stakes tests. Concretely, this manifests in teachers teaching content knowledge in isolated bits and pieces in preparation for the bits and pieces of knowledge required by the tests. The fragmentation of knowledge exhibits strong classification in two ways. First, it establishes thickly insulated boundaries between acceptable and unacceptable knowledge forms. The fragmented knowledge forms required by the tests establish the acceptable knowledge forms to teach in the classroom. Second, the tests establish strong classification regarding epistemology, or how we "know" the world. This is essentially strong classification within specific knowledge domains, where each piece of information is insulated from other pieces of information within any one tested subject area. In this epistemological classification, knowledge does not integrate with or relate to other knowledge. In other words, knowledge learned for the tests exists in strongly classified, isolated pieces, not in integrated wholes.

By extension high-stakes testing also exhibits strong classification of pedagogy. Pedagogy that matches the content knowledge and knowledge forms required by the tests is favored. It is assumed that if children learn this knowledge and these forms, then they will demonstrate improved test scores. Therefore, what is deemed to be good pedagogy or bad pedagogy, effective pedagogy or ineffective pedagogy, is strongly classified by the tests. Most compellingly, strong classification is reflected in the results of individual studies where teachers clearly distinguished between their use of test-focused pedagogies and pedagogies that they felt were not defined by the tests (see, e.g., Brimijoin, 2005; Gerwin & Visone, 2006; Passman, 2001; Perreault, 2000).

High-stakes testing policies also manifest qualities of strong classification. Through bureaucratic control, educational authorities have the power to define the categories and limits of who is passing and failing in regards to scores on high-stakes tests. Policies erect a series of categories to define various groups (in this case, students and schools), so there is, in Bernstein's words, a "full stop" between good and bad, passing and failing, "meets standard" and "does not meet standard," functional and dysfunctional in the assessing and ranking of schools, students, and teachers (Lipman, 2004; M. L. Smith, 2004). Clearly, these labels are powerful. As Apple (1979/2004) explains:

> Usually the 'deviant' label has an *essentializing* quality in that a person's (here, a student's) entire relationship to an institution is conditioned by the category applied to [them]. He or she *is* this and only this…Thus, such labels are not neutral, at least not in their significance for the person. By the very fact that the labels are tinged with moral significance—not only is the child different but also inferior—their application has a profound impact… [T]he effect of these labels is immense for they call forth forms of 'treatment' which tend to confirm the persons in the institutionally applied category. (p. 128, original emphasis)

The strongly classified delineations associated with high-stakes testing policies demonstrate strong insulation, where students are either passing or failing, and schools are either meeting standard or not meeting standard. Such strong classification means that, within the policy design, there is no tangible middle ground, and in the case of high-stakes testing, research has found that this has led to increased educational stratification (Kim & Sunderman, 2005).

Classification, it must be remembered, is the translation of power at the level of the individual. This is because social power is expressed through the development and maintenance of definitive categories and their relationships between each other. As I explained earlier, those with power have the material economic and social means for their definitive categories to become normalized and hegemonic in our consciousness. Thus, the boundaries and boundary strengths that exist in our consciousness—in other words, the classification of knowledge and how we order the world—is a realization of social relations (Vygotsky, 1981, 1987). In terms of education, the above manifestations of classification in both policy and classroom practice are themselves translations of dominant social relations into pedagogic discourse. For instance, the brief discussion of policy categories addressed above outlines an expression of power through educational policy design. These categorizations themselves are often built on the "shaky foundations" (M. L. Smith, 2004, p. 27) of the political aspects of the processes that determine the categories, and as Apple (1979/2004) notes are,

> ...developed out of specific social and historical situations which conform to a specific framework of assumptions and institutions, the use of which categories brings with it the logic of institutional assumptions as well. (p. 127)

In Foucault's (1995) terms, high-stakes testing creates a visible subject as an extension of disciplinary power, and this visibility,

> ...assures the hold of power that is exercised over them. It is the fact of being constantly seen, of being able always to be seen, that maintains the disciplined individual in his subjection. And the examination is the technique by which power, instead of emitting the signs of its potency, instead of imposing its mark on its subjects, holds them in a mechanism of objectification. In this space of domination, disciplinary power manifests its potency, essentially, by arranging objects. (p. 187)

The ability to construct categories that can be and are applied to others, and that others can potentially internalize as part of their own identities, is thus an expression of power (Apple, 1979/2004).

Even leaving the policy categories aside, power is also evident in the knowledge and pedagogic domains discussed above. Setting the boundaries of content knowledge through high-stakes tests is an act of power. Further, it must also be recognized that, similar to policy categories, the tests themselves are a part of complex political, social, and ideological processes that mainly function as a socioeconomic sorting mechanism. Thus we see particular worldviews, particular epistemological assumptions, and particular images of "correct" teaching and learning (as well as "correct" teachers and learners), being transmitted through the tests and their accompanying policies. Through the lens of classification we can see that, contrary to the hegemonic assumptions that these policies and tests are neutral, hierarchies of power are evident at every step of the educational process. The question, of course, is: How is power operationalized and communicated in pedagogic discourse in the classroom? The answer to this question is explained by "framing" (Bernstein, 1977, 1990, 1996; Bernstein & Solomon, 1999).

FRAMING AND HIGH-STAKES TESTING

As discussed earlier, power creates boundaries and determines the relationships *between* categories. Control, on the other hand, is concerned with how patterns of communication socialize individuals into the boundary relations defined by power. Classification correlates with power, cognitively translating it at the level of individual consciousness, at the level of pedagogic discourse. Framing is the counterpart to classification, and it correlates with control. Framing is how control is communicated within pedagogic discourse. Bernstein (1996) defines framing as the,

> ...form of control which regulates and legitimizes communication in pedagogic relations ... [F]raming refers to the controls on communication in local, interactional pedagogic relations: between parents/children, teacher/pupil, social worker/client, etc... (p. 26)

Whereas classification establishes the cognitive boundaries or limits of understanding within pedagogic discourse, framing establishes the way those boundaries or limits are communicated between people within pedagogic discourse. As Bernstein explains, "Classification refers to *what*, framing is concerned with *how* meanings are to be put together, the forms by which they are to be made public, and the nature of the social relationships that go with it" (p. 27, original emphasis). Put more simply, framing refers to the communicative and discursive interactions between individuals within pedagogic discourse. Within pedagogic discourse in the classroom, we are then looking at two things—classification between teachers and students and the communication of this relationship within pedagogic discourse. It is the communication of this classification that constitutes framing. Thus, in pedagogic discourse, framing is about operationalizing both *how* meaning is communicated and *who* has control over what happens in the classroom, that is, who has control over the ways in which meanings are communicated. Framing is therefore about control, control over the selection of knowledge, its sequencing, its pacing, the criteria of selection, and the social interactions[1] that make transmission possible (Bernstein, 1996; Morais, 2002).

Like classification, Bernstein's conception of framing is meant to denote a range of possibilities. Pedagogic discourse can exhibit strong framing as well as weak framing. Strong framing exists, for example, when a teacher has tight control over the selection, sequencing, pacing, criteria, and social interactions within the curriculum. Strong framing is therefore associated with teacher-centered pedagogies of lecture and direct instruction. Framing may also be weak, however, such as when the students have more control over the selection, sequencing, pacing, criteria, and social interactions within the curriculum. Weak framing is associated with student-centered or constructivist pedagogies where students are encouraged to "discover" knowledge, learn "on their own," have input in the direction and content of their learning experiences, and bring their own lives into the classroom.

An application of framing to high-stakes testing explains how the power relations embodied in classification are communicated and operationalized within classroom discourse.[2] Indeed, it could be argued that the types of control outlined in Chapter 4 are manifestations of how power is "framed" or communicated *within* the test-influenced pedagogic discourse, because high-stakes testing strongly frames the curriculum. This means that, in addition to strongly classifying valid and invalid, tested and nontested subjects, high-stakes testing demonstrates strong framing (or control) over the selection, sequencing, pacing, criteria for selection, and classroom social interactions *within* the tested subjects. As I discussed in the previous chapter, numerous studies point to instances of teachers rushing the teaching of specific content knowledge or skills in order to make sure they have covered the appropriate facts and knowledge forms before test dates. This has often also coincided with learning knowledge in small pieces within the context of the tests themselves (see, e.g., Fickel, 2006; Firestone, Mayrowetz, & Fairman, 1998; Luna & Turner, 2001; A. M. Smith, 2006; van Hover, 2006). Thus, in their pedagogic discourse, teachers are communicating particular boundary relationships that exist between content knowledge subject areas and between content knowledge subject forms.

The above point mainly focuses on aspects of *content* and *formal* control as they manifest in strong framing of tested content. Strong framing, however, is generally also evident in the *pedagogic* and *Discursive* controls of high-stakes testing. I argued in Chapter 4 that teachers generally change their pedagogies to fit the demands of the tests, thus demonstrating a strong classification of pedagogy. This strong classification is operationalized and communicated in practice through pedagogic discourse where test-induced changes are characterized by increases in teacher-centered instruction associated with lectures to aid in the coverage of large amounts of tested information. Relative to the students, this increase in teacher-centered pedagogy is a reflection of strong framing, because the students make almost no decisions regarding selection, sequencing, pacing, criteria for selection, and classroom social relations of content knowledge and knowledge forms.

Strong framing is perhaps most evident in *Discursive control*. Earlier in this chapter, I discussed how the strong classification exhibited by high-stakes testing defines and limits content knowledge, knowledge forms, and pedagogies. In addition to the above manifestations, this strong classification is also framed, that is, operationalized and communicated, through *Discursive control* of both teachers and students. As I outlined in Chapter 4, when the curriculum is narrowed, the limits of acceptable identities are also narrowed. It is through such narrowing that not only "good" and "bad" teaching are established, but "good" and "bad" *teachers* are determined. This phenomenon is communicated through teacher responses to this framing, where teachers have undergone personal and pedagogic identity shifts (Agee, 2004; Costigan III, 2002; Passman, 2001) and felt both that they and their practice were being reduced to mere numbers (Booher-Jennings, 2005).

In Bernsteinian terms, teachers are "agents of symbolic control" (Bernstein, 1990, p. 138) whose role within the process of the regulation of consciousness, within the communication of pedagogic discourse, is that of "reproducer" of particular forms of consciousness. In this sense, high-stakes testing frames teaching in a way that regulates the consciousness of teachers themselves, placing relative limits on the types of pedagogic identities they are encouraged to maintain, which in turn places relative limits on the pedagogic discourse that students are allowed to experience (therefore also placing limits on the forms of consciousness students are introduced to and encouraged to maintain). As I've noted previously, these limits are not universal or automatic, and teachers (and students) do resist them. However as teachers have shifted their pedagogic identities, the overall effect of such pedagogic regulation has been a substantial decreases in teacher morale and motivation (B. D. Jones & Egley, 2004; Nichols & Berliner, 2005, 2007; Perreault, 2000; Taylor et al., 2001). Teachers are thus feeling the effects of high-stakes testing on their practices, and these effects are a product of the framing asserted by high-stakes testing—what Ball (2003b) refers to as the "terrors of performativity."

Similarly, the strong classification of the curriculum results in the strong framing of student identity, or *Discursive control* of the learner. The power to determine officially tested knowledge manifests through the classification of tested and non-tested subjects. This is another way of viewing the process of the standardization of knowledge. Some knowledge falls within the standard, while knowledge deemed less important or unnecessary falls outside the boundaries of the standard. Strong framing produces pedagogic discourses that extend from the strong classification produced by standardization. These discourses actively exclude the identities, cultures, histories, and material realities of some students' lives (see, e.g., Goodson & Foote, 2001; McNeil, 2000, 2005; Rex, 2003). As I discussed in Chapter 4, students of color are generally not reflected in curricular form and content as multicultural knowledge is not tested and therefore not deemed worth teaching (see, e.g., Agee, 2004; Anagnostopolous, 2003; Berlak, 2000; Bigelow, 1999, 2001; Darder & Torres, 2004; McNeil, 2000; McNeil & Valenzuela, 2001; Themba-Nixon, 2000). Bernstein (1996) refers to this phenomenon in terms of the "Distribution of Images," where he remarks:

> A school metaphorically holds up a mirror in which an image is reflected. There may be several images, positive and negative. A school's ideology may be seen as a construction in a mirror through which images are reflected. The question is: who recognizes themselves as of value? What other images are excluded by the dominant image of value so that some students are unable to recognize themselves? (p. 7)

The strong framing associated with high-stakes testing literally communicates that some students should not be considered as a valuable part of the curriculum, thereby increasing their alienation from the process of education as a whole.

Thus, the types of control outlined in Chapter 4 illustrate how teachers are operationalizing, or framing, the test-determined categories of knowledge, pedagogy, and identity at the individual and classroom level. However, I must also add a twist to this formulation. In many cases, it is assumed that if there is strong framing in relation to students, then the teacher dominates the classroom discourse. By and large, this assumption can and should be held as true. A rise in test-induced, teacher-centered pedagogy is just that—*teacher-centered*. Students have little power or control in the relationship. The twist I would like to add is that high-stakes testing (or, in reality, the authority implementing high-stakes testing) also exhibits strong framing in relation to the teachers: Teachers' shifts toward more teacher-centered pedagogies are being driven by the tests, not necessarily by teacher choice (see, e.g., Gerwin & Visone, 2006; Landman, 2000; Passman, 2001; Perreault, 2000; Segall, 2003). Thus, to some degree, teacher control over pedagogy is relatively illusory because the strong pedagogic framing does not come from teachers alone. Rather, in large part it originates from sources above the teachers in the highly stratified social relations outside of the classroom. In this way, teachers are themselves strongly classified in relation to policy makers and, subsequently, high-stakes testing policies strongly frame teacher pedagogy and identity.

The above discussion of the framing of both teacher and student identities by high-stakes testing also speaks to Bernstein's (1996) discussion of the relationship between identity and trainability, where he comments that:

> The concept of trainability places emphasis upon "something" the actor must possess in order for that actor to be appropriately formed and re-formed according to technological, organizational and market contingencies. This "something," which is crucial to the survival of the actor, the economy and presumably the society, is the ability to be taught, the ability to respond effectively to concurrent, subsequent, intermittent pedagogics. Cognitive and social processes are to be specially developed for such a pedagogized future. (p. 73)

In the case of high-stakes testing and the framing of teacher/pedagogic and student/learner identities, we see how the strong framing communicated by the testing attempts to form and re-form these identities along the norms embedded and embodied in the tests. And, as I explained in Chapters 2 and 3, high-stakes testing itself is constructed around certain "technological, organizational and market contingencies" —both perceived (in terms of the efficient and fair sorting of people) and real (in terms of the logics of capitalist production). However, as Bernstein (1996) explains:

> [T]he ability to respond to such a [pedagogized] future depends upon a capacity, not an ability. The capacity to enable the actor to project him/herself *meaningfully*...into this future...This capacity is the outcome of a specialized identity and this precedes the ability to respond effectively to concurrent and subsequent retraining. In this sense effective forming and re-forming rests upon... the construction of a specialized identity...This identity arises out of a particular social order, through relations which the identity enters into with other identities of reciprocal recognition, support, mutual legitimization and finally through a negotiated collective purpose. (p. 73, original emphasis)

Indeed, high-stakes testing, in the forming and reforming of classroom identities, essentially seeks the production and reproduction of *specialized identities* around the norms established and enforced by the tests themselves. These identities are then recognized and regarded as legitimate or disregarded as illegitimate through social negotiation. Thus, as Bernstein (Bernstein & Solomon, 1999) notes:

> Underlying this particular approach to identity is the issue of how variations in the distribution of power (classifications) and variations in the principles of control (framings) impose or enable variations in the formation of identities and their change, through differential specialisation of communication and of its social base. (p. 271)

This point lies at the heart of my analysis of high-stakes testing. It rings particularly true as we look at classification and framing and later when my analysis turns toward the "pedagogic device."

It is important to recognize that classification and framing are relatively flexible concepts, and that, therefore, some high-stakes, standardized tests could exhibit weaker classification or weaker framing. For instance, in research on Social Studies instruction in certain high-stakes testing environments, it has been found that some Social Studies teachers have consciously integrated more English/Language Arts into their curriculum. This has particularly been the case English/Language Arts is a tested subject and Social Studies is not. Thus we see that, as Social Studies teachers attempt to maintain their subject matter relevancy in high-stakes testing environments, there is a weakening of the boundaries (or a weakening of the classification) between these two subjects (see, e.g., Vogler, 2003). As another example, as I discussed in Chapter 4 in the section on the "Contradictions of Classroom Control," there are some literacy-focused tests where teachers feel less constrained in terms of pedagogy and content (see, e.g., Clarke et al., 2003; Libresco, 2005; Rex & Nelson, 2004; Wolf & Wolf, 2002; Wollman-Bonilla, 2004; Yeh, 2005). In these cases the high-stakes tests exhibit weaker framing in that they place less restriction on how knowledge is communicated in the classroom and teachers are more "free" (or less controlled) in their instruction.

Thus far in this chapter, I have been concerned with explaining the process of how control operates through high-stakes testing. I used Bernstein's conceptual framework to demonstrate how macro-level power manifests in control at the individual level. As I explained, this happens through classification and framing. Thus, in the above discussion of high-stakes testing, using Bernstein's formulation, I have outlined the way in which macro-social relations manifest in micro-individual relations, how power is manifest in the forms of control outlined in

Chapter 4. But, as Bernstein (1990) notes, there is at least one more problematic in this relationship to address. The analysis completed thus far has once again been largely descriptive. The *what* and the *why* have now been explained, but the *how* has yet to be addressed. While on the one hand we can see macro-social relations here and micro-individual relations there, we still have no sense of the *relay* between the macro and micro, or how power and control, via classification and framing, are communicated and realized at the level of the individual. This relay is explained through the concept of the *pedagogic device* (Bernstein, 1990, 1996; Bernstein & Solomon, 1999).

HIGH-STAKES TESTING AND THE PEDAGOGIC DEVICE

The pedagogic device (Bernstein, 1990, 1996; Bernstein & Solomon, 1999) explains the regulation of consciousness in classrooms as an extension of socioeconomic power relations that exist externally to schools. Contrary to the popular usage of the term, "device," it is important not to think of the pedagogic device as a physically existing machine. Rather, the pedagogic device refers to a process whereby a set of rules for the communication and acquisition of school knowledge effectively serves to regulate consciousness in the classroom, and, by extension, serves to legitimate specific identities within pedagogic discourse (pedagogic discourse being the sum of communication and acquisition of knowledge at the classroom level). The concept of the pedagogic device offers a conceptual framework for understanding how "the intrinsic grammar of pedagogic discourse" (Bernstein, 1996, p. 42) is devised through the processes of communication and acquisition of knowledge. The concept of the pedagogic device thus refers to the set of rules that regulate the structures of pedagogic discourse. These rules are the distributive rules, recontextualizing rules and evaluative rules. These rules relate to each other hierarchically: The distributive rules are the most fundamental; they produce the recontextualizing rules, which in turn produce the evaluative rules. My analysis of high-stakes testing will move through each of the rules of the pedagogic device, beginning with the distributive rules.

HIGH-STAKES TESTING AND THE DISTRIBUTIVE RULES

Bernstein (1996) explains that "The distributive rules mark and distribute who may transmit what to whom and under what conditions, and... attempt to set the outer limits of legitimate discourse" (p. 46). Or, in the words of Wong and Apple (2003), the distributive rules "mediate the social order through distributing different forms of knowledge and consciousness to diverse social groups" (p. 84). In performing this function, the distributive rules, according to Bernstein, regulate the gap between that which is understood to be possible and that which is considered to be impossible, the gap between what is understood as existing reality and what might be understood as potential or imagined reality. Bernstein (1996) refers to this gap between the knowable and unknowable, between material reality and our consciousness of that reality, as the "potential discursive gap" (p. 44). This gap is very important because it "can become (not always) a site for alternative possibilities, for alternative realizations of the relation between the material and immaterial... It is the crucial site of the *yet to be thought*" (p. 44, original emphasis). The potential discursive gap exists as the site where consciousness can change, where new material realities can be imagined, where new identities are envisioned, where new social relations might be realized.

The distributive rules, as part of the pedagogic device, describe the process of the regulation of the potential discursive gap, attempting to place limits of possibility on consciousness, identity, and social relations via pedagogic discourse. The distributive rules operate, for instance, through the teacher's curricular planning, textbook creation by publishers, textbook adoption by educational institutions, and state mandated content standards, where, through the social and political process of content selection, the limits of legitimate knowledge and forms this knowledge takes are established and regulated. Thus, as Bernstein (1996) notes, the distributive rules are directly linked to relations of power in society more generally since, "Any distribution of power will regulate the potential of this gap in its own interest, because the gap itself has the possibility of an alternative order, an alternative society, and an alternative power relation" (p. 45). Consequently, the distributive rules also seek to regulate not only *what* is thought of as possible or impossible, but also *who* has the right or power to set the limits of possibility. As Bernstein (1990) explains, "Through its distributive rules the pedagogic device is both the control on the 'unthinkable' and the control on those who may think it" (p. 183).

The distributive rules of the pedagogic device operate through high-stakes testing in several key ways. Perhaps most glaring among these ways is the fact that, within the political power structures of the United States, including federal and state institutions as well as well-funded think tanks that inform policy, high-stakes testing is taken as an a priori assumption in educational policy. An educational system without high-stakes testing is nearly unthinkable, unimaginable, that the tests are "here to stay." The origins of the distribution of this form of consciousness, that high-stakes testing are inevitable in public education, can be traced through earlier chapters of this book: Those in power communicate their power through policy language and structures that not only regulate what we think is normal or necessary in education, but also regulate what we think is possible in education. High-stakes tests are a manifestation of this power, and they have been normalized through the passing of NCLB since all U.S. states are now required to administer high-stakes tests. From this vantage point, one sees that, because of the increased federal powers of NCLB (Sunderman & Kim, 2005), the potential discursive gap between the reality of high-stakes testing and the potential for alternative visions of education has shrunk considerably in recent years. For all of the technical, political, economic, and social difficulties outlined in this book, instead of working toward an educational system without high-stakes testing, many educators and educational reformers (those in the "commonsense" mainstream in particular) end up working on ways to merely cope with high-stakes testing and its surrounding policies (Karp, 2006a; Pahl, 2003; Popham, 2001; Vogler, 2003; Yeager & Davis, 2005). Hence, as an evidence of the distributive rules at work, high-stakes testing is hegemonic within education.

This is not to say that the distributive rules mean that our consciousness about high-stakes testing is completely and totally regulated or subject to someone else's control. Any hegemonic alliance is the product of negotiation and struggle amongst powerful elites (Apple, 2006a), and likewise, the hegemony of high-stakes testing is a product of such negotiation and struggle. Thus, as I discussed at the end of Chapter 3, there are those associated with power, such as Robert Reich, who seriously question the efficacy and worth of high-stakes testing on the grounds that they do not meet the needs of the changing economy. Further, there are pockets of organized resistance to high-stakes testing that exist at the school or community level, and these resisters often envision educational systems without high-stakes testing (see, e.g., FairTest, 2005; Meier, Cohen, & Rogers, 2000; Rethinking Schools, 2008).

Clearly, consciousness regarding the hegemony of high-stakes testing is mixed, but this does not mean that the distributive rules do not operate through high-stakes testing. Rather, the above examples of organized resistance to high-stakes, standardized testing illustrate the pedagogic device in action. Those with power, those who use the distributive rules to regulate consciousness regarding what is possible or impossible, attempt to isolate these critiques as impractical, wrong, extreme, radical, or nonsensical—even if such attempts result in limited success in regulation. This point illustrates the distributive rules at work in the bureaucratic control discussed in Chapter 4. The vertical power hierarchies associated with systems of education, economics, and politics in the United States, provide the structure upon which the distributive rules operate. Within high-stakes testing regimes, those at the bottom of the system are held accountable to those on top, while those on top define the rules and regulations of accountability (Apple, 2000; Gibson, 2001; Hanson, 2000; G. M. Jones et al., 2003; Madaus, 1988; McNeil, 2000, 2005; Natriello & Pallas, 2001; Sloan, 2005; Sunderman & Kim, 2005). Thus, the distributive rules also regulate consciousness regarding *who* has the "legitimate" power to consider what's possible within education.

The distributive rules operate through the curriculum as well. As I outlined in Chapter 4, the distributive rules operate to regulate what is knowable, what is possible in terms of knowledge, where when tested and non-tested subject areas are strongly classified through content control. The distributive rules are also in operation when knowledge is learned and understood in strongly classified, isolated fragments associated with the formal control exerted by high-stakes testing. Here they operate at the level of epistemology, regulating how the world is "known" (fragmented, decontextualized, isolated, reified), thus also placing limits other, alternative ways that humans "know" the world (integrated wholes, processes, and interrelations). The distributive rules also regulate pedagogy as well, where, through high-stakes testing, limits are placed on ways of teaching, or pedagogic control. Finally, we see the distributive rules at work in Discursive control, in that certain identities are regulated as being possible or impossible, valued or devalued within high-stakes testing environments.

The distributive rules operate at a particular level of abstraction, however, and in order to work downwards toward the materiality of classroom practice, the pedagogic device operates through two more sets of rules. The following section deals with the next, lower order of rules, the recontextualizing rules.

THE RECONTEXTUALIZING RULES AND HIGH-STAKES TESTING

According to Bernstein (1996), the recontextualizing rules of the pedagogic device are derived from the distributive rules. They refer the process in which pedagogic discourse "selectively appropriates, relocates, refocuses and relates other discourses to constitute its own order" (p.

47). Thus, pedagogic discourse can be seen as a retranslation, a rearticulation, and a recontextualization of other discourses associated with knowledge domains outside of education into pedagogic discourse. Put differently, what takes place within pedagogic discourse is essentially a recontextualization of knowledge forms that are developed outside of education. Consequently, whether it is through teachers' own consciousness vis-à-vis curricular planning, textbook creation and adoption, or state-mandated content standards, subject matter content knowledge from discourses outside of education are in essence being appropriated, relocated, refocused, and related into pedagogic discourse. For instance, a history teacher teaches history. History as a discipline, however, consists of knowledge that is developed and maintained within the discourse of the discipline itself, by "historians." Education, or even history education, exists as its own discourse as well. Thus, generally speaking, a history teacher takes a discourse that exists outside of education—in this case, history—and recontextualizes it within pedagogic discourse.[3]

Because pedagogic discourse is a recontextualizing discourse, and because the form in which knowledge is recontextualized into pedagogic discourse also carries with it implications for pedagogic delivery (Apple, 1995; Au, 2007b; Segall, 2004b), in Bernstein's (1996) formulation the recontextualizing rules also dictate *how* knowledge is communicated within pedagogic discourse by providing a "theory of instruction" (p. 49) embedded within the recontextualized content. Thus the process of recontextualization in pedagogic discourse also carries socioeconomic power relations with it. In part, as a derivative of the distributive rules which seek to regulate both what is thinkable and who has the power to think it, the recontextualizing rules explain how that power is immediately translated into pedagogic discourse, particularly in terms of who has the power to determine what knowledge is recontextualized and the form that recontextualized knowledge takes. Again, whether it is through teachers' own consciousness vis-à-vis curricular planning, textbook creation and adoption, or state-mandated content standards, the recontextualization of knowledge into pedagogic discourse is ultimately connected to extant socioeconomic relations that grant teachers, schools, districts, and governing bodies the power to make decisions regarding the content and form of knowledge. These decisions are, in effect, a manifestation of the recontextualizing rules.

The recontextualizing rules of pedagogic discourse clearly operate through high-stakes testing. As I argued in Chapter 4, high-stakes testing exerts content control over the curriculum (Au, 2007b), and as I explained, the tests exhibit strong framing of content knowledge. The rule at work in the process of this framing is that of recontextualization, where we see the high-stakes tests recontextualizing content knowledge. The subject knowledge areas exist as discourses of their own. High-stakes testing "selectively appropriates, relocates, refocuses and relates" (Bernstein, 1996, p. 47) these other discourses and reconstitutes them for test-defined pedagogic discourse. The content knowledge that exists in other fields of study (i.e., other discourses of disciplines that exist outside of education) is recontextualized for the classroom by high-stakes testing. Similarly, the tests recontextualize content knowledge forms as well, as the recontextualizing rules of the tests operate to appropriate, relocate, refocus, and relate the forms of knowledge from outside of education into the pedagogic discourse as isolated fragments. A very concrete example of this comes from Social Studies education, where researchers have found that high-stakes history tests have promoted the learning of a collection of historical "facts" (see, e.g., Fickel, 2006; Grant et al., 2002; van Hover & Heinecke, 2005; Vogler, 2005), as opposed to promoting what those who study social studies education suggest should be the purpose of the social studies—the teaching of historical thinking (Pahl, 2003; VanSledright, 2004).

We can also see the recontextualizing rules of the pedagogic device operating within Discursive control. As discussed earlier, because of the strong classification of knowledge content, knowledge forms, and pedagogies, high-stakes testing exerts control over the types of identities that "fit" into high-stakes testing educational environments. This control manifests through the framing of student and teacher identities in instruction: Home cultures, home languages, home Discourses, and local knowledge are left out of the curricular content and neglected in curricular form (see, e.g., Agee, 2004; Anagnostopolous, 2003; Berlak, 2000; Bigelow, 2001; Darder & Torres, 2004; Goodson, CARE, & Foote, 2001; McNeil, 2000, 2005; McNeil & Valenzuela, 2001; Rex, 2003). High-stakes testing thus recontextualizes students' and teachers' identities within the Discursive norms of pedagogic discourse operating through the tests. As I discussed in previous chapters, this recontextualization has had deleterious effects on students of color in particular.

Further, Bernstein observes that the recontextualizing rules of the pedagogic device produce two social fields: the *official recontextualizing field* (ORF) and the *pedagogic recontextualizing field* (PRF). The ORF is created by and consists of the state and its agents. The PRF, on the other hand, consists of teachers in schools and colleges, as well as journals, research foundations, and publishing houses. Staying with the above example of history, state committees that draw up and establish history education standards or adopt particular textbooks are a part of the ORF. History textbook publishers or curriculum developers outside of the state's institutional power structures are examples of the PRF (see Singh, 2002 for further discussion).

Bernstein's conception of the official recontextualizing field and the pedagogic recontextualizing field further aids in sorting through some of the relationships in systems of standardized, high-stakes testing. Regarding the relationship between the ORF and the PRF, Bernstein (1996) observes that:

> If the PRF can have an effect on pedagogic discourse independently of the ORF, then there is both some autonomy *and* struggle over pedagogic discourse and its practices. But, if there is only the ORF, then there is no autonomy. (p. 48, original emphasis)

High-stakes testing presents an interesting case regarding the relationship between the ORF and the PRF. Broadly speaking, high-stakes testing, as part of a policy design, is a product of the ORF. Both federal and state governments, as official bodies of the state, are involved in the legitimation of high-stakes testing as the preferred reform. However, the entirety of the test industry (test designers, test administrators, test score interpreters and reporters, and makers of test-preparation materials) is all part of the PRF. Here, we see a weakening of the autonomy of the PRF, as many parts of this field are nearly indistinguishable from their promoters in the ORF, as demonstrated by the relationship between private industry and high-stakes testing discussed in Chapter 3. This helps to explain the power relations of high-stakes testing, as the decreased autonomy of the PRF also simultaneously denotes decreased struggle over pedagogic discourse and increased control. This relationship is illustrated through the above application of the recontextualizing rules to high-stakes testing, where we see "the state is attempting to weaken the PRF through its ORF, and thus attempting to reduce relative autonomy over the construction of pedagogic discourse and over social contexts" (Bernstein, 1996, p. 48).[4]

However, at the level of the recontextualizing rules, control over pedagogic discourse is always contested. This is the case for two reasons. As Wong and Apple (2003) explain, "First, when the PRF is strong and has a certain level of autonomy from the state, the discourse it creates can impede official pedagogic discourse" (p. 85). For instance, discourses of social equality often promoted in education sometimes rub up against and contradict the official pedagogic discourses that effectively reproduce social power relations. Second, as Wong and Apple (2003) assert:

> ...[B]ecause of the manifold agents within the ORF and PRF—the former includes a core consisting of officials from state pedagogic agencies and consultants from the educational system and fields of economy and symbolic control, whereas the latter comprises agents and practices drawn from universities, colleges of education, schools, foundations, journals and publishing houses, and so on—there is the potential for conflict, resistance, and inertia both within and between these two fields. (p. 85)

This second point is basic, but important. It acknowledges that, because individuals exist in both the ORF and PRF, there may be differing interpretations, appropriations, implementations, and political interests within fields. This creates the potential for conflict both within and between fields. Such struggles are apparent surrounding high-stakes testing. For instance, 47 of the 50 states have introduced legislation that rejects all or part of NCLB (Karp, 2006a), a policy constructed around high-stakes testing. Even though most of this introduced legislation is not likely to be passed into law, the fact of its introduction demonstrates conflict within the ORF, as state agencies and agents have increasingly shown signs of revolt against NCLB as a federal policy. Similarly, there is conflict within the ORF, as researchers and classroom teachers have demonstrated opposing views of high-stakes testing and policies like NCLB (see, e.g., Grant, 2006; Meier & Wood, 2004; Ravitch, 2002b; Valenzuela, 2005b). Additionally, as I've touched upon elsewhere in this book, there are researchers, teachers, and activist organizations in the PRF who continue to struggle for the relative autonomy of pedagogic discourse (as well as struggle for social justice) by challenging official pedagogic discourse through research and classroom practice (see, e.g., Karp, 2003; J. Lee, 2006).

However, in order to fully understand how the process of control reaches down into the classroom, it is necessary to explore the set of rules that are derived from the recontextualizing rules. These are the evaluative rules.

THE EVALUATIVE RULES AND HIGH-STAKES TESTING

According to Bernstein (1996), "Evaluation condenses the whole meaning of the device" (p. 50). Thus, the final set of rules of the pedagogic device are the evaluative rules, which,

> ...regulate pedagogic practice at the classroom level, for they define the standards which must be reached. Inasmuch as they do this, then evaluative rules act selectively on contents, the form of

transmission, and their distribution to different groups of pupils in different contexts. (p. 118)

This order of rules focuses on pedagogic discourse at the classroom level, as knowledge is communicated and acquired between teachers and students. They illustrate how evaluation influences pedagogic discourse through the regulation of the selection of content and form of transmission, as well as the selective distribution of both form and content to students in the classroom. The evaluative rules perform this function because they "specify the transmission of suitable contents under proper time and context and perform the significant function of monitoring the adequate realization of the pedagogic discourse" (Wong & Apple, 2003, p. 85). Pedagogic discourse is realized in the classroom, in practice, through the evaluative rules. Thus, as the lowest order of rules of the pedagogic device, the evaluative rules—as a derivative of the recontextualizing rules, which themselves are a derivative of the distributive rules—provide the final step of the relay of dominant social relations in pedagogic discourse.

The evaluative rules are central to the analysis done in this book. While the distributive rules attempt to regulate boundaries of consciousness, and the recontextualizing rules attempt to regulate how knowledge is recontextualized within pedagogic discourse generally, the evaluative rules attempt to regulate how knowledge is selected, formed and distributed in the classroom. The controls of the curriculum outlined in Chapter 4 (content, formal, and pedagogic controls) are the evaluative rules at work within pedagogic discourse. Because of the high-stakes tests, which as a form of evaluation are literally a manifestation of the evaluative rules, classroom practice has changed and altered. Contents, knowledge forms, and pedagogies have generally shifted toward that contained in the tests. This shift also carries with it a shift in classroom identities embodied by the content, knowledge forms, and pedagogies associated with the tests (Discursive control). The curriculum is thus being regulated by high-stakes testing (Au, 2007b), and this regulation is a manifestation of the evaluative rules in operation. Consequently, through the evaluative rules, we see how high-stakes testing selects for certain contents, knowledge forms, pedagogies, and identities, and selectively distributes them to different students. This is the control of classroom practice that I detailed in Chapter 4. As Bernstein (1996) says, "Evaluation condenses the whole meaning of the device" (p. 50). High-stakes testing as a form of evaluation, and its affect on classroom practice, epitomize the functioning of the pedagogic device.

The whole of the device, however, cannot be reduced to the evaluative rules alone. The three sets of rules of the pedagogic device are hierarchical and interrelated, and they identify how three different processes operate as dominant social relations are communicated within pedagogic discourse. The distributive rules operate through and provide the structural basis for the control over acceptable content, knowledge forms, and pedagogy, as I discussed in detail in Chapter 4. In a sense, it is this power that defines the distributive rules, for it is this manifestation of power and social relations that attempts to regulate what is viewed as being possible (or impossible) within pedagogic discourse. The recontextualizing rules explain a different, yet related, process. Based on the distributive rules, which determine both what is legitimate and who can determine legitimacy, the recontextualizing rules selectively take other discourses (e.g., disciplines of knowledge, political discourses) and appropriates, relocates, and relates them into pedagogic discourse. Thus, the recontextualizing rules explain the process of how knowledge is selected, distributed, and communicated into pedagogic discourse, the authority and boundaries of which are granted vis-à-vis the distributive rules. However, the recontextualizing rules only explain how knowledge is translated *into* pedagogic discourse, not how it is communicated *within* pedagogic discourse as it happens in the classroom. The evaluative rules then explain this process, and this process alone, by addressing how knowledge, knowledge forms, and identities are selected and distributed amongst students and teachers within actual classroom practice.

THE PEDAGOGIC DEVICE AND THE NEW MIDDLE CLASS

In Chapter 2, following Meiksins (1984) I discussed how the rise of scientific management was connected to the rise of an insurgent class of engineers. This discussion prefigured that which I undertook in Chapter 3, where I argued that the modern day progeny of this class of engineers can be found in what Apple (2006a) calls the professional and managerial new middle class, who essentially provide the technical know-how to develop, maintain, interpret, and manage complex systems of educational "accountability" and high-stakes testing. The role of the new middle class also figures strongly both in Bernstein's work (Power & Whitty, 2002) and the present analysis of high-stakes testing and the pedagogic device. Bernstein (1977) observes that:

The new middle class...are caught in a contradiction; for their theories are at variance with their objective class relationship.... On the one hand, they stand for variety against inflexibility, expression against repression, the inter-personal against the inter-positional; on the other hand, there is a grim obduracy of the division of labour and the of the narrow pathways to its positions of power and prestige....Thus, if the new middle class is to repeat its position in the class structure, then appropriate secondary socialization into privileged education becomes crucial. But as the relation between education and occupation becomes more direct and closer in time, then the classifications and frames increase in strength. (pp. 126–127)

This contradiction in many ways still exists today in that the professional and managerial new middle class often exhibits liberal ideologies while actively propagating rigid systems of efficiency and accountability upon which their upward mobility depends upon (Apple, 2006a). Such positioning means that this class fraction oftentimes maintains a more moderate social agenda, but also exhibits more conservative politics in order to support the upward mobility of their own children (see, e.g., Au, 2005a; Oakes, Welner, Yonezawa, & Allen, 1998).

Clearly, however, there have been significant shifts in both education and the economy over the last 30 years. As I noted in Chapter 3, such shifts are marked by increased globalization and the reconfiguration of certain aspects of the economy, including working- and middle-class labor. Indeed, many workers in the United States are now essentially "working class without work" (Weis, 1990, 2004), and the increased interknitting of the global economy has lead to increased competition (and falling wages) for white collar, technical work in the United States as well (Brown & Lauder, 2006). Hence, under current economic conditions the "relation between education and occupation" has become "more direct and closer in time," in Bernstein's words, as educational credentials take on increased importance relative to increased occupational competition for the new middle class. Thus, in agreement with Bernstein's above comment, regimes of high-stakes testing exhibit increased strength in classification and framing as the professional and managerial new middle class seeks to "enhance the chances that [their] children will have *less competition* from other students," while simultaneously enhancing "the value of credentials that the new middle class is more likely to accumulate" (Apple, 2006a, p. 107, original emphasis).

This last point speaks to Bernstein's more implicit acknowledgement of the importance of the new middle class in his later work. As

I've shown here, within the pedagogic device, the evaluative rules are extremely important and powerful because they are the final arbiter of how pedagogic discourse is shaped in the classroom (and, by extension, an arbiter of the shaping of consciousness as well). As the designers of the standardized tests, as well as the systems for the calibration and interpretation of test results themselves, the professional and managerial new middle class has a direct hand in the articulation of the evaluative rules, for, as agents of symbolic control (Bernstein, 2001), they in part determine the forms and structures through which the evaluative rules are themselves expressed. Thus, even though Bernstein does not explicitly name the role of the new middle class in his conception of the pedagogic device, this class fraction is implicitly present due to their pivotal role within regimes of high-stakes testing. I must be clear, however, that the new middle class is only but one group within the conservative modernization (Apple, 2006a), and as such, they only partly determine how the pedagogic device shapes consciousness.

THE PEDAGOGIC DEVICE AND THE REGULATION AND DISTRIBUTION OF KNOWLEDGE

The above analysis shows that high-stakes testing is a manifestation of the pedagogic device in operation. Through this analysis, we can see how the classification and framing of knowledge, as extensions of power and control, are operationalized in pedagogic discourse. It is through the distribution of power, recontextualization in pedagogic discourse, and evaluation, that social relations manifest in classroom practice via high-stakes testing. Thus, we see the device attempting to limit and regulate consciousness itself through pedagogic discourse. This is why Bernstein (1996) refers to the device as a "symbolic regulator of consciousness" (p. 53). It is not that the device itself is symbolic, or that its control is symbolic of something else. Rather, the device regulates consciousness through the control of symbols, codes, and sign systems, through the control of meaning making. One could read this in a simplistic manner, and suggest that Bernstein's (and my) formulation is just a reiteration of mechanistic, overly deterministic analyses of the relationship between capitalism and inequality in education. However, I would argue that this conceptual framework provides a much more fluid way of understanding social reproduction in education.

Bernstein (1996) himself offers two reasons why his model of the pedagogic device is not overly deterministic. First, the device creates its own inherent contradiction, one that subverts the device itself. He states that,

Although the device is there to control the unthinkable, in the process of controlling the unthinkable it makes the possibility of the unthinkable available. Therefore, internal to the device is its own paradox: it cannot control what it has been set up to control. (p. 52)

Here, Bernstein is pointing out an internal contradiction of the device: As soon as you delineate what is "unthinkable," you automatically make "the possibility of the unthinkable available." Put differently, once boundaries are established in our consciousness defining what "is" a cognitive structure is immediately established for thinking about what "is not" or what "might be."

As an example, I will use the "teacher" and "student" categories from the earlier discussion of classification and framing. These two categories co-exist with each other. "Teacher" implies the existence of the other category, "student," just as "student" implies the existence of "teacher." "Teacher," to varying degrees, has a relatively distinct identity as "not-student." Likewise, also to varying degrees, "student" has a relatively distinct identity as "not-teacher." The very existence of these relational categories in our consciousness creates the possibility for us to ask particular questions: Why is a teacher not a student? Why is a student also not a teacher? What is the basis for these categories? What is the relationship between the teachers and students? What is the basis of the relationship between students and teachers? The existence of these categories automatically creates potential to critically challenge and subvert the categories themselves. Thus, as Bernstein (1990) observes, "[F]rom a purely formal perspective, the pedagogic device cannot but be an instrument of order and of transformation of that order" (p. 206). Our sense of alternatives (e.g., alternative forms of education, alternative social and economic relations) is immediately conditioned by our sense of how things are now, and a source of that conditioning is that which is working to regulate our consciousness of such possibilities— the pedagogic device itself.

Further, as Bernstein (1996) explains, the second reason why the device cannot be deterministic exists externally to the device:

[T]he distribution of power which speaks through the device creates potential sites of challenge and opposition. The device creates in its realizations an arena of struggle between different groups for the appropriation of the device, because whoever appropriates the device has the power to regulate consciousness. Whoever appropriates the device appropriates a crucial site of symbolic control. The device itself creates an arena of struggle for those who are to appropriate it. (p. 52)

Here Bernstein identifies another contradictory tension of the device. Its very existence means that it can be struggled over by forces both within and outside of education. A clear example exists regarding high-stakes testing. As soon as high-stakes testing is established as a force within pedagogic discourse, the possibility of the realization of an anti-high-stakes testing movement is automatically created. Forces both within and outside of education can now unite around their opposition to high-stakes testing because, as Bernstein points out above, "[t] he device itself" has created "an arena of struggle for those who are to appropriate it."[5]

I would add a third reason the pedagogic device does not slip into determinism. At every level of the device, through the operation of every set of its rules, there are individual actors involved in interpretation and implementation. This guarantees that the transmission of power and control via the device is an imperfect operation, that the device cannot transmit a mirror reflection of power relations external to education. Thus, for instance, at the level of the classroom, at the level of the evaluative rules, teachers are taking up active resistance to high-stakes testing and the controls it attempts to exert on their practice, even if that resistance is limited by circumstance and evokes punishment by educational and political authorities.

RELATIVE AUTONOMY AND THE PEDAGOGIC DEVICE

Bernstein's formulation of the pedagogic device has its political roots in the concept of "relative autonomy" (Apple, 2002), a concept usually credited to Althusser (1971) that in reality was originally conceived of by Marx and Engels (Au, 2006a; Engels, 1968a, 1968b; Marx, 1968b). The concept of relative autonomy asserts that the social relations associated with capitalist society are relatively autonomous from the economic relations of capitalist production i.e., that what we see happening at the level of the "superstructure" is not totally and perfectly determined by the "economic base" of capitalism (see my discussion in Chapter 1). A relatively autonomous educational system "may...ultimately...reproduce capitalist relations, but it cannot be reduced to them" alone (Apple, 2002, p. 609). As Bernstein (1990) explains:

> [T]he concept of relative autonomy plays an important role in defining the space available to agents, and agencies in recontextualizing fields, and so a crucial role in the construction and relaying of pedagogic discourse. Relative autonomy here...points to *all* pedagogic discourse as an arena of conflict, a site of struggle

and appropriation. Relative autonomy refers to the constraints on the realizations of the pedagogic device as symbolic ruler. Whose ruler, what consciousness, is revealed by the discourses' privileging texts and the procedures of evaluation such texts presuppose. (p. 209, original emphasis)

Consequently, even though the pedagogic device is about the communication of social power relations and the regulation of consciousness, the negotiation, interpretation, and acquisition of such communication and regulation always holds the potential for resistance, disruption, and even critical intervention because of its relatively autonomous relationship to social and economic conditions.

Bernstein's formulation, however, does pose an important question. Just what is exactly does the pedagogic device (re)produce? At the most surface level, Bernstein appears to be talking about culture. For instance, in his summation of the pedagogic device, Bernstein (1996) explains that, "The pedagogic device...is a condition for the production, reproduction and transformation of culture" (p. 53). This conclusion points to the possibility that, for Bernstein, power relations are not economic and class relations, but are essentially cultural relations (Apple, 1992; Bernstein, 1977). Such a "culturalist" position, however, can prove to be problematic if one is interested in social change. If power relations are essentially cultural relations, then socioeconomic transformation (and educational transformation) is mainly a matter of cultural transformation, thus leaving the inequality of capitalist economic relations untouched. This is the critique made by Kelsh and Hill (2006), and, although I disagree with their particular reading of Bernstein and Apple, I do share this particular political concern regarding more culturalist analyses of power and education.

However, an argument can be made that, even though Bernstein did focus on culture in his analysis, one need not assume that his position was necessarily solely focused on culture alone. The issue at hand is the nature of the relationship between culture and power. As Apple (2002) explains, Bernstein's concept of relative autonomy,

> ...argues that education is not reducible to a mere reflection of unmediated economic needs. It is not simply a mirror image of capitalist *economic* relations... The educational system provides and reproduces critical resources within the field of symbolic control. (p. 609, original emphasis)

Hence, Bernstein's analysis is concerned with culture, but not necessarily because culture is the hinge upon which social and economic transformation is made. Indeed, Bernstein (1977) has consistently maintained that, while there is some level of relative autonomy between education and capitalist production:

> Education is a class-allocatory device, socially creating, maintaining and reproducing non-specialized and specialized skills, and specialized dispositions which have an *approximate* relevance to the mode of production...The state, historically, has gained increasing control over the *systemic* relationships whilst maintaining the educational system in its essential role as a class distributor of the social relationships of production. The class-based distribution of power and modalities of control are made substantive in the form of transmission/acquisition *irrespective* of variations in the systemic relationships between modes of education and production. In this way, the educational system maintains the dominating principle of the social structure.
>
> It is clear that the *systemic* relationships between education and production create for education the form of its economic or material base. (pp. 185–186, original emphasis)

Hence, Bernstein's focus is on a specific unit of analysis—pedagogic discourse. Relative to this specific unit of analysis, Bernstein's thesis is that, *in education*, power is transmitted via cultural codes and that the pedagogic device is the relay for this transmission—leaving open the possibility that both culture and education have much of their grounding in the materiality of macro-economic configurations of capitalist production. Thus, while the structure of education is generally bound by the social relations associated with capitalist economic relations, this binding is at least in part communicated through the transmission of cultural codes (symbolic control). Again, relative autonomy figures prominently here because, since culture is not stagnant or ossified but embodied in the relative chaos of individual and group actions and interactions, this transmission is *imperfect at best*. At every step of the way, along every relay, the pedagogic device simultaneously regulates consciousness and creates space for resistance to that regulation because of such built-in imperfection. Despite such imperfection, however, systems of high-stakes, standardized testing are *unequal by design* in that they inherently (re)produce inequalities associated with socioeconomic relations external to education through the selective regulation and distribution of consciousness and identities.

6

STANDARDIZING INEQUALITY
The Hidden Curriculum of High-Stakes Testing

> We should understand what we are up against: not that tests are
> arbitrary, but a class society that requires such tests. No attack on
> these rites of passage can be finally successful unless it overturns
> bourgeois culture, itself, and the rule of our dominant classes.
>
> **Richard Ohmann (1976, p. 65)**

Promoters of federal education policy assert that high-stakes testing
leads to increased achievement (Ravitch, 2002a) and that "No Child
Left Behind Is *Working*" (U.S. Department of Education, 2006, original emphasis). These promoters argue that student achievement is
improving generally and that achievement gaps between Whites and
other students are closing because of high-stakes testing used in policies like NCLB. However, such arguments do not necessarily match
the data. Analyses of NCLB have found that the high-stakes testing
has not improved reading and math achievement across states and has
not significantly narrowed national and state level achievement gaps
between White students and students of color nor gaps between rich
and poor students (J. Lee, 2006; Mathis, 2006). Additionally, studies
which compare test score results of the Texas high-stakes testing system
(the blueprint for NCLB) with four other standardized tests commonly
taken by students in Texas and nationally—the American College Test
(ACT), the Scholastic Achievement Test (SAT), the National Assessment of Educational Progress (NAEP), and the Advanced Placement

(AP) test—finds that the Texas high-stakes testing in early grades either was indeterminate, had no impact, or had a negative impact on student achievement in relation to the other tests. Thus, the implementation of high-stakes testing in Texas could not be shown to improve learning (Amrein & Berliner, 2002b; Nichols, Glass, & Berliner, 2006).[1] These findings correlate with other research nationally (Harris & Herrington, 2004) and raise the question of the overall effectiveness of high-stakes tests in improving achievement generally.

If the correlation between high-stakes testing and increased learning is questionable, empirically unproven, and possibly even false, what does this indicate about the validity of using such testing to measure learning, teaching effectiveness, as well as to allocate financial sanctions? First and foremost, it may indicate that the tests themselves are not valid. For instance, in their research on the statistical validity of standardized high-stakes tests, Kane and Staiger (2002) found that between 50% to 80% of any change in individual test scores from year to year and test to test occurs due to completely random factors. This means that 50% to 80% of any improvement or decline in individual test scores may be due to any number of randomly occurring events— whether a child taking a test ate breakfast that morning, population changes from year to year, who was in attendance the day the test was taken, who was proctoring that test, whether or not a dog was barking outside of the school window, the physical conditions of the space where the test is being taken, and so on.

Other research has also found that the testing industry does not have the infrastructure necessary to keep up with the enormous technical and administrative demands created by NCLB's high-stakes testing provisions, which has lead to many widely reported scoring errors (Toch, 2006), and that some districts, principals, teachers, and students are cheating on the tests in response to the immense pressures created by the high-stakes policies (Nichols & Berliner, 2005), thus raising further questions about test-score validity in general. Putting this evidence together with the fact that it is a statistical impossibility for all students to reach 100% proficiency on high-stakes tests (Darling-Hammond, 2007; Linn, 2003), in part because standardized test require that a certain percentage of students fail in order to be considered valid and reliable (Popham, 2001) and in part because bias can be structured into test criterion and test question language, and considering that it is also financially impossible to reach 100% proficiency on the tests since the monetary investment curve increases exponentially the closer one approaches 100% proficiency (Haas, Wilson, Cobb, & Rallis, 2005), it seems more than reasonable to question the use of these tests to make important decisions regarding the lives of children, teachers, administrators, and their communities.

If the tests do not necessarily measure learning, then, what do they do? Based on the evidence and analysis presented in this book, they sort human populations along socially, culturally, and economically determined lines. Madaus and Horn (2000) speak to the elitism that is often involved with testing when they state:

> In addition to the basic proposition that testing is a technology, there is an additional characteristic of technologies that must be recognized and addressed. It is that technological endeavours tend to be directed by elites who isolate themselves from those who are not members of that elite... (p. 52)

From this vantage, high stakes testing can be seen as a form of regulated elitism (Gibson, 2001), where, on the most basic level, there is an extremely close correlation between high standardized test scores and the wealth of students' parents and grandparents (Sacks, 1999). This may be a vulgar assertion, but based on the available evidence regarding the achievement gaps between rich and poor students and between White students and students of color, high-stakes tests are incredibly efficient at sorting for race and economic class in the United States. Indeed, as I noted earlier, this outcome demonstrates a remarkable affinity to the outcomes of the I.Q. tests associated with the eugenics and social efficiency movements of the early 20th century. Thus, De Lissovoy and McLaren (2003) may not be overreaching when they assert that:

> If the main tool of accountability initiatives, the norm-referenced standardized test, is racist...in its use, and if these initiatives are touted both as a means of restructuring schools and understanding the truth of what goes on in them, then what is confronted in this [standardized testing] movement is really a large-scale *staging* of the failure of students of colour. In other words, it is not simply that students of colour compete on an unequal playing field. The field is more than unequal. In fact, the field is constructed so that the responses of these students will come to *constitute* what is called failure. (p. 135, original emphasis)

Given the striking evidence I cited in previous chapters regarding test-based achievement gaps and the racialized bias constructed into the psychometric heart of college entrance exams like the SAT, De Lissovoy and McLaren's above conclusion, that high-stakes standardized tests not only *sort* for race and class, but that the tests *define failure* by race and class as well, speaks to the material realities of test-defined achievement gaps in public education.

Putting the arguments of this book together, we can begin to see how systems of high-stakes, standardized testing, both at the policy and conceptual levels, contribute to the (re)production of educational inequality, and that the ideological justification of the "American meritocracy" works as cover for this phenomenon. Inequality is literally *built-into* our systems of testing, and the tests operate as a mechanism for the (re)production of socioeconomic and educational inequality. High-stakes, standardized tests are simply unequal by design. This, I would argue, is the *hidden curriculum of high-stakes testing*.

There is a long history and much literature devoted to discussion of what has been called the hidden curriculum (for an excellent review of this literature, see, Margolis, Soldatenko, Acker, & Gair, 2001). The hidden curriculum refers to the "…the tacit teaching of social and economic norms and expectations to students in schools…" (Apple, 1979/2004, p. 42), where these "norms and values … are related to working in this unequal society" (Apple, 1995, p. 87). What is evident in the implementation of high-stakes testing is that the tests tacitly enforce educational inequality, standardization, disempowerment, and alienation. This hidden curriculum, however, is not the manifestation of complete economic determinism in the classroom. Rather, the hidden curriculum of high-stakes testing has more to do with establishing the boundaries of validity and legitimacy and enforcing these borders through bureaucratic and institutional hierarchies. In this way we can see the hidden curriculum not as completely deterministic, but more as setting acceptable limits that "at the level of practice are often mediated by…the informal…action of groups of people…" (Apple, 1995, p. 82).

RESISTING THE HIDDEN CURRICULUM

Educational inequality in the United States has been persistent, and it seems to be matched only by the persistence of social inequalities (Anyon, 2005; Barton, 2003). For the reasons outlined in this book, high-stakes testing and policies such as NCLB that are erected around the tests contribute to this persistence by hurting, rather than helping students—poor students and students of color in particular. In this way, high-stakes testing only works to enact inequality by increasing the educational and social stratification of students, and by extension, their communities. As the contradictions surrounding both NCLB and high-stakes testing heighten, and as the critical issues come into sharper focus, resistance, from the more critical Left to the muted mainstream, continues to build (Karp, 2006b). But, given the powerful hegemonic alliance aligned against social justice and equality and in support of these systems that are unequal by design (Apple, 2006a), it will take a substantial social movement to end educational inequality (Anyon, 2005). However, it is my belief that we are up to this critical task.

There are several notable instances of increasing organizing and resistance in the contemporary era, where people are in the process of both consciously challenging existing inequalities and envisioning new policies and new systems of relations. In 1999, when the World Trade Organization met in Seattle, activists from around the world converged in that Northwest city to protest the neoliberal economic policies being advanced under the "new" capitalism (Carnoy, Castells, Cohen, & Cardoso, 1993; Greider, 1997; Hardt & Negri, 2000). This event affected many regionally, nationally, and internationally, and many students were involved and participated in the protests (see, e.g., Au, 2000). Similar protests have followed in major cities around the globe, as workers, peasants, activists, environmentalists, farmers, and indigenous peoples have convened to voice their opposition to privatization and deregulation of public services and natural resources. This growing global movement affected education in dramatic ways as well. Internationally, the "Citizen Schools" in Porto Alegre, Brazil, illustrate the growing, popular movement against privatization and toward more democratic participation of Brazilian workers in their school governance (Gandin & Apple, 2003).

Curricular examples of social justice educators challenging both high-stakes testing and the inequalities associated with public education in the United States also abound, and these examples realize and operationalize a vision of critical education within the potential discursive gap. Among others, these include: *Rethinking Our Classrooms: Teaching for Equity and Justice* (Au, Bigelow, & Karp, 2007), *Beyond Heroes and Holidays* (E. Lee, Menkhart, & Okazawa-Rey, 1998), *Putting the Movement Back Into Civil Rights Teaching* (Menkhart, Murray, & View, 2004), *Rethinking Globalization* (Bigelow & Peterson, 2002), *Teaching About Asian Pacific Americans* (Chen & Omastu, 2006), *Resistance In Paradise* (Wei & Kamel, 1998), *Reading, Writing, and Rising Up* (Christensen, 2000), *Rethinking Mathematics* (Peterson & Gutstein, 2005), *The Line Between Us* (Bigelow, 2006), and *Democratic Schools* (Apple & Beane, 2007). All of these publications, as well as many others not mentioned here, are united by their collective focus on classroom practice and a firm belief that teachers, as active resisters of the forces of inequality in society and education, can make a significant and powerful difference in the lives (and futures) of students and the world (Au,

2006b; Au & Apple, 2004). Further, much of the research cited here, such as Apple (2006a), Lipman (2004), McNeil (2000), Sleeter (2005), M.L. Smith (2004), and Valenzuela (2005a), represent scholarly interrogations of this same space, where the works of these academic-activists perform as political and ideological intervention in the process of social (re)production in education.

Increasing numbers of networks of educators working for social justice (and against inequality) in education exist as well. A few examples include: Education Not Incarceration (2006), a San Francisco Bay Area-based group that challenges the State of California's spending priorities; Teachers 4 Social Justice (2006), a San Francisco collective of teachers holds an annual conference regularly drew well over 1,000 educators in 2007 and continues to work on issues of equity and equality in education; Chicago Teachers for Social Justice (Teachers for Social Justice, 2005), a collective of midwestern teachers very similar to their San Francisco counterparts; and the New York Collective of Radical Educators (2006), which holds regular meetings and study groups, organizes around social justice issues, and develops critical curricula both in New York City and the northeastern region of the United States. Additionally, there are collections of teachers in the Seattle, Washington, and the Portland, Oregon (Portland Area Rethinking Schools, 2006) areas that unite around the publication *Rethinking Schools* (2008) and convene to promote social justice education, build curricula, and take part local organizing efforts. Indeed, on a national level, publications like *Rethinking Schools* and organizations like FairTest (2005) and the Rouge Forum (Gibson, Queen, Ross, & Vinson, 2007) have played key roles in critiquing both high-stakes testing and the No Child Left Behind legislation while simultaneously offering alternative visions of what social justice education can look like. As was true early in the 1900s, the hegemonic control of education is not won easily, and these organizations and publications represent the legacy of popular resistance to the imposition of social inequality that is wrought through influence of capitalist ideology in education.

UNEQUAL BY DESIGN

I hope that in this book I have not presented myself as a dogged structural-functionalist. I know that I have made strong assertions regarding high-stakes testing, the curriculum, and inequalities associated with dominant socioeconomic relations. However, as part of my analysis, I have tried to consistently side with complexity over simplicity because the relationship between schools and social reproduction is complex.

Although we see incredible levels of educational inequality, we cannot simply reduce them to a mere function of capitalist production—even if the end results generally present themselves that way (and in this regard, perhaps Bowles & Gintis (1976) were at least partially correct). As I have tried to show here, there are always tangled and sometimes contradictory tendencies at work within nearly all aspects of education, high-stakes, standardized testing included. For example, as I touched on in Chapter 3, not everyone on the Right, not even all neoliberals, agree with high-stakes testing, even though the logics and policies associated with the tests are generally aligned with free-market, capitalist production and consumption. Furthermore, as I talked about at great length in Chapter 2, the rise and eventual triumph of the production model in public education in the United States was *not* simply a matter of big industrial capital telling educators how to structure the system. While there were significant and influential elements of big business present, there were also other factors involved, such as the rise of a new class of engineers in education, along with capacity issues that schools were having to face. Further, there was resistance to this production model by educational leaders from its very inception. For that matter, none of the history relayed in this book, nor the educational policies and outcomes related to high-stakes testing outlined here, were/are foregone conclusions. They, like the curriculum and education generally, are representative of social processes, representatives of relationships between humans operating in concert with each other as individuals and as representatives of broader social structures.

Thus, through my analysis I have hoped to outline how systems of high-stakes, standardized testing are *unequal by design*. I've chosen wording very explicitly to describe the phenomenon of educational inequality. *Design* implies conscious action. It denotes a process. It implies actors and relations between actors, and therefore simultaneously implies groups (classes, communities, cultures) and social relations. *Design*, then, frames the creation of inequality as a process, as a product of human social and material relations. This process, however, is "over determined" in the sense which Althusser (1969) uses the term. What I mean is that the process by which inequality is produced is, in fact, inseparable from the social and economic structures within which it is found, inseparable from the very conditions in which it exists. As such, the production of inequality not only dramatically affects social and economic relations as a determinant, but is also determined by the social and economic relations themselves. Thus, the (re)production of inequality is "over determined" in a dialectical sense, as aspects of the economic, political, and cultural spheres push and pull in this process

(Au, 2006a). This conception of over determination is extremely important for my analysis because it recognizes that inequality does not exist as a presumption of human social and economic life. Rather, inequality is brought into the world as part and parcel of these relations. It is produced. It is *designed*, and to ignore the intentional elements of this production is to ignore the historical, political, conceptual, empirical, and sociological analyses I've provided here. Conversely, however, such over determination also means that inequality, socioeconomic, cultural, or educational, can be stopped. If inequality is the product of design, then collective conscious action can be taken to change that inequality. It can literally be designed out of existence.

Although I did not refer to it in Chapter 5, this conclusion is one of the central implications of Bernstein's conceptual framework. If, as I demonstrated, social relations are carried in the structure of knowledge and translated into pedagogic discourse, and if, under current socio-economic conditions, this process (re)produces educational inequality, then, *different social and economic relations are capable of producing different structures of knowledge and are therefore also capable of producing different educational outcomes*. Further, because there is space within education to subvert dominant social relations, pedagogic discourse can also play a role in developing consciousness that sees different social relations as both possible and necessary (Anyon, 2005; Apple, 1995). It is for this reason that Bernstein's theoretical framework proves so useful.

This last point is important because it speaks to one of the overall aims of this book. My focus in this analysis has been that of critique. This focus means that I have neglected offering concrete solutions in favor of devoting the bulk of this study to detailing what is wrong with high-stakes testing, and by extension, what is wrong with education and education policy in the United States. However, I would argue that this focus is not misplaced because there are at least two relevant conclusions to be drawn. The first is that, this book is part of pedagogic discourse and is therefore also part of the pedagogic device itself (as am I, as an educator). By exploring and examining high-stakes testing as part of a broader analysis of educational control, my analysis has highlighted and defined the sometimes-hidden limits of the tests in historical, social, economic, cultural, political, and technical terms. As we've learned from Bernstein's formulation, this critique in and of itself is absolutely necessary because it lays the conscious groundwork for contemplating what might yet exist. Put differently, this book is an attempt to trace the limits of the possible, what we see as the limits of the thinkable. This act allows for a conception of—and movement into—what might be thought of as impossible or unthinkable, occupying the "potential discursive gap" (Bernstein, 1996, p. 44) between what we consciously conceive of what "is" and what "may be." The second conclusion to draw from this analysis is that, whatever the future forms of assessment implemented in education policy and practice may be, they are intimately and inextricable intertwined with social relations external to education and schools, external to pedagogic discourse. Systems of high-stakes assessment, of test-and-punish, are *unequal by design*, and therefore hold the potential to be *equal by design* should we so choose. This fact must be kept in mind as many of us work to envision new policies and new systems of relations in education and society.

AFTERWORD

In 2004 I wrote the essay, "Critical Social Theory and Transformative Knowledge" as part of an attempt to describe the beginnings of a critical social theory program in education. Part of my goal was to make the case for building a tradition of educational criticism as part of quality education. Criticism is not new to many disciplines, such as literature, where literary criticism is a specialization with a long history. In political science, philosophy, and film studies, we again see that a tradition of criticism exists, if not thrives. Often, work in these areas is high in theoretical content. Criticism is associated with but different from philosophy, which exists as a specialization in education and enjoys a long tradition dating back to John Dewey. Job descriptions may be indicative, where one may find calls for "philosophy of education," but never for "educational criticism." Seen through the prism of Critical Social Theory (CST), educational criticism utilizes interdisciplinary knowledge. As I have defined it, criticism is not only deconstructive, but reconstructive. That is, it serves the function of building possibilities through synthesis rather than incommensurability, or leaving tensions as tensions.

Wayne Au's excellent and Marxist-inspired criticism of standards-based education in general and No Child Left Behind in particular, showcases the uses of criticism that I would like to emphasize here. In educational theory, there is much attention to notions of difference as launching points for criticism. Difference has all been but associated with poststructuralism as part of an overall problematization of both modernism and Marxism. I want to argue that *Unequal By Design* is positioned not only to highlight difference as a form of maximizing the tensions among discourses, but difference as a point of mutual entry among apparently incompatible discourses, a process I will call "synthesis." In other words, Au's brand of Marxism takes back the concept of difference and reclaims it as part of the Marxist project, arguing that capitalism has the uncanny ability to subvert living with difference as the economy standardizes basically all aspects of social and educational life. Under the current regime, students become variations within a model as they are manufactured by an educational system that does not misinterpret their differences; it sincerely does not care about their differences. Any discourse on difference that does not take capitalism seriously subverts its own claims about its valued status as well as undertheorizes the conditions of its production (Ebert, 1996). Here Au argues not only for the necessity of Marxism, but its indispensability for educational criticism that values difference not only at the level of discourse but at the material plane of social intercourse where educational labor is not valorized for its capacity to generate high API scores but as part of a dynamic life that is educative and dialectical at its core. What is profound about a materialist understanding has been all but profaned and Au's task is to put educational criticism back on its feet.

As part of this synthesis, Au shows educators the ability of CST, which is largely an academic production, to respond to historical conditions outside the university, making it difficult radically to separate the academic from public life. His framework proceeds from a hermeneutics of suspicion as well as a language of transcendence, that is, neither caught up in the distortions of the Right nor the pessimism of the Left. CST often targets larger structural issues, which is arguably its dominant modus operandi. As a result, it has been criticized for lacking concrete utility in schooling practices, often citing its highly specialized language. Although the excesses of such criticism should be avoided, Au's intervention clearly provides a concrete analysis that takes the larger framework of economic life as intimate with educational life. By doing so, Au does not argue that schools are outside of "society" as an abstraction, but completely immersed in their sociality.

It is through synthesis—of combining competing discourses to open up an alternative path—that further criticism is made possible, which is ultimately what generative criticism produces: more criticism. However, it is not criticism that is part of a sophistic exercise of generating criticism for its own sake. Compelling, theoretical production in the university and the disciplines arises out of a recursive relationship with the empirical world and responds to real institutional conditions. It may be abstract in the first sense—that is, conceptual—but not abstract in the second sense—that is, a mystification. Au does not draw a radical distinction between theoretical production in the disciplines and the empirical state of the world "out there." He does not return theory to a false dichotomy between "school life" and "real life." Thus, synthesis is not just among theories, but equally between theory and empirical life. Although much of CST can be characterized as theoretical, it is a constellation of responses to institutional arrangements like racism, sexism, and class exploitation. In Au's analysis, CST is not comprised of theories about abstract notions like black holes—interesting for another occasion—but responds to the exigencies of concrete social conditions. In the process, both academic discourse and community-specific discourse are transformed as they interact with each other. Moreover, intellectual knowledge does not just travel beyond the academy in the form of language *qua* language, but *language as social practice*, language as analysis and carrier of ideologies.

In our search for the beginnings of educational criticism, tensions among competing discourses should not be neglected. In my own work, I have tried to account for some of these jockeying for supremacy by marking the productive debates between materialism and discourse analysis, between race-based perspectives and class-first philosophies, and between determinist modernisms and vertiginous strains of postmodern thought. Ricoeur (1981) reminds us that the rubbing together of two apparently irreconcilable discourses is conducive to producing new knowledge. Ricoeur uses Max Black's insight that metaphor happens at the level of the sentence rather than the word, through "semantic innovation" when two unlikely words are paired and violate the original environment of meaning, thereby changing it. Likewise, knowledge production frequently comes from the act of juxtaposing two different worlds, giving rise to an even more different third world. In the wake of serious questions about the utility of Marxism, Au's book injects new hope in historical materialism by reinvigorating our interests in social (re)production, not by returning to Bowles and Gintis' (1976) context-bound insights but taking stock of current conditions, that is, how human beings today make history.

In criticism, there is always the danger of reducing, of caricaturing and truncating competing discourses in order to make one's point. Consensus building may institutionalize a symbolic form of violence (Bourdieu, 1991) when the different are made to look identical, as when all iterations of Marxism are cut from the same cloth. Emphasizing difference brings the adversarial process to its highest form as discourses are pushed to their limit or breaking point through criticism. That said, the adversarial process is too strong where it promotes the mutual exclusion of discourses through differences that are hopelessly incommensurate (Flecha, 1999). This position diverges from the construction of competing discourses as lacking any common ground. We may go a long way with what Lyotard and Thebaud (1994) call the "agonistics" of discourse, something that they promote as the standard for criticism in order to preserve the differences among discourses—their "singularity." However as Au shows us, *the opposite of difference does not suggest consensus but synthesis.* The negation of difference is not sameness but *different again.* With several decades of criticism laid at the doorsteps of Marxism, Au's reconstruction of Marxist discourse affirms its ability to respond to demands for difference, of being different even from itself. He succeeds in raising Marxism out of the ashes of criticism to rise once again in full view. He does not respond with Marxism's strength, but rather its weakness, or its ability to flex and accommodate rather than its orthodoxy.

Focusing on synthesis allows for the creation of an alternative, interpenetrating discourse that happens precisely at the weak points of discourses, precisely where they are uncertain. But it is one thing to expose the weak point in order to subvert its certainty, its "general politics of truth" (Foucault, 1980, p. 131), and quite another to provide an entry point through criticism as an act of reconstruction, of creation not in the sense of originality but edification and discovering a larger "truth." The weak point is where discursive dogma and polemics end, and where synthesis is possible because frameworks that previously seemed irreconcilable now appear mutually porous and enter each other's horizon. As a result, both poles of the dialogue are changed and mutually transformed. This method of criticism does not suggest taking the middle ground as a convenient position, but suggests that dialectical criticism appropriates "true ideas" (Freire, 1993) for the purpose of moving synthesis forward.

Synthesis enables Au to move beyond limitations evident in traditional paradigms. The Frankfurt School merged Freudian analysis and Marxian thought to arrive at useful concepts like repressive desublimation (Marcuse, 1991), Hegel and Nietszche to produce negative dialectics (Adorno, 1973), and Mead and Saussure to come up with insights on the pragmatics of communication (Habermas, 1984, 1987). More recently, Michael Peters and Walter Humes (2003) linked education with the contours of "knowledge economy" by combining Marxian analyses of political economy with insights on information society and the proliferation of knowledge, a condition "characterized in terms of the economics of abundance (as opposed to scarcity), the annihilation of distance, the deterritorialization of the state, and investment in human capital" (p. 5). Like Ricoeur and Black's insights, these concepts were made possible through what I am calling a *discursive innovation*, of leveraging two or more unlikely discourses against each other to produce a fresh theoretical pathway. In the end, this creative process is less about establishing consensus among competing discourses, but joining them at their weak points where they can find mutual expression. Au joins insights from Marxism and the politics of recognition without losing sight of a specific intellectual project centered on an analysis of capitalism as the driving force behind high stakes testing. To some, this may risk a form of conceptual violence that reduces a complex whole to a simple origin.

I would argue that the space between discursive violence and innovation is where educational criticism finds itself, of risking violence in order to arrive at new insights. Stuart Hall (1996) performed such an operation when he tapped Gramsci's relevance for the study of race and ethnicity. Although Hall admits that Gramsci's ideas (e.g., hegemony) come out of a Marxist problematic, Hall was able take an inventory of race and discuss racial hegemony, or the saturation of society with the contradictions of race. Elsewhere, I (2006) attempted a similar maneuver by applying Althusser's theory of ideology to the study of racial interpellation and the school as a racial state apparatus. Charles Mills (1997) accomplishes generative insights on race and white supremacy by appropriating the concept of the social contract, criticizing its failure to capture the terms of the racial contract.[1] Educational criticism pays respect to the competing claims among discourses not only to maximize their tension but to optimize the possibility of higher and more critical forms of understanding, a process which is at the heart of criticism if it is tied not only to generating new knowledge, but to building new theories (Althusser, 2003).

The educator-as-critic is key in Au's rearticulation of the purpose of criticism. In building a tradition of criticism, one must avoid reifying the traditional notion of the critic. Just as the traditional intellectual was transformed through Gramsci's (1971) insistence that the intellectual was less of a social position and more of a social function, we may argue that the educational critic is less a bureaucratic description and more of a political vocation. Although a critic may function as an official title (e.g., "professor of educational criticism"), it is more accurately a political position that teachers and educators take up. In this sense, criticism is tied less to its current elitist tendencies, which is monopolized by academics in the popular imagination, without neglecting the fact that the academy serves a special function in the production of criticism. In building a tradition of criticism in education, Au recognizes that rethinking schools requires a new subject position for teachers and educators in the figure of the critic.

The critic takes part in the public sphere that Habermas (1989) once valorized without falling prey to the excesses of a romantic idealism about direct or face-to-face communication. Criticism may be driven by the regulative ideal of consensus building but with the demands of solidarity as a concrete political process. It requires the risk of deciding in the midst of a profound conceptual undecidability, which is less about universal agreement but a provisional solidarity to recognize a problem and determine a path to action. CST may be the academic version of Frankenstein's creature but its practice is determined by concrete circumstances, where high theory meets Main Street. Ultimately and with no guarantees, CST may be used in the service of real communities. As is often the case, the academy figures largely into this project, not as something separate from "real life" but part of the synthesis that is life. Au's fruitful analysis gets us one step closer to the reality of putting educational criticism in its rightful place.

Zeus Leonardo, PhD

Visiting Associate Professor
University of California
Graduate School of Education

NOTE

1. For an earlier appropriation of the social contract's inability to grasp patriarchal relations, see Pateman's (1988) analysis in *The Sexual Contract*.

BIBLIOGRAPHY

Adorno, T. (1973). *Negative dialectics*. E. B. Ashton (Trans.). New York: Continuum.

Althusser, A. (2003). *The humanist controversy and other writings*. London: Verso.

Bourdieu, P. (1991). *Language and symbolic power*. J. B. Thompson (Ed.). G. Raymond & M. Adamson (Trans.). Cambridge, MA: Harvard University Press.

Bowles, S., & Gintis, H. (1976). *Schooling in capitalist America*. New York: Basic Books.

Ebert, T. (1996). *Ludic feminism and after*. Ann Arbor: University of Michigan Press.

Flecha, R. (1999). Modern and postmodern racism in Europe: Dialogical approach and anti-racist pedagogies. *Harvard Educational Review, 69*(2), 150–171.

Foucault, M. (1980). *Power/knowledge*. C. Gordon (Ed.). C. Gordon, L. Marshall, J. Mepham, & K. Soper (Trans.). New York: Pantheon Books.

Freire, P. (1993). *Pedagogy of the oppressed*. M. Ramos (Trans.). New York: Continuum.

Gramsci, A. (1971). *Selections from prison notebooks*. Q. Hoare & G. Smith (Eds. & Trans.). New York: International Publishers.

Habermas, J. (1984). *The theory of communicative action*. Vol. 1. T. McCarthy (Trans.). Boston: Beacon Press.

Habermas, J. (1987). *The theory of communicative action*. Vol. 2. T. McCarthy (Trans.). Boston: Beacon Press.

Habermas, J. (1989). *The structural transformation of the public sphere*. T. Burger with F. Lawrence (Trans.). Cambridge, MA: The MIT Press.

Hall, S. (1996). Gramsci's relevance for the study of race and ethnicity. In D. Morley & K. Chen (Eds.), *Stuart Hall* (pp. 411–440). London: Routledge.

Leonardo, Z. (2004). Critical social theory and transformative knowledge: The functions of criticism in quality education. *Educational Researcher, 33*(6), *11–18*.

Leonardo, Z. (2006). Through the multicultural glass: Althusser, ideology, and race relations in post-Civil Rights America. *Policy Futures in Education, 3*(4), 400–412.

Lyotard, J., & Thebaud, J. (1994). *Just gaming*. W. Godzich (Trans.). Minneapolis: University of Minnesota Press.

Marcuse, H. (1991). *One-dimensional man: Studies in the ideology of advanced industrialized society* (2nd ed.). Boston: Beacon Press.

Mills, C. (1997). *The racial contract*. Ithaca, NY: Cornell University Press.

Pateman, C. (1988). *The sexual contract*. Stanford, CA: Stanford University Press.

Peters, M., & Humes, W. (2003). Editorial: Education in the knowledge economy. *Policy Futures in Education, 1*(1), 1–19.

Ricoeur, P. (1981). *Hermeneutics and the human sciences*. J. B. Thompson (Ed. & Trans.). Cambridge, UK: Cambridge University Press.

NOTES

CHAPTER 1

1. Please note that this is not to be overly critical of the faculty, staff, and students at Berkeley high. I have many friends and colleague there whom I love and respect greatly, and whom I know are working very hard to help all of their students succeed. Further, I believe that some of the best education possible can and does take place there. Finally, Berkeley High's students are a politically conscious, intellectual, intelligent, and lively bunch whom I enjoyed working with.

2. I recognize that the term "students of color" is problematic for several reasons, one of which is that it normalizes Whiteness. However, other racial signifiers, such as the commonly used "non-White," are also problematic. "Non-White," for instance, does now allow for "mixed-race" individuals who are "half-White," such as myself (my father is Chinese American and my mother is European American), and therefore upholds notions of racial purity (in addition normalizing Whiteness as well). Further, to use such phrases as "racialized as White" or "racialized as not White" seems too cumbersome and overly academic, particularly when most community and education activists I know who are not academics use the term "students of color." Therefore, given that we are somewhat shackled by the imperfection and power relations in language, I use the term "students of color" to refer to students who have been racialized as not White.

3. I must note that, for the purposes of this book, I will use "high-stakes, standardized tests," "High-stakes tests," "testing," "testing policies," and their grammatical derivatives fairly interchangeably. Specifically, within the context of this book, these terms all refer to "high-stakes, standardized testing."

4. Despite such criticism, I do want to acknowledge that critical education theorists have used these concepts fruitfully to analyze the relationship between schools and socioeconomic inequalities in nondeterministic ways (see, e.g., Apple, 1992; Apple, 1995; Bernstein, 1990, 1996).

CHAPTER 2

1. Additionally, while I draw heavily upon the works of Kliebard (2004), Cuban (2004), for instance, my overall orientation and view of this history includes a specific focus on economics, social power, and class relations that these other authors do not.

2. Despite the fact that this chapter tells a somewhat linear story of the rise and dominance of social efficiency in public schooling in the United States, to assume that this history, or any history for that matter, proceeds in such a linear manner would be a mistake. As I try to make clear at certain points in this narrative, the application of the principles of industrial management and capitalist production to education was never predestined or predetermined. The era in U.S. history I touch upon here was in fact marked by resistance offered by the growing labor and populist movements. While it is true that the captains of industry ultimately out maneuvered and eventually co-opted the interests of organized labor in particular (Boyer & Morais, 1975; Noble, 1977), a hard fought struggle between "robber barons and rebels" (Zinn, 1995) certainly took place.

3. As Noble (1977) reminds us, however, Taylor's original vision of scientific management ultimately proved too rigid of a labor structure for most capitalists. So, while the original intension of controlling the labor process was ultimately maintained, scientific management underwent some revision after Taylor's death as corporations attempted to "humanize" their relations with workers. It should be noted, however, that this move toward recognizing some of the workers' needs as humans was largely as a result of the massive labor protests, strikes, and organizing that began during the late 1800s and continued through the 1920s, both in the United States and around the world.

4. For instance, Callahan (1964) notes that the median class size in high schools of cities with populations greater than 100,000 people during the 1930–1931 school year was 34.1 students in junior high and 30.5 students in senior high. These numbers are surprisingly consistent with current urban classroom size averages.

5. Indeed, the social programs associated with the New Deal could be seen as somewhat of a capitulation to the demands of labor on the part of big capitalists. This included some capitalists motions to accept the fact of the existence of organized labor that included various attempts to "humanize" the labor process.

6. Cuban's (2004) silence regarding these particular influences is notable.

7. It should be noted that Counts actually collected data on 1,654 school boards total, 974 of which were rural. Counts' intent for this study was to analyze the composition of mainly the 532 city school boards.

8. Apple (1986) attributes this shift of several factors. Women were increasingly being called into factory work. Compulsory schooling was growing, and the population was generally shifting away from factory work. With the rapidly increasing demand for teachers as school size increased, school boards turned to women to fill the need.

9. It should be noted that certain aspects of Taylorism were adopted by Lenin in the Soviet Union with mixed results and with much political tension and struggle. At times Lenin and other socialists advocated for its use to increase worker productivity, but within a framework of worker collectivity and to serve the working class generally (Sochor, 1981), causing some scholars to argue that these substantial differences ultimately meant the Soviet Union did *not* actually use Taylorism (see, e.g., Van Atta, 1986). I raise this mainly to complicate how we think about Taylorism and "scientific" approaches to production and to raise the issue of how such a system is in fact put to very specific use—control and increased profits—within the capitalist economic system.

10. It should be noted that educational tracking and guidance counseling also have their origins within the milieu of standardized testing, scientific management, and social efficiency (Chapman, 1988).

11. This is not to say, however, that capital and capitalism are mechanically deterministic with regards to systems standardized testing. Rather, the overarching point is that systems of standardized testing are constructed upon the *logics* of capitalist production, even if the reality is that individuals, classrooms, and schools may at times be challenging these very same logics.

12. Bisseret (1979) makes a very provocative and convincing argument that the concept of naturally occurring aptitude was one of the ideological tools developed by the ascendant bourgeoisie in Europe to justify its recently acquired position of social and economic power while maintaining that all individuals were equal under the eyes of the law.

13. It should be noted that in recent years the SAT has come under increasing critique, and the list of universities that have stopped using it as an entrance requirement has grown substantially. At one point, because of the critiques, the entire University of California system was going to stop using SAT scores as an entrance requirement. Soon after the UC system made its threat, ETS changed the verbal portion of the SAT that was receiving the bulk of the criticism (the analogy section). The UC system subsequently backed down and returned to using the SAT as an entrance requirement.

14. It should be noted that the SAT is consists of 138 test questions in six categories, including 60 math questions and 78 verbal questions.

CHAPTER 3

1. Two things must be noted about the claims to falling educational achievement made in *A Nation At Risk*. First, the report used test scores for the vast majority of indicators of the educational decline of the United States. Second, later research demonstrated that the report's claims to the falling levels of educational achievement of U.S. students were inaccurate (Amrein & Berliner, 2002b; Berliner & Biddle, 1995).

2. It is also worth noting that, during the 1980s, the Reagan administration used this crisis to attack ESEA through funding cuts and structural changes to the program, including an unsuccessful attempt by President Reagan for the complete repeal of the program (Jennings, 2000).

3. Once again, it must be pointed out that these changes had developed, in part, as a continued attack on ESEA and its funding of programs aimed at helping poor children succeed in school—since the tests were now being used to hold schools "accountable" for the federal monies they were receiving (Jennings, 2000).

4. This conversion strategy of the professional and managerial new middle class, however, does not require an active, intentional consciousness as a class. Rather, as Bourdieu (1984) argues, this class fraction only needs to act out of its class *habitus*, that is, it only needs to act out of its cultural and physical embodiment as a class fraction to achieve its upward mobility.

5. I must make it clear, however, that I am *not* implying that our educational system is working as it should. As this book demonstrates, our system of education does have a crisis of race and class inequality, and it is a crisis that in inextricably tied to society. What I am saying here is that the crisis that has been defined in the past—that of a correlation between economic competitiveness and education—is a falsely constructed crisis that merely demonstrates the power that industry and industrial logic wield over public education in the United States today.

6. It is worth noting that the Office of the Inspector General of the U.S. Federal Government released a report regarding the internal operations and granting standards of the Department of Education's (DOE) Reading First initiative. Among others, this report found that the DOE did not screen for conflicts of interest in the constitution of its Reading First panel, did not follow guidance for peer review of their granting process, and awarded monies to states without getting full approvals (Office of the Inspector General, 2006).

7. While teacher resistance to such scripted reading programs does exist, the intent and structure of these policies makes resistance a difficult and increasingly risky process because resistant teachers face the prospects of public scrutiny and potential job loss (see, e.g., Jaeger, 2006).

8. In reality this means that advanced capitalist economies have mainly shipped their factory-like production to impoverished countries around the globe.

9. This process is reminiscent of the various "curriculum accords" (Apple, 1988b, 2000) offered to dispossessed/oppressed groups as state social studies content standards have been developed, and provide an parallel illustration of how hegemony operates in education. In such curriculum accords, states like California and New York ultimately had to include multicultural, counter-hegemonic content in their textbook standards (Cornbleth & Waugh, 1995).

10. However, it remains to be seen just how much influence *Tough Choices* will ultimately have. It may fizzle, and produce no lasting change in public education. It also may spark a national debate, evoke significant shifts in education policy, and truly become this generation's *A Nation At Risk*. As of this writing, it is simply too early to tell. Given the varying and sometimes competing interests of the coalition of Rightist forces that currently maintains hegemonic control of education and politics in this country (Apple, 2006a), we cannot be exactly sure about what direction public education will head in the future, because new proposals for public education such as the *Tough Choices* report have already created some fissures in the rightist alliance. For instance, noted neoconservative Diane Ravitch recently attacked the *Tough Choices* report because, in her opinion, it recommends completely dismantling public education by reducing local control and too relying too much on privatization (Ravitch, 2007).

11. Indeed, this contradiction might be considered to be an expression of the tension which the new middle class and neoliberals (who are more closely aligned with knowledge workers) on one side struggling against the tendencies associated with neoconservatives (who are more closely aligned with the control over knowledge associated with traditional schooling).

CHAPTER 4

1. I concede that the concept of curricular form is somewhat elusive, but basically it refers to how knowledge is organized. When we select content knowledge to communicate to and with students, we also make decisions regarding what form that knowledge takes. This includes specific decisions about whether or not to teach content knowledge in connected, integrated wholes (e.g., theme based curriculum that integrates different subject domains) or in fragmented, isolated pieces (collections of individual facts or operations).

2. It is true that there are several takes on even this definition, including concepts of the "hidden curriculum"(Apple, 1979/2004, 1980–81; Margolis, Soldatenko, Acker, & Gair, 2001) or "intended" vs. "operational" curriculum (Eisner, 1994). Such distinctions are powerful, useful, and fruitful avenues for analyzing the impacts and implications (both explicit and implicit) of the curriculum. However, a thorough about these distinctions is outside of the purview of the present discussion.

3. While it is true that Apple frames his definition of bureaucratic control in terms of "*hierarchical* social relations," but this too is somewhat misleading. Bureaucracy by definition implies institutional structure. While it is true that these institutional relationships have certain correspondences with social relations, it seems more precise to discuss bureaucratic control in terms of the hierarchical *institutional* relations of the workplace to denote the differences of power that exist at different levels of the institutions where bureaucracies exist. Indeed, it is often the hierarchical bureaucracy of an institution that creates the structural levels of power, which in turn allows for those above to exert "simple" control over those below.

4. As NCLB requires that science be tested by 2008, the research suggests that we can expect an increase in the teaching of science in preparation for the high-stakes tests.

5. This finding in some ways contradicts Spillane's (2004) research in Michigan, which essentially posits that state-mandated reforms, due to the various interpretations as different levels of the implementation process, do not necessarily reach the classroom level. It seems likely, however, that since Spillane specifically addresses standards reform and Segall (2006) specifically addresses high-stakes testing, that the differing nature of each study allows for the possibility of contradiction.

6. In one nationwide survey of over 5,000 teachers, 95% of the respondents agreed or strongly agreed with statement that high-stakes testing policies associated with No Child Left Behind are contributing to "teacher burnout" (Teachers Network, 2007).

7. While I am opposed to using the term "minority" to refer to non-White people or people of color, I use it here, in quotes, because that is the term that the researchers use in the two reports referred to in the text.

CHAPTER 5

1. I am taking liberty with one piece of Bernstein's formulation here. He uses the term "social base" where I have used the term "social interactions." Unfortunately, Bernstein is absolutely unclear about what he means by "social base." He offers no definition, and even excludes it elsewhere when he just lists selection, sequencing, pacing, and criteria in reference to "framing." I take Bernstein to mean that, since pedagogic discourse

implies social relations, at least in the classroom (social relations between students and social relations between students and teacher), then framing must also communicate some social norms regarding interactions between people. Thus, I use the term "social interactions" to connote the relationships that are embedded in any pedagogic discourse.

2. In order to avoid confusion, I have to note that in the following discussion both of the terms "discourse" and "Discourse" will be used. "Discourse" (with a big "D") refers back to Chapter 4 and the idea of Discursive control. This is a very specific use of the term, which, as I outlined in that chapter refers to how identities and power are communicated via all manner of markers (dress, culture, mannerisms, language, etc.). Bernstein does not use the concept of "Discourse" at all. Rather, he uses the term "discourse" more generally, particularly within the context of linguistics and the sociology of language. Thus, in Bernstein's use, "discourse" (with a small "d") is the term generally used to refer to language and interactions around that language.

3. I realize that the boundaries of any discourse are problematic, and that the maintenance of any field, such as history, is wrapped up in politics, power, and social relations—just as pedagogic discourse is as well. I also realize that it is possible that a history teacher also may be a historian, as might be the case in the university or possibly in secondary education. However, the discourse of education operates as a separate discourse from history, with its own rules, norms, and politics. Thus, my point, which is really Bernstein's point, still holds that pedagogic discourse operates on a principle of recontextualization of an outside discourse into the classroom.

4. A similar argument could be made regarding the above example of state committees that determine history standards. These committees have state-sanctioned power, and operate at the behest of the state as a political and educational institution. Thus, they are a part of the ORF. However, these committees also are usually made up of state officials, as well as history teachers and experts from the field of history—constituents of the PRF. Thus, in the case of such standards committees, we see a weakening of the autonomy of the PRF in relation to the ORF.

5. The above two points may be Bernstein's version of Marx's (1967) conclusion that capitalism, like the pedagogic device, creates its own grave diggers.

CHAPTER 6

1. Although this finding was challenged on methodological grounds (see, Braun, 2004; Rosenshine, 2003), it was later confirmed to hold up both in Texas and nationally through an analysis of greater detail (Nichols et al., 2006).

BIBLIOGRAPHY

Abrams, L. M., Pedulla, J. J., & Madaus, G. F. (2003). Views from the class-room: teachers' opinions of statewide testing programs. *Theory Into Practice, 42*(1), 18–29.

Agee, J. (2004). Negotiating a teaching identity: An African American teach-er's struggle to teach in test-driven contexts. *Teachers College Record, 106*(4), 747–774.

Allman, P. (1999). *Revolutionary social transformation: Democratic hopes, political possibilities and critical education.* Westport, CT: Bergin & Garvey.

Allman, P., McLaren, P., & Rikowski, G. (2000). After the box people: The labour-capital relation as class constitution — and its consequences for Marxist educational theory and human resistance. Retrieved May 1, 2004, from http://www.ieps.org.uk.cwc.net/afterthebox.pdf

Althusser, L. (1969). *For Marx.* New York: Pantheon Books.

Althusser, L. (1971). *Lenin and philosophy and other essays* (B. Brewster, Trans.). New York: Monthly Review Books.

Altwerger, B. (Ed.). (2005). *Reading for profit: How the bottom line leaves kids behind.* Portsmouth, NH: Heinemann.

Altwerger, B., & Strauss, S. L. (2002). The business behind testing. *Language Arts, 79*(3), 256–263.

Amrein, A. L., & Berliner, D. C. (2002a). *An analysis of some unintended and negative consequences of high-stakes testing.* Tempe: Arizona State University, College of Education, Language Policy Research Unit, Educational Policy Studies Laboratory.

Amrein, A. L., & Berliner, D. C. (2002b). High-stakes testing, uncertainty, and student learning. *Education Policy Analysis Archives, 10*(18). Retrieved September 27, 2005, from http://epaa.asu.edu/epaa/v10n18

Anagnostopolous, D. (2003). Testing and student engagement with literature in urban classrooms: A multi-layered perspective. *Research in the Teaching of English, 38*(2), 177–212.

Anderson, P. (1980). *Arguments within English Marxism.* London: Verso.

Anyon, J. (2005). *Radical possibilities: Public policy, urban education, and a new social movement.* New York: Routledge.

Apple, M. W. (1979/2004). *Ideology and curriculum* (3rd ed.). New York: RoutledgeFalmer.

Apple, M. W. (1980–81). The other side of the hidden curriculum: Correspondence theories and the labor process. *Interchange, 11*(3), 5–22.

Apple, M. W. (1986). *Teachers and texts: A political economy of class and gender relations in education.* New York: Routledge & Kegan Paul.

Apple, M. W. (1988a). Facing the complexity of power: For a parallelist position in critical educational studies. In M. Cole (Ed.), *Bowles and Gintis revisited: Correspondence and contradiction in educational theory* (pp. 112–130). New York: The Falmer Press.

Apple, M. W. (1988b). Social crisis and curriculum accords. *Educational Theory, 38*(2), 191–201.

Apple, M. W. (1992). Education, culture, and class power: Basil Bernstein and the neo-Marxist sociology of education — beyond the automaticity thesis. *Educational Theory, 42*(2), 127–145.

Apple, M. W. (1995). *Education and power* (2nd ed.). New York: Routledge.

Apple, M. W. (2000). *Official knowledge: Democratic education in a conservative age* (2nd ed.). New York: Routledge.

Apple, M. W. (2002). Does education have independent power? Bernstein and the question of relative autonomy. *British Journal of Sociology of Education, 23*(4), 607–616.

Apple, M. W. (2006a). *Educating the "right" way: Markets, standards, god, and inequality* (2nd ed.). New York: Routledge.

Apple, M. W. (2006b). Rhetoric and reality in critical educational studies in the United States. *British Journal of Sociology of Education, 27*(5), 679–687.

Apple, M. W., & Au, W. (in press). Politics, theory and reality in critical pedagogy. In A. Kazamias & R. Cowen (Eds.), *Handbook on comparative education.* Dordrecht, The Netherlands: Springer.

Apple, M. W., & Beane, J. A. (Eds.). (2007). *Democratic schools* (2nd ed.). Portsmouth, NH: Heinemann.

Apple, M. W., & Beyer, L. E. (1988). Social evaluation of curriculum. In L. E. Beyer & M. W. Apple (Eds.), *The curriculum: Problems, politics, and possibilities* (pp. 334–349). Albany: State University of New York Press.

Apple, M. W., & Buras, K. L. (2006a). Introduction. In M. W. Apple & K. L. Buras (Eds.), *The subaltern speak: Curriculum, power, and educational struggles* (pp. 1–39). New York: Routledge.

Apple, M. W., & Buras, K. L. (Eds.). (2006b). *The subaltern speak: Curriculum, power, and educational struggles.* New York: Routledge.

Apple, M. W., & Pedroni, T. C. (2005). Conservative alliance building and African American support of vouchers: the end of *Brown's* promise or a new beginning? *Teachers College Record, 107*(9), 2068–2105.

Arnot, M., David, M., & Weiner, G. (1999). *Closing the gender gap: Postwar education and social change.* Cambridge, UK: Polity Press.

Arnot, M., & Whitty, G. (1982). From reproduction to transformation: Recent radical perspectives on the curriculum from the USA. *British Journal of Sociology of Education, 3*(1), 93–103.

Au, W. (2000). Teaching about the WTO. *Rethinking Schools, 14*(3), 4–5.

Au, W. (2004). The NCLB zone: Where 'highly qualified' can mean low quality teaching. *Rethinking Schools, 19*(1), 11–13.

Au, W. (2005a). Power, identity, and the third rail. In P. C. Miller (Ed.), *Narratives from the classroom: An introduction to teaching* (pp. 65–85). Thousand Oaks, CA: Sage.

Au, W. (2005b). Small is volatile. *Rethinking Schools, 19*(4), 7–8.

Au, W. (2006a). Against economic determinism: Revisiting the roots of neo-Marxism in critical educational theory. *Journal for Critical Education Policy Studies, 4*(2). Retrieved December 12, 2006, from http://www.jceps.com/?pageID=article&articleID=66

Au, W. (2006b, November 29). *Rethinking Schools: Subaltern cosmopolitan multiculturalism in practice.* Paper presented at the Annual meeting of the College University and Faculty Assembly (CUFA) of the National Council of the Social Studies, Washington, DC.

Au, W. (2007a). Epistemology of the oppressed: the dialectics of Paulo Freire's theory of knowledge. *Journal for Critical Education Policy Studies, 5*(2). Retrieved November 2, 2007, from http://www.jceps.com/index.php?pageID=article&articleID=100

Au, W. (2007b). High-stakes testing and curricular control: A qualitative metasynthesis. *Educational Researcher, 36*(5), 258–267.

Au, W. (2007c). Vygotsky and Lenin on learning: The parallel structures of individual and social development. *Science & Society, 71*(3), 273–298.

Au, W. (in press). Social studies, social justice: W(h)ither the social studies in high-stakes testing? *Teacher Education Quarterly.*

Au, W., & Apple, M. W. (2004). Interrupting globalization as an educational practice. *Educational Policy, 18*(5), 784–793.

Au, W., & Apple, M. W. (2007). Freire, critical education, and the environmental crisis. *Educational Policy, 21*(3), 457–470.

Au, W., Bigelow, B., & Karp, S. (Eds.). (2007). *Rethinking our classrooms: Teaching for equity and justice* (2nd ed., Vol. 1). Milwaukee, WI: Rethinking Schools.

Augustine, N. R., Lupberger, E., & Orr III, J. F. (1996). *A common agenda for improving education in America* (Position Statement). Washington, DC: Business Roundtable.

Baker, B. (2002). The hunt for disability: The new eugenics and the normalization of school children. *Teachers College Record, 104,* 663–703.

Baker, K. (2007). Are international tests worth anything? *Phi Delta Kappan, 88*(8), 101–104.

Ball, S. J. (2003a). *Class strategies and the education market: The middle classes and social advantage.* New York: RoutledgeFalmer.

Ball, S. J. (2003b). The teacher's soul and the terrors of performativity. *Journal of Education Policy, 18*(3), 215–228.

Baltodano, M. (2006). The accreditation of schools of education and the appropriation of diversity. *Cultural Studies/Critical Methodologies, 6*(1), 123–142.

Barrow, L., & Rouse, C. E. (2006). The economic value of education by race and ethnicity. *Economic Perspectives, 30*(2), 14–27.

Barton, P. E. (2003). *Parsing the achievement gap: Baselines for tracking progress.* Princeton, NJ: Policy Information Center, Educational Testing Service.

Beatty, A., Neisser, U., Trent, W. T., & Heubert, J. P. (2001). *Understanding dropouts: Statistics, strategies, and high-stakes testing.* Retrieved September 27, 2005, from http://www.nap.edu/catalog/10166.html

Beauchamp, G. A. (1982). Curriculum theory: Meaning, development, and use. *Theory Into Practice, 21*(1), 23–27.

Bebray, E., Parson, G., & Avila, S. (2003). Internal alignment and external pressure. In M. Carnoy, R. Elmore, & L. S. Siskin (Eds.), *The new accountability: High schools and high-stakes testing* (pp. 55–85). New York: RoutledgeFalmer.

Benjamin, S. (2001). Challenging masculinities: disability and achievement in testing times. *Gender and Education, 13*(1), 39–55.

Benton, T., & Craib, I. (2001). *Philosophy of social science: The philosophical foundations of social thought.* New York: Palgrave.

Berlak, H. (2000). Cultural politics, the science of assessment and democratic renewal of public education. In A. Filer (Ed.), *Assessment: Social practice and social product* (pp. 189–207). New York: RoutledgeFalmer.

Berlak, H. (2003). *The 'no child left behind act' and teaching reading.* Tempe: Arizona State University, College of Education, Language Policy Research Unit, Educational Policy Studies Laboratory.

Berliner, D. C., & Biddle, B. J. (1995). *The manufactured crisis: Myths, fraud, and the attack on America's public schools.* Reading, MA: Addison-Wesley.

Bernstein, B. B. (1971). *Class, codes and control.* London: Routledge and Kegan Paul.

Bernstein, B. B. (1975). *Class, codes, and control; theoretical studies towards a sociology of language.* New York: Schocken Books.

Bernstein, B. B. (1977). *Class codes and control volume 3: Towards a theory of educational transmissions* (2nd ed., Vol. 3). London: Routledge and Kegan Paul.

Bernstein, B. B. (1990). *The structuring of pedagogic discourse* (1st ed., Vol. IV). New York: Routledge.

Bernstein, B. B. (1996). *Pedagogy, symbolic control, and identity: Theory, research, critique.* London: Taylor & Francis.

Bernstein, B. B. (1999). Official knowledge and pedagogic identities. In F. Christie (Ed.), *Pedagogy and the shaping of consciousness: Linguistic and social processes* (pp. 246–261). New York: Cassell.

Bernstein, B. B. (2001). Symbolic control: Issues of empirical description of agencies and agents. *The International Journal of Social Research Methodology, 4*(1), 21–33.

Bernstein, B. B., & Solomon, J. (1999). 'Pedagogy, identity, and the construction of a theory of symbolic control': Basil Bernstein questioned by Joseph Solomon. *British Journal of Sociology of Education, 20*(2), 265–279.

Bigelow, B. (1999). Why standardized tests threaten multiculturalism. *Educational Leadership, 56*(7), 37–40.

Bigelow, B. (2001). Standards and multiculturalism. In J. L. Kincheloe & D. Weil (Eds.), *Standards and schooling in the United States: An encyclopedia* (Vol. 2, pp. 695–702). Denver, CO: ABC-CLIO.

Bigelow, B. (2006). *The line between us: Teaching about the border and Mexican immigration.* Milwaukee, WI: Rethinking Schools.

Bigelow, B., & Peterson, B. (Eds.). (2002). *Rethinking globalization: Teaching for justice in an unjust world.* Milwaukee, WI: Rethinking Schools.

Bisseret, N. (1979). *Education, class language and ideology.* Boston: Routledge & Kegan Paul.

Blackmore, J. (2002). Leadership for socially just schooling: More substance and less style in high-risk, low-trust times? *Journal of School Leadership, 12*, 198–222.

Blount, J. M. (1999). Manliness and the gendered construction of school administration in the USA. *International Journal of Leadership in Education, 2*(2), 55–68.

Bobbitt, J. F. (1909). Practical eugenics. *Pedagogical Seminary, 16*, 385–394.

Bobbitt, J. F. (1912). The elimination of waste in education. *The Elementary School Teacher, 12*(6), 259–271.

Bobbitt, J. F. (1913). *The supervision of city schools: The twelfth yearbook of the National Society for the Study of Education.* Bloomington, IL: Public School Pub.

Bobbitt, J. F. (2002). The objectives of secondary education. In J. R. Gress (Ed.), *Curriculum: frameworks, criticism, and theory* (pp. 135–144). Richmond, CA: McCutchan. (Original published 1920)

Bolgatz, J. (2006). Using primary documents with fourth-grade students: Talking about racism while preparing for state-level tests. In S. G. Grant (Ed.), *Measuring history: Cases of state-level testing across the United States* (pp. 133–156). Greenwich, CT: IAP-Information Age.

Booher-Jennings, J. (2005). Below the bubble: "educational triage" and the Texas accountability system. *American Educational Research Journal, 42*(2), 231–268.

Bourdieu, P. (1984). *Distinction: A social critique of the judgment of taste* (R. Nice, Trans.). Cambridge, MA: Routledge & Kegan Paul.

Bourdieu, P., & Passeron, J. (1977). *Reproduction in education, society, and culture.* Beverly Hills, CA: Sage.

Bowles, S., & Gintis, H. (1976). *Schooling in capitalist America: Educational reform and the contradictions of economic life.* New York: Basic Books.

Bowles, S., & Gintis, H. (1988). Schooling in capitalist America: Reply to our critics. In M. Cole (Ed.), *Bowles and Gintis revisted: Correspondence and contradiction in educational theory.* Philadelphia: The Falmer Press.

Boyer, R. O., & Morais, H. M. (1975). *Labor's untold story* (3d ed.). New York: United Electrical, Radio & Machine Workers of America.

Braun, H. (2004). Reconsidering the impact of high-stakes testing. *Education Policy Analysis Archives, 12*(1). Retrieved March 29, 2006, from http://epaa.asu.edu/epaa/v12n1

Braverman, H. (1974). *Labor and monopoly capital: The degradation of work in the twentieth century.* New York: Monthly Review Press.

Brimijoin, K. (2005). Differentiation and high-stakes testing: An oxymoron? *Theory Into Practice, 44*(3), 254–261.

Brosio, R. A. (1994). *A radical democratic critique of capitalist education.* New York: Peter Lang.

Brown, P., & Lauder, H. (2006). Globalisation, knowledge and the myth of the magnet economy. *Globalisation, Societies and Education, 4*(1), 25–27.

Burch, P. E. (2006). The new educational privatization: educational contracting and high stakes accountability. *Teachers College Record, 108*(12), 2582–2610.

Burch, P. E. (2007). Educational policy and practice from the perspective of institutional theory: crafting a wider lens. *Educational Researcher, 36*(2), 84–95.

Bush, G. W. (1999, October 5). The future of educational reform. Retrieved February 11, 2006, from http://www.manhattan-institute.org/html/bush_speech.htm

Callahan, R. E. (1964). *Education and the cult of efficiency: A study of the social forces that have shaped the administration of the public schools* (First Phoenix ed.). Chicago: University of Chicago Press.

Carlson, D. L. (1988a). Beyond the reproductive theory of teaching. In M. Cole (Ed.), *Bowles and Gintis revisited: Correspondence and contradiction in educational theory* (pp. 158–173). New York: The Falmer Press.

Carlson, D. L. (1988b). Curriculum planning and the state: the dynamics of control in education. In L. E. Beyer & M. W. Apple (Eds.), *The curriculum: Problems, politics, and possibilities* (pp. 98–115). Albany: State University of New York Press.

Carnoy, M., Castells, M., Cohen, S. S., & Cardoso, F. H. (1993). Introduction. In M. Carnoy, M. Castells, S. S. Cohen & F. H. Cardoso (Eds.), *The new global economy in the information age: Reflections on our changing world* (pp. 1–13). University Park: The Pennsylvania State University Press.

Carnoy, M., & Levin, H. M. (1985). *Schooling and work in the democratic state.* Stanford, CA: Stanford University Press.

Castells, M. (1993). The informational economy and the new international division of labor. In M. Carnoy, M. Castells, S. S. Cohen & F. H. Cardoso (Eds.), *The new global economy in the information age: Reflections on our changing world* (pp. 15–43). University Park: The Pennsylvania State University Press.

CEP. (2007). *Choices, changes, and challenges: Curriculum and instruction in the NCLB era.* Washington, DC: Center on Education Policy.

Chabran, M. (2003). Listening to talk from and about students on accountability. In M. Carnoy, R. Elmore, & L. S. Siskin (Eds.), *The new accountability: High schools and high-stakes testing* (pp. 129–145). New York: RoutledgeFalmer.

Chapman, P. D. (1988). *Schools as sorters: Lewis M. Terman, applied psychology, and the intelligence testing movement, 1890–1930.* New York: New York University Press.

Chen, E., & Omastu, G. (Eds.). (2006). *Teaching about Asian Pacific Americans.* New York: Rowman & Littlefield.

Chenoweth, K. (2004). 50 years later: Can current education policy finish the work started with *Brown*? *Black issues in higher education, 21*(9), 40–42.

Christensen, L. M. (2000). *Reading, writing, and rising up: Teaching about social justice and the power of the written word.* Milwaukee, WI: Rethinking Schools.

Clarke, M., Madaus, G. F., Horn, C. L., & Ramos, M. A. (2000). Retrospective on educational testing and assessment in the 20th century. *Journal of Curriculum Studies, 32*(2), 159–181.

Clarke, M., Shore, A., Rhoades, K., Abrams, L. M., Miao, J., & Li, J. (2003). *Perceived effects of state-mandated testing programs on teaching and learning: Findings from interviews with educators in low-, medium-, and high-stakes states.* Boston: National Board on Educational Testing and Public Policy, Lynch School of Education, Boston College.

Cole, M. (Ed.). (1988). *Bowles and Gintis revisited: Correspondence and contradiction in educational theory.* Philadelphia: The Falmer Press.

Coleman, J. S., Campbell, E. Q., Hobson, C. J., McPartland, J., Mood, A. M., & Weinfield, F. D. (1966). *Equality of educational opportunity.* Washington, DC: U.S. Government Printing Office.

Coles, G. (2000). *Misreading reading: The bad science that hurts children.* Portsmouth, NH: Heinemann.

Coles, G. (2003). *Reading the naked truth: Literacy, legislation, and lies.* Portsmouth, NH: Heinemann.

Collin, R., & Apple, M. W. (2007). Schooling, literacies, and biopolitics in the global age. *Discourse: Studies in the Cultural Politics of Education, 28*(4), 433–454.

Cornbleth, C., & Waugh, D. (1995). *The great speckled bird*. New York: St. Martin's Press.

Costigan III, A. T. (2002). Teaching the culture of high stakes testing: Listening to new teachers. *Action in Teacher Education, 23*(4), 28–34.

Counts, G. S. (1927/1969). *The social composition of boards of education: A study in the social control of public education*. New York: Arno Press & The New York Times.

Creaven, S. (2000). *Marxism and realism: A materialistic application of realism in the social sciences*. London: Routledge.

Cuban, L. (2004). *The blackboard and the bottom line: Why schools can't be businesses*. Cambridge, MA: Harvard University Press.

Cubberley, E. P. (1916). *Public school administration*. Boston: Houghton Mifflin.

Dance, J. L. (2002). *Tough fronts: the impact of street culture on schooling*. New York: RoutledgeFarmer.

Darder, A., & Torres, R. D. (2004). *After race: Racism after multiculturalism*. New York: New York University Press.

Darling-Hammond, L. (2004). From "separate but equal" to "no child left behind": the collision of new standards and old inequalities. In D. Meier & G. Wood (Eds.), *Many children left behind: How the no child left behind act is damaging our children and our schools* (pp. 3–32). Boston: Beacon Press.

Darling-Hammond, L. (2007). Race, inequality and educational accountability: The irony of 'no child left behind'. *Race, Ethnicity, and Education, 10*(3), 245–260.

Darling-Hammond, L., McClosky, L., & Pecheone, R. (2006). *Analysis and recommendations for alternatives to the Washington Assessment of Student Learning*. Palo Alto, CA: School Redesign Network, Stanford University School of Education.

Davis, J. E. (2006). Research at the margin: mapping masculinity and mobility of African-American high school dropouts. *International Journal of Qualitative Studies in Education, 19*(3), 289–304.

De Lissovoy, N., & McLaren, P. (2003). Educational 'accountability' and the violence of capital: a Marxian reading. *Journal of Educational Policy, 18*(2), 131–143.

Debray, E., Parson, G., & Avila, S. (2003). Internal alignment and external pressure. In M. Carnoy, R. Elmore, & L. S. Siskin (Eds.), *The new accountability: High schools and high-stakes testing* (pp. 55–85). New York: RoutledgeFalmer.

Dewey, J. (1916). *Democracy and education* (Free Press Paperback, 1966 ed.). New York: The Free Press.

Dorn, S. (1998). The political legacy of school accountability systems. *Education Policy Analysis Archives, 6*(1). Retrieved February 10, 2006, from http://epaa.asu.edu/epaa/v6n1/

DuBois, W. E. B. (1903). The talented tenth. In *The Negro problem* (pp. 31–76). New York: James Pott and Company.

Education Not Incarceration. (2006). Homepage. Retrieved March 4, 2006, from http://www.ednotinc.org

Edwards, T. (1980). Schooling for change: Function, correspondence and cause. In L. Barton, R. Meighan, & S. Walker (Eds.), *Schooling, ideology, and the curriculum* (pp. 67–79). Sussex, UK: The Falmer Press.

Eisenhart, M., & Town, L. (2003). Contestation and change in national policy on "scientifically based" education research. *Educational Researcher, 32*(7), 31–38.

Eisner, E. W. (1994). *The educational imagination: on the design and evaluation of school programs* (3rd ed.). New York: Macmillan.

Ellis, M. W. (2008). Leaving no child behind yet allowing none too far ahead: Ensuring (in)equity in mathematics education through the science of measurement and instruction. *Teachers College Record, 110*(4). Retrieved November 19, 2007, from http://www.tcrecord.org/content. asp?contentid=14757c

Emery, K., & Ohanian, S. (2004). *Why is corporate America bashing our public schools?* Portsmouth, NH: Heinemann.

Engels, F. (1940). *Dialectics of nature* (C. Dutt, Trans.). New York: International Publishers.

Engels, F. (1968a). Engels to H. Borgius in Breslau. In *Karl Marx & Frederick Engels: Their selected works* (pp. 704–706). New York: International Publishers.

Engels, F. (1968b). Engels to J. Bloch in Konigsberg. In *Karl Marx & Frederick Engels: Their selected works* (pp. 692–693). New York: International Publishers.

Engels, F. (1968c). Ludwig Feuerbach and the end of classical German philosophy. In I. Publishers (Ed.), *Karl Marx & Frederick Engels selected works* (pp. 596–618). New York: International Publishers.

Erevelles, N. (2005). Understanding curriculum as normalizing text: Disability studies meet curriculum theory. *Journal of Curriculum Studies, 37*(4), 421–439.

Evers, W. M., & Walberg, H. J. (2004). Introduction and overview. In W. M. Evers & H. J. Walberg (Eds.), *Testing student learning, evaluating teaching effectiveness* (pp. vii–xiii). Stanford, CA: Hoover Institution Press.

FairTest. (2005). FairTest Homepage. Retrieved July 11, 2005, from http://www.fairtest.org

Ferguson, K. E. (1984). *The feminist case against bureaucracy.* Philadelphia: Temple University Press.

Fickel, L. H. (2006). Paradox of practice: Expanding and contracting curriculum in a high-stakes climate. In S. G. Grant (Ed.), *Measuring history: Cases of state-level testing across the United States* (pp. 75–103). Greenwich, CT: IAP-Information Age.

Firestone, W. A., Mayrowetz, D., & Fairman, J. (1998). Performance-based assessment and instructional change: The effects of testing in Maine and Maryland. *Educational Evaluation and Policy Analysis, 20*(2), 94–113.

Foucault, M. (1995). *Discipline and punish: The birth of the prison* (A. Sheridan, Trans., 2nd ed.). New York: Vintage Books.

Franzway, S., Court, D., & Connell, R. W. (1989). *Staking a claim: Feminism, bureaucracy and the state.* Cambridge, UK: Polity Press.

Fraser, N. (1995). From redistribution to recognition? dilemmas of justice in a 'post-Socialist' age. *New Left Review, 212*, 68–93.

Fraser, S. (1995). *The bell curve wars race, intelligence, and the future of America.* New York: BasicBooks.

Freeman, E. (2005). No child left behind and the denigration of race. *Equity & Excellence in Education, 38*(3), 190–199.

Freire, P. (1974). *Pedagogy of the oppressed* (M. B. Ramos, Trans.). New York: Seabury Press.

Freire, P. (1982). *Education for critical consciousness.* New York: Continuum.

Fritzell, C. (1987). On the concept of relative autonomy in educational theory. *British Journal of Sociology of Education, 8*(1), 23–35.

Gandin, L. A., & Apple, M. W. (2003). Education the state, democratizing knowledge: the citizen school project in Porto Alegre, Brazil. In M. W. Apple (Ed.), *The state and the politics of knowledge* (pp. 193–220). New York: RoutledgeFalmer.

Garan, E. M. (2005). Scientific flimflam: A who's who of entrepreneurial research. In B. Altwerger (Ed.), *Reading for profit: How the bottom line leaves kids behind* (pp. 21–32). Portsmouth, NH: Heinemann.

Gay, G. (2007). The rhetoric and reality of NCLB. *Race, Ethnicity, and Education, 10*(3), 279–293.

Gayler, K. (2005). *How have exit exams changed our schools? Some perspectives from Virginia and Maryland.* Washington, DC: Center on Education Policy.

Gee, J. P. (1996). *Social linguistics and literacies: Ideology in discourses* (2nd ed.). New York: RoutledgeFalmer.

Gee, J. P. (2000). New people in new worlds: networks, the new capitalism and schools. In B. Cope & M. Kalantzis (Eds.), *Multiliteracies: Literacy learning and the design of social futures* (pp. 43–68). New York: Routledge.

Gerstl-Pepin, C. I., & Woodside-Jiron, H. (2005). Tensions between the "science" of reading and a "love of learning": One high-poverty school's struggle with NCLB. *Equity & Excellence in Education, 38*(3), 232–241.

Gerwin, D. (2004). Preservice teachers report the impact of high-stakes testing. *The Social Studies, 95*(2), 71–74.

Gerwin, D., & Visone, F. (2006). The freedom to teach: Contrasting history teaching in elective and state-tested course. *Social Education, 34*(2), 259–282.

Gibson, R. (2001). Outfoxing the destruction of wisdom. *Theory and Research in Social Education, 29*(2), 308–329.

Gibson, R., Queen, G., Ross, E. W., & Vinson, K. D. (2007). "I participate, you participate, we participate...they profit," notes on revolutionary educational activism to transcend capital: the Rouge Forum. *Journal for Critical Education Policy Studies, 5*(2). Retrieved November 2, 2007, from http://www.jceps.com/index.php?pageID=article&articleID=97

Giordano, G. (2005). *How testing came to dominate American schools: The history of educational assessment.* New York: Peter Lang.

Giroux, H. A. (1980). Beyond the correspondence theory: Notes on the dynamics of educational reproduction and transformation. *Curriculum Inquiry, 10*(3), 225–247.

Giroux, H. A. (1983a). Ideology and agency in the process of schooling. *Journal of Education, 165*(1), 12–34.

Giroux, H. A. (1983b). Theories of reproduction and resistance in the new sociology of education: A critical analysis. *Harvard Educational Review, 53*(3), 257–293.

Goodson, I., CARE, & Foote, M. (2001). Testing times: a school case study. *Education Policy Analysis Archives, 9*(2). Retrieved February 8, 2006, from http://epaa.asu.edu/epaa/v9n2/

Goodson, I., & Foote, M. (2001). A sword over their heads: the standards movement as a disciplinary device. In J. L. Kincheloe & D. Weil (Eds.), *Standards and schooling in the United States: an encyclopedia* (Vol. 2, pp. 703–709). Denver, CO: ABC-CLIO.

Gould, S. J. (1996). *The mismeasure of man* (Rev. ed.). New York: Norton.

Gradwell, J. M. (2006). Teaching in spite of, rather than because of, the test: A case of ambitious history teaching in New York State. In S. G. Grant (Ed.), *Measuring history: Cases of state-level testing across the United States* (pp. 157–176). Greenwich, CT: IAP-Information Age.

Gramsci, A. (1971). *Selections from the prison notebooks* (Q. Hoare & G. N. Smith, Trans.). New York: International Publishers.

Grant, S. G. (2001). When an 'A' is not enough: Analyzing the New York State global history and geography exam. *Education Policy Analysis Archives, 9*(39). Retrieved February 8, 2006, from http://epaa.asu.edu/epaa/v9n39/

Grant, S. G. (2003). *History lessons: teaching, learning, and testing in U.S. high school classrooms.* Mahwah, NJ: Erlbaum.

Grant, S. G. (Ed.). (2006). *Measuring history: Cases of state-level testing across the United States.* Greenwich, CT: IAP-Information Age.

Grant, S. G., Gradwell, J. M., Lauricella, A. M., Derme-Insinna, A., Pullano, L., & Tzetzo, K. (2002). When increasing stakes need not mean increasing standards: The case of the New York state global history and geography exam. *Theory and Research in Social Education, 30*(4), 488–515.

Greider, W. (1997). *One world, ready or not: The manic logic of global capitalism.* New York: Simon & Schuster.

Groves, P. (2002). 'Doesn't it feel morbid here?': High-stakes testing and the widening of the equity gap. *Educational Foundations, 16*(2), 15–31.

Grubb, N. W., & Oakes, J. (2007). *'Restoring value' to the high school diploma: The rhetoric and practice of higher standards.* East Lansing, MI: The Great Lakes Center for Education Research and Practice.

Grundy, S. (1987). *Curriculum: Product or praxis?* New York: The Falmer Press.

Guthrie, R. V. (1998). *Even the rat was white: A historical view of psychology* (2nd ed.). Boston: Allyn and Bacon.

Haas, E., Wilson, G., Cobb, C., & Rallis, S. (2005). One hundred percent proficiency: A mission impossible. *Equity & Excellence in Education, 38*(3), 180–189.

Hampton, E. (2005). Standardized or sterilized? Differing perspectives on the effects of high-stakes testing in West Texas. In A. Valenzuela (Ed.), *Leaving children behind: How 'Texas-style' accountability fails Latino youth* (pp. 179–199). Albany: State University of New York.

Haney, W. (1984). Testing reasoning and reasoning about testing. *Review of Educational Research, 54*(4), 597–654.

Haney, W. (2000). The myth of the Texas miracle in education. *Education Policy Analysis Archives, 8*(41). Retrieved October 8, 2005, from http://epaa. asu.edu/epaa/v8n41

Haney, W., Madaus, G. F., & Lyons, R. (1993). *The fractured marketplace for standardized testing.* Boston: Kluwer.

Hanson, A. F. (2000). How tests create what they are intended to measure. In A. Filer (Ed.), *Assessment: Social practice and social product* (pp. 67–81). New York: RoutledgeFalmer.

Harden, R. M. (2001). The learning environment and the curriculum. *Medical Teacher, 23*(4), 335–336.

Hardt, M., & Negri, A. (2000). *Empire.* Cambridge, MA: Harvard University Press.

Harris, D., & Herrington, C. (2004, March). *Accountability, standards, and the growing achievement gap: lessons from the past half-century.* Paper presented at the American Education Finance Association Meeting, Salt Lake City, Utah.

Herrnstein, R. J., & Murray, C. A. (1996). *The bell curve: Intelligence and class structure in American life.* New York: Simon & Schuster.

Hill, P. T., & Lake, R. J. (2002). Standards and accountability in Washington state. In D. Ravitch (Ed.), *Brookings papers on educational policy: 2002* (pp. 199–234). Washington, DC: Brookings Institution Press.

Hillocks Jr., G. (2002). *The testing trap: How state writing assessments control learning*. New York: Teachers College Press.

Hinchey, P. H., & Cadiero-Kaplan, K. (2005). The future of teacher education and teaching: Another piece of the privatization puzzle. *Journal for Critical Education Policy Studies*, 3(2). Retrieved October 25, 2005, from http://www.jceps.com/?pageID=aricle&articleID=48

Hoffman, B. (1962). *The tyranny of testing*. New York: The Crowell-Collier Press.

Horn, C. L. (2006). The technical realities of measuring history. In S. G. Grant (Ed.), *Measuring history: Cases of state-level testing across the United States* (pp. 57–74). Greenwich, CT: IAP-Information Age.

Howell, W. G. (2005). Introduction. In W. G. Howell (Ed.), *Besieged: School boards and the future of education politics* (pp. 1–23). Washington, DC: Brookings Institutions Press.

Hunter, R. C., & Bartee, R. (2003). The achievement gap: Issues of competition, class, and race. *Education and Urban Society*, 35(2), 151–160.

Hursh, D. W. (2005). The growth of high-stakes testing in the USA: Accountability, markets and the decline in educational quality. *British Educational Research Journal*, 31(5), 605–622.

Hursh, D. W. (2007). Exacerbating inequality: The failed promise of the no child left behind act. *Race, Ethnicity, and Education*, 10(3), 295–308.

Hursh, D. W., & Ross, E. W. (2000). Democratic social education: social studies for social change. In D. W. Hursh & E. W. Ross (Eds.), *Democratic social education: Social studies for social change* (pp. 1–22). New York: Falmer Press.

Jackson, J. M., & Bassett, E. (2005). *The state of the K-12 state assessment market*. Boston: Eduventures.

Jackson, P. W. (1996). Conceptions of curriculum and curriculum specialists. In P. W. Jackson (Ed.), *Handbook of research on curriculum: A project of the American Educational Research Association* (pp. 3–40). New York: Simon & Schuster.

Jaeger, E. (2006). Silencing teachers in an era of scripted reading. *Rethinking Schools*, 20(3), 39–41.

Jennings, J. F. (2000). Title I: its legislative history and its promise. *Phi Delta Kappan*, 81(7), 516–522.

Johnson, D. D., & Johnson, B. (2006). *High stakes: Children, testing, and failure in American schools* (2nd ed.). New York: Rowman & Littlefield.

Jones, B. D. (2007). The unintended outcomes of high-stakes testing. *Journal of Applied School Psychology*, 23(2), 65–86.

Jones, B. D., & Egley, R. J. (2004). Voices from the frontlines: teachers' perceptions of high-stakes testing. *Education Policy Analysis Archives, 12*(39).
Retrieved February 8, 2005, from http://epaa.asu.edu/epaa/v12n39/

Jones, G. M., Jones, B. D., & Hargrove, T. Y. (2003). *The unintended consequences of high-stakes testing.* New York: Rowman & Littlefield.

Kalantzis, M., & Cope, B. (2000). Changing the role of schools. In B. Cope &
M. Kalantzis (Eds.), *Multiliteracies: Literacy learning and the design of
social futures* (pp. 121–148). New York: Routledge.

Kane, T. J., & Staiger, D. O. (2002). Volatility in school test scores: Implications for test-based accountability systems. In D. Ravitch (Ed.), *Brookings papers on education policy 2002* (pp. 235–284). Washington, DC:
Brookings Institution Press.

Karier, C. J. (1967). *Man, society, and education: A history of American educational ideas.* Glenview, IL: Scott, Foresman.

Karp, S. (2003). Let them eat tests: NCLB and federal education policy. In L.
Christensen & S. Karp (Eds.), *Rethinking school reform* (pp. 199–213).
Milwaukee, WI: Rethinking Schools.

Karp, S. (2006a). Bandaids or bulldozers?: What's next for NCLB. *Rethinking
Schools, 20*(3), 10–13.

Karp, S. (2006b). Leaving public education behind: The Bush agenda in American education. *Our Schools/Our Selves, 15*(3), 181–196.

Kelsh, D., & Hill, D. (2006). The culturalization of class and the occluding of
class consciousness: The knowledge industry in/of education. *Journal for
Critical Education Policy Studies, 4*(1). Retrieved August 8, 2006, from
http://www.jceps.com/?pageID=article&articleID=59

Kidder, W. C., & Rosner, J. (2002–2003). How the SAT creates "built-in head-
winds": An educational and legal analysis of disparate impact. *Santa
Clara Law Review, 43*, 131–212.

Kim, J. S., & Sunderman, G. L. (2005). Measuring academic proficiency under
the no child left behind act: Implications for educational equity. *Educational Researcher, 34*(8), 3–13.

Kincheloe, J. L. (2001). From positivism to an epistemology of complexity:
Grounding rigorous teaching. In J. L. Kincheloe & D. Weil (Eds.), *Standards and schooling in the United States: An encyclopedia* (Vol. 2, pp.
325–396). Denver, CO: ABC-CLIO.

King, J. (2006). *Gender equity in higher education: 2006.* Washington, DC:
American Council on Education.

Kliebard, H. M. (1975). Bureaucracy and curriculum theory. In W. F. Pinar
(Ed.), *Curriculum theorizing: The reconceptualists* (pp. 51–69). Berkeley,
CA: McCutchan.

Kliebard, H. M. (2002). The drive for curriculum change in the United States,
1890–1920. Part I - the ideological roots of curriculum as a field of specialization. In J. R. Gress (Ed.), *Curriculum: Framework, criticism, and
theory* (pp. 67–81). Richmond, CA: McCutchan. (Original published
1979)

Kliebard, H. M. (1988). The effort to reconstruct the modern American curriculum. In L. E. Beyer & M. W. Apple (Eds.), *The curriculum: problems, politics, and possibilities* (pp. 19–31). Albany: State University of New York.

Kliebard, H. M. (1989). Problems of definition in curriculum. *Journal of Curriculum and Supervision, 5*(1), 1–5.

Kliebard, H. M. (2004). *The struggle for the American curriculum, 1893–1958* (3rd ed.). New York: RoutledgeFalmer.

Kohn, A. (2004). NCLB and the effort to privatize public education. In D. Meier & G. Wood (Eds.), *Many children left behind: How the no child left behind act is damaging our children and our schools* (pp. 79–100). Boston: Beacon Press.

Kornhaber, M. L., & Orfield, G. (2001). High-stakes testing policies: examining their assumptions and consequences. In G. Orfield & M. L. Kornhaber (Eds.), *Raising standards or raising barriers?: Inequality and high-stakes testing in public education* (pp. 1–18). New York: Century Foundation Press.

Krueger, A. B. (1998). Reassessing the view that American schools are broken. *Federal Reserve Board of New York Economic Policy Review,* 29–43.

Ladson-Billings, G. (1994). *The dreamkeepers: successful teachers of African American children.* San Francisco: Jossey-Bass.

Ladson-Billings, G. (1995). Toward a theory of culturally relevant pedagogy. *American Educational Research Journal, 32*(3), 465–491.

Ladson-Billings, G. (2006). From the achievement gap to the education debt: Understanding achievement in U.S. schools. *Educational Researcher, 35*(7), 3–12.

Laird, J., Lew, S., DeBell, M., & Chapman, C. (2006). *Dropout rates in the United States: 2002 and 2003* (No. NCES 2006-062). Washington, DC: U.S. Department of Education: National Center for Education Statistics.

Land, R., & Moustafa, M. (2005). Scripted reading instruction: help or hindrance? In B. Altwerger (Ed.), *Reading for profit: How the bottom line leaves kids behind* (pp. 63–77). Portsmouth, NH: Heinemann.

Landman, J. (2000). *A state-mandated curriculum, a high-stakes test: One Massachusetts high school history department's response to a very new policy context* (No. ED 440 915). Cambridge, MA: Harvard Graduate School of Education.

Lankshear, C. (1997). Language and the new capitalism. *The International Journal of Inclusive Education, 1*(4), 309–321.

Lapayese, Y. V. (2007). Understanding and undermining the racio-economic agenda of no child left behind: Using critical race methodology to investigate the labor of bilingual children. *Race, Ethnicity, and Education, 10*(3), 309–321.

Lauder, H., Hughes, D., Watson, S., Waslander, S., Thrupp, M., Strathdee, R., et al. (1999). *Trading in futures: Why markets don't work for education.* Philadelphia: Open University Press.

Lee, E., Menkhart, D., & Okazawa-Rey, M. (Eds.). (1998). *Beyond heroes and holidays*. Washington, DC: Network of Educators on the Americas.

Lee, J. (2006). *Tracking achievement gaps and assessing the impact of NCLB on the gaps: An in-depth look into national and state reading and math outcome trends*. Cambridge, MA: Harvard Civil Rights Project.

Lemann, N. (1999). *The big test: The secret history of the American meritocracy*. New York: Farrar, Straus, and Giroux.

Lenin, V. I. (1975). *What is to be done?: Burning questions of our movement*. Peking: Foreign Language Press.

Libresco, A. S. (2005). How she stopped worrying and learned to love the test... sort of. In E. A. Yeager & J. Davis, O. L. (Eds.), *Wise social studies teaching in an age of high-stakes testing* (pp. 33–49). Greenwich, CT: Information Age.

Linn, R. L. (2003). *Accountability, responsibility and reasonable expectations* (No. 601). Los Angeles: Center for the Study of Evaluation, National Center for Research on Evaluation, Standards, and Student Testing, Graduate School of Education & Information Studies, University of California, Los Angeles.

Lipman, P. (2000). Bush's education plan, globalization, and the politics of race. *Cultural Logic*, 4(1). Retrieved March 28, 2006, from http://www.eserver.org/clogic/4-1/lipman.html

Lipman, P. (2004). *High stakes education: Inequality, globalization, and urban school reform*. New York: RoutledgeFalmer.

Lomax, R. G., West, M. M., Harmon, M. C., Viator, K. A., & Madaus, G. F. (1995). The impact of mandated standardized testing on minority students. *Journal of Negro Education, 64*(2), 171–185.

Luna, C., & Turner, C. L. (2001). The impact of the MCAS: Teachers talk about high-stakes testing. *English Journal, 91*(1), 79–87.

Madaus, G. F. (1988). The influence of testing on the curriculum. In L. N. Tanner (Ed.), *Critical issues in curriculum: Eighty-seventh yearbook of the national society for the study of education* (pp. 83–121). Chicago: University of Chicago Press.

Madaus, G. F. (1994). A technological and historical consideration of equity issues associated with proposals to change the nation's testing policy. *Harvard Educational Review, 64*(1), 76–95.

Madaus, G. F., & Clarke, M. (2001). The adverse impact of high-stakes testing on minority students: evidence from one hundred years of test data. In G. Orfield & M. L. Kornhaber (Eds.), *Raising standards or raising barriers?: Inequality and high-stakes testing in public education* (pp. 85–106). New York: Century Foundation Press.

Madaus, G. F., & Horn, C. (2000). Testing technology: The need for oversight. In A. Filer (Ed.), *Assessment: Social practice and social product* (pp. 47–66). New York: RoutledgeFalmer.

Madaus, G. F., & Kelleghan, T. (1993). Testing as a mechanism of public policy: A brief history and description. *Measurement & Evaluation in Counseling & Development, 26*(1), 6–11.

Maher, F. (2002). The attack on teacher education and teachers. *Radical Teacher, 64*(2–4), 5–8.

Maran, M. (2000). *Class dismissed: A year in the life of an American high school, a glimpse into the heart of a nation.* New York: St. Martin's Griffin.

Marchant, G. J., & Paulson, S. E. (2005). The relationship of high school graduation exams to graduation rates and SAT scores. *Education Policy Analysis Archives, 13*(6). Retrieved February 8, 2006, from http://epaa.asu.edu/epaa/v13n6/

Margolis, E., Soldatenko, M., Acker, S., & Gair, M. (2001). Peekaboo: Hiding and outing the curriculum. In E. Margolis (Ed.), *The hidden curriculum in higher education* (pp. 1–22). New York: Routledge.

Marx, K. (1967). *Capital: A critique of political economy* (S. Moore & E. Aveling, Trans. & Eds. Vol. 1). New York: International Publishers.

Marx, K. (1968a). Preface to a contribution to the critique of political economy. In *Karl Marx & Frederick Engels: Their selected works* (pp. 181–185). New York: International Publishers.

Marx, K. (1968b). The eighteenth brumaire of Louis Bonaparte. In *Karl Marx & Frederick Engels: Their selected works* (pp. 95–180). New York: International Publishers.

Marx, K., & Engels, F. (1848/1977). *Manifesto of the communist party.* Peking: Foreign Language Press.

Mathis, W. J. (2006). *The accuracy and effectiveness of adequate yearly progress, NCLB's school evaluation system.* East Lansing, MI: The Great Lakes Center for Education Research & Practice.

McEwan, H., & Bull, B. (1991). The pedagogic nature of subject matter knowledge. *American Educational Research Journal, 28*(2), 316–334.

McGuire, M. E. (2007). What Happened to Social Studies? *Phi Delta Kappan, 88*(8), 620–624.

McLaren, P., & Farahmandpur, R. (2005). *Teaching against global capitalism and the new imperialism: A critical pedagogy.* New York: Rowman and Littlefield.

McNeil, L. M. (1986). *Contradictions of control: School structure and school knowledge.* New York: Routledge & Kegan Paul.

McNeil, L. M. (2000). *Contradictions of school reform: Educational costs of standardized testing.* New York: Routledge.

McNeil, L. M. (2005). Faking equity: High-stakes testing and the education of Latino youth. In A. Valenzuela (Ed.), *Leaving children behind: How 'Texas-style' accountability fails Latino youth* (pp. 57–112). Albany: State University of New York.

McNeil, L. M., & Valenzuela, A. (2001). The harmful impact of the TAAS system of testing in Texas: Beneath the accountability rhetoric. In G. Orfield & M. L. Kornhaber (Eds.), *Raising standards or raising barriers?: Inequality and high-stakes testing in public education* (pp. 127–150). New York: The Century Foundation Press.

McWhorter, J. (2005). *Winning the race: Beyond the crisis in Black America.* New York: Gotham Books.

Meier, D., Cohen, J., & Rogers, J. (2000). *Will standards save public education?* Boston: Beacon Press.

Meier, D., & Wood, G. (Eds.). (2004). *Many children left behind: How the no child left behind act is damaging our children and our schools.* Boston: Beacon Press.

Meiksins, P. F. (1984). Scientific management and class relations: A dissenting view. *Theory and Society, 13*(2), 177–209.

Menkhart, D., Murray, A. D., & View, J. L. (Eds.). (2004). *Putting the movement back into civil rights teaching.* Washington, DC: Teaching for Change.

Menter, I., Muschamp, Y., Nicholl, P., Ozga, J., & Pollard, A. (1997). *Work and identity in the primary school.* Philadelphia: Open University Press.

Metcalf, S. (2002, January 28). Reading between the lines. *The Nation,* 18–22.

Miner, B. (2003). For-profits target education. In L. Christensen & S. Karp (Eds.), *Rethinking school reform: Views from the classroom* (pp. 176–183). Milwaukee, WI: Rethinking Schools.

Miner, B. (2006). Exploding the privatization myth: Charter and private schools are no better than public schools and sometimes worse. *Rethinking Schools, 21*(1), 28–29.

Moe, T. M. (2003). Politics, control, and the future of school accountability. In P. E. Peterson & M. R. West (Eds.), *No child left behind?: The politics and practice of school accountability* (pp. 80–106). Washington, DC: Brookings Institution Press.

Moore, R. (1988). The correspondence principle and the Marxist sociology of education. In M. Cole (Ed.), *Bowles and Gintis revisited: Correspondence and contradiction in educational theory* (pp. 51–85). New York: The Falmer Press.

Morais, A. M. (2002). Bernstein at the micro level of the classroom. *British Journal of Sociology of Education, 23*(4), 559–569.

Murillo Jr., E. G., & Flores, S. Y. (2002). Reform by shame: Managing the stigma of labels in high-stakes testing. *Educational Foundations, 16*(2), 93–108.

National Center for Education Statistics. (2004). Digest of education statistics, 2004: Chapter 2. elementary and secondary education. Retrieved February 24, 2006, from http://nces.ed.gov/programs/digest/d04/ch_2.asp#2

National Center on Education and the Economy. (2006). Tough choices or tough times: The report of the *New* Commission on the Skills of the American Workforce — executive summary. Retrieved December 15, 2006, from http://www.skillscommission.org/pdf/exec_sum/Tough-Choice_EXECSUM.pdf

National Commission on Excellence in Education. (1983). *A nation at risk: The imperative for educational reform.* Washington DC: United States Department of Education.

Natriello, G., & Pallas, A. M. (2001). The development and impact of high-stakes testing. In G. Orfield & M. L. Kornhaber (Eds.), *Raising standards or raising barriers?: Inequality and high-stakes testing in public education* (pp. 19–38). New York: Century Foundation Press.

Nearing, S. (1917). Who's who on our boards of education. *School and Society, V.*

New York Collective of Radical Educators. (2006). Homepage. Retrieved March 4, 2006, from http://www.nycore.org/

Nichols, S. L., & Berliner, D. C. (2005). *The inevitable corruption of indicators and educators through high-stakes testing* (No. EPSL-0503-101-EPRU). Tempe: Education Policy Research Unit, Education Policy Studies Laboratory, College of Education, Division of Educational Leadership and Policy Studies, Arizona State University.

Nichols, S. L., & Berliner, D. C. (2007). *Collateral damage: How high-stakes testing corrupts America's schools.* Cambridge, MA: Harvard Education Press.

Nichols, S. L., Glass, G. V., & Berliner, D. C. (2005). *High-stakes testing and student achievement: Problems for the no child left behind act* (No. EPSL-0509-105-EPRU). Tempe: Education Policy Research Unit, Education Policy Studies Laboratory, College of Education, Division of Educational Leadership and Policy Studies, Arizona State University.

Nichols, S. L., Glass, G. V., & Berliner, D. C. (2006). High-stakes testing and student achievement: Does accountability pressure increase student learning? *Education Policy Analysis Archives, 14*(1). Retrieved February 8, 2006, from http://epaa.asu.edu/epaa/v14n1/

Noble, D. F. (1977). *America by design: Science, technology, and the rise of corporate capitalism.* New York: Knopf.

Noguera, P. (2001). Racial politics and the elusive quest for excellence and equity in education. *Education and Urban Society, 34*(1), 18–41.

Noguera, P. (2003a). *City schools and the American dream: Reclaiming the promise of public education.* New York: Teachers College Press.

Noguera, P. (2003b). The trouble with Black boys: The role and influence of environment and cultural status on the academic performance of African-American males. *Urban Education, 38*, 431–459.

Nordgren, R. D. (2002). Globalization and education: What students will need to know and be able to do in the global village. *Phi Delta Kappan, 84*(4), 318–321.

Oakes, J., Welner, K., Yonezawa, S., & Allen, R. L. (1998). Norms and politics of equity-minded change: researching the "zone of mediation". In M. Fullan (Ed.), *International handbook of educational change* (pp. 953–975). Norwell, MA: Kluwer.

Office of the Inspector General. (2006). *The reading first program's grant application process: Final inspection report* (No. ED-OIG/I13-F0017). Washington, DC: U.S. Department of Education.

Ohmann, R. M. (1976). *English in America: A radical view of the profession*. New York: Oxford University Press.

Ollman, B. (2003). *Dance of the dialectic: Steps in Marx's method*. Chicago: University of Illinois Press.

Omi, M., & Winant, H. (1994). *Racial formation in the United States: From 1960's to 1990's*. New York: Routledge.

Orfield, G., & Wald, J. (2000). Testing, testing: The high-stakes testing mania hurts poor and minority students the most. *The Nation, 270*(22), 38–40.

Orlich, D. C. (2004). No child left behind: An illogical accountability model. *Clearing House, 78*(1), 6–11.

Owens, M. (2006, February 6). Education mobilization. *The Nation, 282*, 24.

Pahl, R. H. (2003). Assessment traps in K-12 social studies. *The Social Studies, 94*(5), 212–215.

Paige, R. (2003, October 6). Letter to the editor. *New Yorker, 79*, 12.

Paris, S. G., & Urdan, T. (2000). Policies and practices of high-stakes testing that influence teachers and schools. *Issues in Education, 6*(1/2), 83–108.

Passman, R. (2001). Experiences with student-centered teaching and learning in high-stakes assessment environments. *Education, 122*(1), 189–199.

Pedroni, T. C. (2007). *Market movements: African American involvement in school voucher reform*. New York: Routledge.

Pedulla, J. J., Abrams, L. M., Madaus, G. F., Russell, M. K., Ramos, M. A., & Miao, J. (2003). *Perceived effects of state-mandated testing programs on teaching and learning: Findings from a national survey of teachers*. Boston: National Board on Educational Testing and Public Policy, Lynch School of Education, Boston College.

Perreault, G. (2000). The classroom impact of high-stress testing. *Education, 120*(4), 705–710.

Peterson, B., & Gutstein, E. (Eds.). (2005). *Rethinking mathematics: Teaching social justice by the numbers*. Milwaukee, WI: Rethinking Schools.

Popham, W. J. (2001). *The truth about testing: an educator's call to action*. Alexandria, VA: Association for Supervision and Curriculum Development (ASCD).

Portland Area Rethinking Schools. (2006). Homepage. Retrieved March 4, 2006, from http://web.pdx.edu/~bgds/PARS/

Posner, G. J. (1988). Models of curriculum planning. In L. E. Beyer & M. W. Apple (Eds.), *The curriculum: Problems, politics, and possibilities* (pp. 77–97). Albany: State University of New York Press.

Power, S., & Whitty, G. (2002). Bernstein and the middle class. *British Journal of Sociology of Education, 23*(4), 595–606.

Provasnik, S., & Dorfman, S. (2005). *Mobility in the teacher workforce: Findings from the conditions of education 2005.* Washington, DC: National Center for Education Statistics, Institute of Educational Sciences, U.S. Department of Education.

Ravitch, D. (2002a). Introduction. In D. Ravitch (Ed.), *Brookings papers on education policy 2002* (pp. 1–11). Washington, DC: Brookings Institution Press.

Ravitch, D. (Ed.). (2002b). *Brookings papers on education policy 2002.* Washington, DC: Brookings Institution Press.

Ravitch, D. (2007). "Tough choices": radical ideas, misguided assumptions. *Education Week, 26*(19), 32–33, 44.

Reese, W. J. (1998). American high school political economy in the nineteenth century. *History of Education, 27*(3), 255–265.

Reich, R. B. (2001). Standards for what? *Education Week, 20*(41), 64–65.

Reich, R. B. (2007). *Supercapitalism: The transformation of business, democracy, and everyday life.* New York: Knopf.

Renter, D. S., Scott, C., Kober, N., Chudowsky, N., Joftus, S., & Zabala, D. (2006). *From the capital to the classroom: Year 4 of the no child left behind act.* Washington, DC: Center on Education Policy.

Rethinking Schools. (2008). Homepage. Retrieved January 1, 2008, from http://www.rethinkingschools.org

Rex, L. A. (2003). Loss of the creature: The obscuring of inclusivity in classroom discourse. *Communication Education, 52*(1), 30–46.

Rex, L. A., & Nelson, M. C. (2004). How teachers' professional identities position high-stakes preparation in their classrooms. *Teachers College Record, 106*(6), 1288–1331.

Roderick, M., & Nagaoka, J. (2005). Retention under Chicago's high-stakes testing program: helpful, harmful, or harmless? *Educational Evaluation and Policy Analysis, 27*(4), 309–340.

Rosenbusch, M. H. (2005). The no child left behind act and teaching and learning languages in U.S. schools. *The Modern Language Journal, 89*(2), 250–261.

Rosenshine, B. (2003). High-stakes testing: Another analysis. *Education Policy Analysis Archives, 11*(24). Retrieved March 29, 2006, from http://epaa.asu.edu/epaa/v11n24

Rosner, J. (2003). On white preferences. *The Nation, 276*(14), 24.

Rushton, P. J., & Jensen, A. R. (2005). Thirty years of research on race differences in cognitive ability. *Psychology, Public Policy, and Law, 11*(2), 234–294.

Sacks, P. (1999). *Standardized minds: The high price of America's testing culture and what we can do to change it.* Cambridge, MA: Perseus Books.

Salinas, C. (2006). Teaching in a high-stakes testing setting: What becomes of teacher knowledge. In S. G. Grant (Ed.), *Measuring history: Cases of state-level testing across the United States* (pp. 177–193). Greenwich, CT: IAP-Information Age.

Sayers, S. (1990). Marxism and the dialectical method: A critique of G.A. Cohen. In S. Sayers & P. Osborne (Eds.), *Socialism, feminism, and philosophy: A radical philosophy reader* (pp. 140–168). New York: Routledge.

Schneider, A. L., & Ingram, H. (1997). *Policy design for democracy.* Lawrence: University of Kansas.

Segall, A. (2003). Teachers' perceptions of the impact of state-mandated standardized testing: The Michigan Educational Assessment Program (MEAP) as a case study of consequences. *Theory and Research in Social Education, 31*(3), 287–325.

Segall, A. (2004a). Blurring the lines between content and pedagogy. *Social Education, 68*(7), 479–482.

Segall, A. (2004b). Revisiting pedagogical content knowledge: The pedagogy of content/the content of pedagogy. *Teaching and Teacher Education, 20,* 489–504.

Segall, A. (2006). Teaching in the age of accountability: Measuring history or measuring up to it? In S. G. Grant (Ed.), *Measuring history: Cases of state-level testing across the United States* (pp. 105–132). Greenwich, CT: IAP-Information Age.

Selden, S. (1983). Biological determinism and the ideological roots of student classification. *Journal of Education, 165,* 175–191.

Selden, S. (1999). *Inheriting shame: The story of eugenics and racism in America.* New York: Teachers College Press.

Sharp, R., & Green, A. (1975). *Education and social control: A study in progressive primary education.* London: Routledge & Kegan Paul.

Shor, I. (1986). *Culture wars: School and society in the conservative restoration 1969–1984.* Boston: Routledge & Kegan Paul.

Shor, I. (1987). *Critical teaching & everyday life.* Chicago: The University of Chicago Press.

Shor, I. (1992). *Empowering education: Critical teaching for social change.* Chicago: The University of Chicago Press.

Shor, I., & Freire, P. (1987). *A pedagogy for liberation: Dialogues on transforming education.* South Hadley, MA: Bergin & Garvey.

Singh, P. (2002). Pedagogising knowledge: Bernstein's theory of the pedagogic device. *British Journal of Sociology of Education, 23*(4), 571–582.

Sirin, S. R. (2005). Socioeconomic status and student achievement: A meta-analytic review of research. *Review of Educational Research, 75*(3), 417–453.

Siskin, L. S. (2003). Outside the core: Accountability in tested and untested subjects. In M. Carnoy, R. Elmore, & L. S. Siskin (Eds.), *The new accountability: High schools and high-stakes testing* (pp. 87–98). New York: RoutledgeFalmer.

Sklair, L. (2002). Democracy and the transnational capitalist class. *Annals of the American Academy of Political and Social Science, 581*, 144–157.

Sleeter, C. E. (2005). *Un-standardizing curriculum: Multicultural teaching in the standards-based classroom.* New York: Teachers College Press.

Sloan, K. (2005). Playing to the logic of the Texas accountability system: How focusing on 'ratings' - not children - undermines quality and equity. In A. Valenzuela (Ed.), *Leaving children behind: How 'Texas-style' accountability fails Latino youth* (pp. 153–178). Albany: State University of New York.

Smith, A. M. (2006). Negotiating control and protecting the private: History teachers and the Virginia standards of learning. In S. G. Grant (Ed.), *Measuring history: Cases of state-level testing across the United States* (pp. 221–247). Greenwich, CT: IAP-Information Age.

Smith, M. L. (1991). Put to the test: The effects of external testing on teachers. *Educational Researcher, 20*(5), 8–11.

Smith, M. L. (2004). *Political spectacle and the fate of American schools.* New York: RoutledgeFalmer.

Sochor, Z. A. (1981). Soviet Taylorism revisited. *Soviet Studies, 33*(2), 246–264.

Spillane, J. P. (2004). *Standards deviation: How schools misunderstand education policy.* Cambridge, MA: Harvard University Press.

Stecher, B. M., & Barron, S. (2001). Unintended consequences of test-based accountability when testing in 'milepost' grades. *Educational Assessment, 7*(4), 259–281.

Stoskopf, A. (1999). The forgotten history of eugenics. *Rethinking Schools, 13*(3), 12–13.

Stoskopf, A. (1999). An untold story of resistance: African-American educators and I.Q. testing in the 1920's and '30's. *Rethinking Schools, 14*(1). Retrieved October 21, 2007, from http://www.rethinkingschools.org/archive/14_01/iq141.shtml

Struble, G. G. (1922). A study of school board personnel. *American School Board Journal, LXV*, 48–49, 137–139.

Sunderman, G. L., & Kim, J. S. (2005, November 3). The expansion of federal power and the politics of implementing the no child left behind act. *Teachers College Record* Retrieved December 2, 2006, from http://www.tcrecord.org/printcontent.asp?contentID=12227

Survey: More pain than gain. (2006). *The Economist, 380*(8495), 14.

Tatum, B. D. (1997). *"Why are all the Black kids sitting together in the cafeteria?" and other conversations about race.* New York: Basic Books.

Taylor, G., Shepard, L., Kinner, F., & Rosenthal, J. (2001). *A survey of teachers' perspectives on high-stakes testing in Colorado: What gets taught, what gets lost.* Boulder: CRESST/CREDE/University of Colorado at Boulder; National Center for Research on Evaluation, Standards, and Student Testing, Graduate School of Education & Information Studies, University of California, Los Angeles; Center for Research on Evaluation, Diversity and Excellence, University of California, Santa Cruz.

Teachers 4 Social Justice. (2006). Homepage. Retrieved March 4, 2006, from http://www.altrue.net/site/t4sj/

Teachers for Social Justice. (2005). Homepage. Retrieved March 4, 2006, from http://www.teachersforjustice.org/

Teachers Network. (2007). A survey of teachers on no child left behind. Retrieved April 4, 2007, from http://www.teachersnetwork.org

Teitelbaum, K. (1993). *Schooling for 'good rebels': Socialist education for children in the United States 1900–1920.* Philadelphia: Temple University Press.

The Education Trust. (2003). Homepage. Retrieved February 16, 2006, from http://www2.edtrust.org/edtrust/

The Education Trust. (2004). *Education watch: The nation: Key education facts and figures: achievement, attainment, and opportunity from elementary school through college.* Washington, DC: The Education Trust.

Themba-Nixon, M. (2000). Testing slights multiculturalism. In K. Swope & B. Miner (Eds.), *Failing our kids: Why the testing craze won't fix our schools* (p. 32). Milwaukee, WI: Rethinking Schools.

Timar, T., & Tyack, D. (1999). *The invisible hand of ideology: Perspectives from the history of school governance* (No. SE-99-3). Denver, CO: Education Commission of the States.

Titus, J. J. (2004). Boy trouble: Rhetorical framing of boys' underachievement. *Discourse: Studies in the cultural politics of education, 25*(2), 145–169.

Toch, T. (2006). *Margins of error: The education testing industry in the no child left behind era.* Washington, DC: Education Sector.

Toussaint, R. (2000/2001). Manifest destiny or cultural integrity? *Rethinking Schools, 15*(2). Retrieved October 21, 2007, from http://www.rethinkingschools.org/archive/15_02/Test152.shmtl

Tyack, D. (1974). *The one best system: A history of American Urban Education.* Cambridge, MA: Harvard University Press.

U.S. Department of Education. (2002). *No child left behind: A desktop reference.* Washington, DC: U.S. Department of Education, Office of the Under Secretary.

U.S. Department of Education. (2006). *No child left behind is working.* Washington, DC: U.S. Department of Education.

Valenzuela, A. (1999). *Subtractive schooling: U.S. Mexican youth and the politics of caring.* Albany: State University of New York Press.

Valenzuela, A. (2005a). Accountability and the privatization agenda. In A. Valenzuela (Ed.), *Leaving children behind: How 'Texas style' accountability fails Latino youth* (pp. 263–294). Albany: State University of New York Press.

Valenzuela, A. (Ed.). (2005b). *Leaving children behind: How 'Texas style' accountability fails Latino youth.* Albany: State University of New York Press.

Van Atta, D. (1986). Why is there no Taylorism in the Soviet Union? *Comparative Politics, 18*(3), 327–337.

van Hover, S. D. (2006). Teaching history in the old dominion: The impact of Virginia's accountability reform on seven secondary beginning history teachers. In S. G. Grant (Ed.), *Measuring history: Cases of state-level testing across the United States* (pp. 195–219). Greenwich, CT: IAP-Information Age.

van Hover, S. D., & Heinecke, W. (2005). The impact of accountability reform on the 'wise practice' of secondary history teachers: The Virginia experience. In E. A. Yeager & J. Davis, O.L. (Eds.), *Wise social studies teaching in an age of high-stakes testing* (pp. 89–105). Greenwich, CT: Information Age.

VanSledright, B. A. (2004). What does it mean to think historically...and how do you teach it? *Social Education, 68*(3), 230–233.

Vavrus, M. (2002). *Transforming the multicultural education of teachers: Theory, research and practice.* New York: Teachers College Press.

Vinson, K. D., & Ross, E. W. (2003). Controlling images: the power of high-stakes testing. In K. J. Saltman & D. A. Gabbard (Eds.), *Education as enforcement: The militarization and corporatization of schools* (pp. 241–258). New York: RoutledgeFalmer.

Vogler, K. E. (2003). An integrated curriculum using state standards in a high-stakes testing environment. *Middle School Journal, 34*(4), 207–211.

Vogler, K. E. (2005). Impact of a high school graduation examination on social studies teachers' instructional practices. *Journal of Social Studies Research, 29*(2), 19–33.

von Zastrow, C. (2004). *Academic atrophy: The condition of the liberal arts in America's public schools.* Washington, DC: Council for Basic Education.

Vygotsky, L. S. (1978). *Mind in society.* Cambridge, MA: Harvard University Press.

Vygotsky, L. S. (1981). The genesis of higher mental functions (J. V. Wertsch, Trans.). In J. V. Wertsch (Ed.), *The concept of activity in Soviet psychology* (pp. 144–188). Armonk, NY: M.E. Sharpe.

Vygotsky, L. S. (1987). Thinking and speech (N. Minick, Trans.). In R. W. Rieber & A. Carton (Eds.), *The collected works of L.S. Vygotsky: Problems of general psychology including the volume thinking and speech* (Vol. 1, pp. 37–285). New York: Plenum.

Washington, B. T. (1903). The industrial education of the Negro. In *The Negro problem* (pp. 7–30). New York: James Pott and Company.

Weber, M. (1964). *The theory of social and economic organizations*. New York: Free Press of Glencoe.

Wei, D., & Kamel, R. (Eds.). (1998). *Resistance in paradise: Rethinking 100 years of U.S. involvement in the Caribbean and the Pacific*. Philadelphia: American Friends Service Committee.

Weil, D. (2001). World class standards? Whose world, which economic classes, and what standards? In J. L. Kincheloe & D. Weil (Eds.), *Standards and schooling in the United States: An encyclopedia* (Vol. 2, pp. 505–533). Denver, CO: ABC-CLIO.

Weiler, K., & Maher, F. (2002). Teacher education and social justice. *Radical Teacher, 64*(2-4), 2–4.

Weis, L. M. (1990). *Working class without work: High school students in a de-industrializing economy*. New York: Routledge.

Weis, L. M. (2004). *Class reunion: The remaking of the American white working class*. New York: Routledge.

Willis, P. (1977). *Learning to labor: How working class kids get working class jobs*. New York: Columbia University Press.

Willis, P. (2003). Foot soldiers of modernity: The dialectics of cultural consumption and the 21st-century school. *Harvard Educational Review, 73*(3), 390–415.

Winick, D. M., & Kress, S. (2004). Accountability works in Texas. In W. M. Evers & H. J. Walberg (Eds.), *Testing student learning, evaluating teaching effectiveness* (pp. 303–322). Stanford, CA: Hoover Institution Press.

Wirt, J., Choy, S., Rooney, P., Provasnik, S., & Tobin, R. (2004). *The condition of education 2004*. Washington, DC: National Council on Education Statistics, U.S. Department of Education, Institute of Educational Sciences.

Wolf, S. A., & Wolf, K. P. (2002). Teaching *true* and *to* the test in writing. *Language Arts, 79*(3), 240.

Wollman-Bonilla, J. E. (2004). Principled teaching to(wards) the test?: Persuasive writing in two classrooms. *Language Arts, 81*(6), 502–511.

Wong, T.-H., & Apple, M. W. (2003). Rethinking the education-state formation connection: The state, cultural struggles, and changing the school. In M. W. Apple (Ed.), *The state and the politics of knowledge* (pp. 81–107). New York: Routledge.

Woodson, C. G. (1990). *The mis-education of the negro*. Trenton, NJ: Africa World Press. (Original published 1933)

Wößmann, L. (2003). Central exit exams and student achievement: International evidence. In P. E. Peterson & M. R. West (Eds.), *No child left behind?: The politics and practice of school accountability* (pp. 292–324). Washington, DC: Brookings Institution Press.

Wright, W. E., & Choi, D. (2005). *Voices from the classroom: A statewide survey of experiences third-grade English language learner teachers on the impact of language and high-stakes testing policies in Arizona.* Tempe: Arizona State University, Language Policy Research Unit, Educational Policy Studies Laboratory.

Yeager, E. A., & Davis, J., O.L. (Eds.). (2005). *Wise social studies teaching in an age of high-stakes testing: Essays on classroom practices and possibilities.* Greenwich, CT: Information Age.

Yeh, S. S. (2005). Limiting the unintended consequences of high-stakes testing. *Education Policy Analysis Archives, 13*(43). Retrieved February 8, 2006, from http://epaa.asu.edu/epaa/v13n43/

Yeh, S. S. (2007). Personal communication received by W. Au, October 11, Fullerton, CA.

Zabala, D. (2007). *State high school exit exams: Gaps persist in high school exit exam pass rates — policy brief 3.* Washington, DC: Center on Education Policy.

Zinn, H. (1995). *A people's history of the United States: 1492–present* (Rev. ed.). New York: HarperPerennial.

INDEX

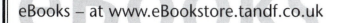